For Better or For Worse

More praise for *For Better or For Worse*

"[Hetherington] has recently accentuated the more positive prognosis for children of divorce. . . . [S]he has brought this long-running argument among social scientists back into the public spotlight. . . . [R]eason for optimism."
—New York Times

"Divorce, it seems, is not predestined. . . . [Hetherington] wants to change the public debate about divorce. Her book offers reassurance to the millions of Americans who don't make it till death does part them."
—Washington Post

"A journey of 30 years and nearly 4,000 people is bound to bring surprises—especially when it involves 2,500 children, and most of them are dealing with divorce. . . . Hetherington has just unveiled her magnum opus: a book on the legacy of divorce, offering fresh hope for 'fragmented' families and a change of pace from the doomsday predictions of recent studies. . . . The recurrent theme in Dr. Hetherington's substantial collection of data is resilience. . . . Hetherington doesn't advocate divorce as a panacea, but she brings a note of cautious optimism to a life course often considered the first perilous misstep on a slippery slope."
—Christian Science Monitor

"The landmark rejoinder to Wallerstein's monochromatically dark view of divorce. . . . [Hetherington] passionately contends that divorce results in a wide spectrum of long-term after-effects, positive as well as negative, even among children. . . . Hetherington's perspective serves to remind us that life is complicated and unpredictable—perhaps especially so in the case of divorce and its consequences."
—Elle

"*For Better or For Worse* deserves a place on everyone's bookshelf . . . it stands as a shining example of what a serious scholar can do when she decides to become a public intellectual. . . . Mavis Hetherington is a shining example to us all."
—Women's Review of Books

"One of the nation's leading family researchers has good news for parents racked by guilt over the break-up of their marriages. . . . [A]lready the two sides in this hot-button debate are squabbling like contentious spouses." —*Philadelphia Inquirer*

"For those waiting for the final word on whether divorce is good or bad, a top expert has now weighed in with a firm 'it depends.'" . . . Praise for Hetherington comes from psychologists who call her research fair, balanced, and, above all, helpful in guiding families toward healthier responses to divorce." —*Minneapolis Star-Tribune*

"Curiously, it's not that anyone is disputing the research methods of Hetherington, one of the most respected family scholars in the country. . . . The controversy is in the interpretation: Is the glass half-full or half-empty?" —*Newark Star-Ledger*

"[A] kind and gentle primer for the newly divorced."
—*CityBooks*, Washington, D.C.

"[A] 'primer' on the 'postnuclear family experience.' . . . With darker realities in mind, the authors offer a series of practical suggestions at the end of each chapter." —*Publishers Weekly*

"[Hetherington] concludes that divorce casts a long shadow, but the focus here includes spouses as well as children. Hetherington confidently argues that divorce, while certainly not desirable, is not necessarily the cataclysm that recent press has made it out to be." —*Library Journal*

For Better or For Worse

DIVORCE RECONSIDERED

by

E. Mavis Hetherington AND *John Kelly*

W.W. Norton & Company
NEW YORK ♦ LONDON

"You Don't Mess Around With Jim." Written by Jim Croce. © 1972 (Renewed) Time In A Bottle/Croce Publishing (ASCAP). All rights reserved. Used by permission.

"For Anne Gregory" reprinted with the permission of Scribner, a Division of Simon & Schuster, Inc., from *The Collected Works of W. B. Yeats, Volume 1: The Poems, Revised*, edited by Richard J. Finneran. Copyright © 1933 by The Macmillan Publishing Company, copyright renewed © 1961 by Bertha Georgie Yeats.

For information about permission to reproduce selections from this book, write to Permissions, W. W. Norton & Company, Inc., 500 Fifth Avenue, New York, NY 10110

The text of this book is composed in Fournier MT
with the display set in Theodoric and Bembo Schoolbook
Composition by Amanda Morrison
Manufacturing by The Maple-Vail Book Manufacturing Group
Book design by Brooke Koven

Library of Congress Cataloging-in-Publication Data

Hetherington, E. Mavis (Eileen Mavis), 1926–
For better or for worse : divorce reconsidered / by E. Mavis Hetherington and John Kelly.
p. cm.
Includes bibliographical references and index.
ISBN 0-393-04862-4
1. Divorce—Psychological aspects. 2. Divorced people—Psychology.
3. Divorce—United States. I. Kelly, John, 1945– II. Title.
HQ814 .H47 2002
306.89—dc21   2001044319

ISBN 0-393-32413-3 pbk.

W. W. Norton & Company, Inc.
500 Fifth Avenue, New York, N.Y. 10110
www.wwnorton.com

W. W. Norton & Company Ltd.
Castle House, 75/76 Wells Street, London W1T 3QT

1 2 3 4 5 6 7 8 9 0

To my husband, John Hetherington, and to my children,
Grant, Eric, and Jason, who taught me about the joys and gratification
of a happy family life

Contents

1

A New Story About Divorce

*N*eighbors, friends, even some of the women in Liddy Pennybaker's* book group knew about James's infidelities, so when
word spread that Liddy had asked for a divorce, everyone thought they
knew why.

James frequently went to social events alone, and just as frequently
left with an attractive female on his arm. But to Liddy, James's affairs
were more in the nature of a last straw than anything else. By the time
receipts from out-of-town hotels began appearing in the Pennybakers'
American Express bills, Liddy was already halfway out of the marriage.
She resented James not spending more time with the children. She had
grown tired of his scowls when she ate anything with more than a hundred calories in it. She was sick of his aloofness and condescension when
she had friends from her church group to the house. She hated James's
social climbing and phony laugh when he was around powerful people.

---

* All names and recognizable details have been changed to protect the privacy of the
participants.

In truth, Liddy felt almost grateful for the affairs—not that she liked being hurt and humiliated, but the affairs finally focused her, forced her to face a truth she had been resisting for two years. The marriage was over!

Before, when Liddy thought about divorce, she thought about it the way a child thinks about being a grown-up—as a kind of fantasy game. Liddy would spend hours trying on new lives, imagining what it would be like to have a career or to be married to someone else. But whenever she sat down and actually analyzed the costs of divorce, the price always seemed too high.

The thought of telling the children was especially frightening. And leaving would mean ignoring, trashing everything she, the minister's daughter, had been brought up to believe. Oddly enough, the marriage itself also made Liddy hesitate. It still had its good moments and so did James, despite all his lies and deceptions. Walking out on her marriage would make Liddy feel as if she were tearing down a home she had built with her own hands, a home a part of her still loved and felt safe in. Besides, what would she be walking out to? She hadn't worked since her marriage and she didn't have a degree. She had dropped out of college to marry James.

The ambivalence, the weighing of hopes against fears, of past happiness against current dissatisfactions that Liddy Pennybaker wrestled with in deciding to divorce occurs in most marital breakups.

Every divorce is a unique tragedy because every divorce brings an end to a unique civilization—one built on thousands of shared experiences, memories, hopes, and dreams. That wonderful Two-for-the-Road summer in Europe, the first day in the new house, the heart-stopping trip to the emergency room—only the people who shared those moments know what it means to lose them forever. So divorce takes a uniquely personal toll on the divorced. But the experience of divorce also has many commonalities. The end of a marriage always, or almost always, produces heartache, fear, self-doubt, confusion, and of course many anxious questions.

What happens to me and my children now? What should I expect, fear, hope for? What kinds of challenges and pitfalls do I face? And how do I go about building a better life? Like other books on divorce, *For Better or For Worse* offers answers to these questions. But the answers you will find here are different. *For Better or For Worse* has a new story to tell about divorce, and it is an important story because it is based on the most comprehensive examination of divorce ever conducted: an in-depth examination of nearly 1,400 families and over 2,500 children, many followed for more than three decades. When I finished my research, the adults I had met as young men and women were now in middle age and most had been remarried for a decade or more, and the children I had met as preschoolers were now teachers, accountants, computer scientists, and engineers; many were married; a few had already gone through a divorce of their own.

The unparalleled scope of my research has produced new and surprising findings about divorce and its immediate aftermath, findings that will make us better able to anticipate the consequences of marital failure for ourselves, our children, and for future partners and marriages.

Among the most important findings to emerge are:

—How divorce changes people's behavior, feelings, friendships, health, and, in the case of adults, their work and sex lives

—Why even people who are eager to leave a marriage often question the decision later

—Why the end of the first year is usually the most painful point in the entire postdivorce period

—Why casual postdivorce sex is more emotionally risky for women than men

—Why divorce heightens vulnerability to psychological problems and physical illness

—Why preadolescent girls usually adjust more easily to divorce than boys

—Why men and women rarely marry the person they leave a marriage for

—Why a familial history of divorce is a greater divorce risk to a woman than a man.

For Better or For Worse also has a second, even more important story to tell. This one is about a new kind of experience created by divorce. Traditionally, marital failure has been viewed as a single event, one that produces temporarily intense but limited effects. People suffer, they heal, and then go on with their lives. What happens to them later, as single parents, in a new romantic relationship, or in a second marriage, is dependent on the conditions they encounter later. Or so the traditional view holds.

But as I followed my families over the years and, in many cases, over the decades, I found this view to be insufficient. Marital failure cannot be understood as a single event; it is part of a series of interconnected transitions on a pathway of life experiences that lead to and issue from divorce. The quality of life in a first marriage influences adults' and children's responses to divorce and experiences in a single-parent family, and these in turn cast a shadow across new romantic relationships, a second marriage, and life in a stepfamily.

Sometimes I saw happy second marriages heal painful, divorce-induced emotional scars. But reactions work the other way around as well. Unhappy second marriages and unhappy stepfamilies can reopen old divorce wounds, and a legacy of fear and mistrust from a first marriage can erode happiness in a remarriage.

As I studied nearly fourteen hundred families across time, I realized that the divorce revolution begun in the 1960s had created entirely new patterns of intimate relations, with less stability and fewer certainties but more options. People were not just marrying and staying with the same partner, the traditional pattern for married life. Half of this new generation were divorcing, and they were taking diverse pathways from marital breakup. Some were opting to cohabit or remain single or to have multiple romantic partners. Others were forming relationships with partners of the same sex. Others again were remarrying, often several times.

On one level, *For Better or For Worse* is a portrait of the new ways Americans have learned to live and love and parent in a divorce-prone society. On another level, the book serves as a primer on what might be called the postnuclear family experience. *For Better or For Worse* explains the options that have become available to the newly divorced over the past few decades. Based on the experiences of my study families, it explains which options are most likely to lead to postmarital success or failure, and why.

At the center of the primer is a new and, I think, more balanced view of divorce and its consequences. After forty years of research, I harbor no doubts about the ability of divorce to devastate. It can and does ruin lives. I've seen it happen more times than I like to think about. But that said, I also think much current writing on divorce—both popular and academic—has exaggerated its negative effects and ignored its sometimes considerable positive effects. Divorce has undoubtedly rescued many adults and children from the horror of domestic abuse, but it is not just a preventative measure. I have seen divorce provide many women and girls, in particular, with a remarkable opportunity for life-transforming personal growth, as we shall see later.

The reason our current view of marital failure is so unremittingly negative is that it is based on studies that have only examined people for a year or two after their divorce, and a year or two is not enough time to distinguish between short- and long-term effects. Additionally, many divorce studies do not employ a comparison group of married couples, and thus are unable to distinguish between problems common to all families and problems unique to divorced families.

Once you remove these distortions by doing what I did, examining men, women, and children for over twenty years and including a comparison group of non-divorced married couples, many of our current beliefs about marital failure turn out to be myths. Six examples of the most common myths follow.

Myth One:
Divorce Only Has Two Outcomes: Win or Lose

Divorce is too complex a process to produce just winners and losers. People adjust in many different ways, and these patterns of adjusting change over time. The most common include:

- *Enhanced.* Two decades after divorce, the 20 percent of individuals who were classified as Enhanced came closest to looking like traditional postdivorce winners. Successful at work, Enhancers also succeeded socially, as parents, and often in new marriages, though in one key aspect the group did depart from the conventional picture of postdivorce winners. The Enhanced flourished *because* of the things that had happened to them during and after divorce, not despite them. Competencies that would have remained latent if they had stayed in a marriage were fostered by the urgent need to overcome the challenges of divorce and single parenthood.

- *Competent Loners.* Men and women who do not remarry are often considered divorce losers. But the 10 percent of men and women in my research who were classified as Competent Loners looked a lot like Enhancers; the only major difference was that they were more emotionally self-sustaining. A Competent Loner did not need—or, in many cases, want—a partner; he or she was fully capable of building a meaningful and happy life without a marriage or a longtime companion.

- *Good Enoughs.* For the people in this category, divorce was like a speed bump in the road. It caused a lot of tumult while the person was going over it, but failed to leave a lasting impression—either positive or negative. Two decades later, Good Enoughs (who represented 40 percent of my study sample and were my largest postdivorce group) had different partners and different marriages, but usually the same problems.

- *Seekers.* Seekers were distinguished by a desire to remarry quickly. Alone, the average Seeker, who was usually a man, felt rootless and insecure. He needed a spouse and a marriage to give his life structure, meaning, and a secure base. Unmarried Seekers often became desperately unhappy and clinically depressed; they also had more drinking problems than other divorced adults.

- *Libertines.* The polar opposites of Seekers, Libertines wanted freedom, not a new set of restrictions. They came out of marriage, as one member of the group said, "ready to live life in the fast lane." Plunging necklines, trendy clothing, tight-fitting jeans, and sports cars were the symbols of their intention. Libertines had the highest rates of casual sex and singles bar patronage in the study.

However, by the end of the first year after divorce many Libertines felt that their life was empty, pointless, a dead end, and they began to seek more stable, committed relationships. As one Libertine said, "After awhile even a sexual smorgasbord gets to be a bit of a bore."

• *The Defeated.* The men and women in this group succumbed to depression, to substance abuse, to a sense of purposelessness. Some of the people in this category lost everything—jobs, homes, second spouses, children, self-esteem; others managed to rebuild a halfway functional new life, but it was joyless. The Defeated often remained embittered over the life they had lost.

Myth Two:
Children Always Lose Out After a Divorce

This is another article of faith in popular wisdom and it contains an undeniable truth. In the short run, divorce usually is brutally painful to a child. But its negative long-term effects have been exaggerated to the point where we now have created a self-fulfilling prophecy. At the end of my study, a fair number of my adult children of divorce described themselves as permanently "scarred." But objective assessments of these "victims" told a different story. Twenty-five percent of youths from divorced families in comparison to 10 percent from non-divorced families did have serious social, emotional, or psychological problems. But most of the young men and women from my divorced families looked a lot like their contemporaries from non-divorced homes. Although they looked back on their parents' breakup as a painful experience, most were successfully going about the chief tasks of young adulthood: establishing careers, creating intimate relationships, building meaningful lives for themselves.

Most unexpectedly—since it has seldom been reported before—a minority of my young adults emerged from divorce and postnuclear family life enhanced. Uncommonly resilient, mature, responsible, and focused, these children of divorce blossomed, not despite the things that had happened to them during divorce and after, but, like Enhanced adults, because of them.

Myth Three:
The Pathways Following Divorce Are Fixed and Unchanging

The effects of divorce are not irrevocable; they do not lock a person into a particular pattern of adjustment. A negative experience at one major transition point, such as divorce, can be offset by a positive experience at another point, transforming a Defeated individual into a Good Enough or a Good Enough individual into Enhanced. But the opposite can happen, too. A person can go from Good Enough to Defeated.

Also, the direction of change is never predetermined. After a divorce, to a great extent individuals influence their own destiny. As we shall see later, a single mother's decision to go back to school to upgrade her work skills, or a divorced man's hurried remarriage, or an adolescent's decision to terminate a pregnancy can close or open the gates to a new life path.

Myth Four:
Men Are the Big Winners in Divorce

In the tabloid press, men always seem to be leaving their wives for younger, slimmer, and prettier women, so-called trophy wives. But in real life, it is usually the women who do the leaving. Indeed, men-as-divorce-winners may be the biggest myth about divorce. In my research, two out of every three marriages ended because the wife walked out.

Furthermore, women did better emotionally after divorce than men did. They were less likely to mope and feel sorry for themselves and also less likely to continue to pine for a former spouse. Women were better at building a new social network of friends and at finding ways to assuage their pain. And while the economic disparity between men and women following divorce continues to be great, with the woman's economic resources declining by about 30 percent and the man's by 10 percent, this difference is beginning to close, thanks to better education of women and stricter enforcement of child support laws. Still, many women, even middle-class women, fall into poverty after divorce.

Myth Five:
The Absence of a Father—and Consequent Poverty—Are the Two
   Greatest Postdivorce Risks to Children

Fathers do contribute vitally to the financial, social, and emotional well-being of a child. But the contribution is not made through a man's sheer physical presence. A child does not automatically become psychologically well adjusted or a competent student just because he or she lives with Dad. Qualities like stability and competency in children have to be nurtured carefully and patiently by active, engaged fathering.

In fact, we found that if a man was psychologically absent before the divorce and a custodial mother is reasonably well adjusted and parents competently following divorce, single-family life often has little enduring negative developmental impact on a child, particularly if that child is a girl. An involved, supportive, firm custodial mother often is able to counter adverse effects of both the lack of a father and poverty.

Myth Six:
Death and Divorce Produce Similar Outcomes

Both death of a father and divorce are associated with the lack of a father in the household, yet children from widowed families show fewer problems than those in divorced, mother-headed families. Why? The conflict associated with the end of a marriage is one reason. Another are the experiences and attitudes of divorced mothers. Widows get more support from families, friends, and in-laws; to some extent there is a "well, you brought it on yourself " attitude to the divorced. Widows also communicate idealized images of their dead husband to their children, whereas divorced women are likely to put down and belittle their ex-spouses, much to the confusion and pain of their children.

However, the death of a marriage, like the death of a loved one, often does produce a mourninglike sadness and grieving. But unlike death, divorce does not provide a sense of closure, of a chapter ending. The unresolved issues of divorce can retain their emotional sting because their source comes by every Saturday morning to pick up the children. Moreover, divorce breeds complicating factors of continued conflict and guilt. Questions like "Was I too selfish?" "Did I try hard enough?" "Could I have done more?" can grate like sandpaper on a guilty conscience.

Although our work uncovered many myths about divorce, on one critical point my research does confirm, resoundingly, the conventional wisdom about divorce:

The end of a marriage is usually brutally painful.

In their worst nightmares, few if any of the middle-class women in my study imagined that they would ever find themselves in a welfare office filling out application forms, or moving back in with a parent; but after divorce a surprisingly large number had to do one or both. Similarly, I don't think that many of the divorced men in my studies ever imagined sitting up night after night watching reruns of *Star Trek* and *M*A*S*H* to avoid an empty bed in a half-furnished apartment. And I know none of them ever thought that talking to their children would become almost as difficult as talking to a stranger.

To the boys and girls in my research, divorce seemed cataclysmic and inexplicable. How could a child feel safe in a world where adults had suddenly become untrustworthy? Marital failure was so outside a child's normal range of experience that the only way many youngsters could make sense of it was to blame themselves. Small wonder, then, that one four-year-old confided to me: "My daddy left my mommy and me because he doesn't like me anymore."

From the Pain of Divorce to the Satisfaction of
the Postnuclear Family

One of our newly divorced men, a geography professor, started worrying about his sanity when he began looking up at birds in the branches of the trees and shouting, "Get off that branch, you God-damned bird!" However, once the confusion of divorce had passed, the man realized that his bizarre behavior had a purpose. "Somehow it gave me something to vent my anger on," he said to me one day. "It gave me a sense of power when everything was so out of control."

Another, a very buttoned-down young banker, was appalled when he found himself crouched behind a boxwood in his old front yard, peering through a window, watching his former wife and a strange man making love on the living-room floor. "I don't know what's happening to me," he told me later. "I've never done anything like that before. I've never even thought of doing anything like that before."

It was easy to understand their concern. Behaviors like Peeping Tomism and harassing birds are worrisome, but they are also fairly normal in the first year after a divorce, as are erratic mood swings, vulnerability to psychological disorders and physical illness, and doubts about the decision to leave.

But very few of the millions of men and women who get divorced each year anticipate these reactions or know that they are usually temporary and self-correcting. The newly divorced also tend to be blind to the long shadow that the past casts over their new lives. Although *For Better or For Worse* is not a self-help book in the conventional sense of the word, it does explain what to expect and when to expect it. It describes what happens to men, women, and children at one and two years after divorce and at five, ten, fifteen, and twenty years.

To guide you through the challenges and options confronted in postdivorce life, I will describe some of the pathways taken by families I studied over the years. Through their experience, you will be introduced to strategies that can ease adjustment to a marital breakup and produce success in a new single family or a second marriage. I think you will be surprised at how commonsensical some of the strategies are and how novel others are. For example:

—Selecting the right kind of school can measurably increase a child's chances of successfully navigating life after divorce.

—Parental monitoring and supervision are particularly critical with adolescents because children from divorced and remarried families are more vulnerable to peer influence.

—Timing is often key to succeeding in a second marriage. Remarriages that occur prior to a child's adolescence succeed more often than those that occur when a youngster is in his or her early teens.

—Marrying a person from an intact family significantly reduces the higher risk of marital instability carried by adult children of divorce.

How the Virginia Longitudinal Study Changed the Way Divorce Is Studied

My interest in divorce grew out of my work in another area of family life. I think I have always had a special interest in the role fathers play in girls' lives because I had the good fortune to have a father who promoted female achievement and independence at a time when fathers rarely encouraged either.

In the late 1960s, my interest in fathers and daughters led to a startling research finding. At the time, informed opinion held that a mother shaped a daughter's gender identity, a father a son's. But a series of studies I did in the 1960s showed that fathers play the more important role in the gender identity of both boys and girls. The finding raised an interesting and important question: What happens to a girl when a father is absent due to death or divorce?

In my first study of families without fathers, I found that peers and especially mothers step in and assume the gender-shaping role men play in two-parent families. But the new study also raised a new question.

Why did girls from divorced families have more social and psychological problems than girls from widowed families? Was there a unique developmental dynamic—perhaps even a uniquely harmful dynamic—in divorced families?

The Virginia Longitudinal Study (VLS), the most comprehensive study of divorce ever conducted, was intended to answer this question. Most earlier research had relied only on the report of a single family member, usually a mother, to study the effects of divorce. The VLS expanded the study base to include not only the mother, father, and one focal child and a sibling in the family, but also people around the family. I also used a vast array of study tools, including interviews, questionnaires, standardized tests, and observations. Some of these instruments had never been used before, though they are now common in family studies. For example, I devised detailed methods of observing family interactions and activities; I and my team of investigators studied families in the home as they solved problems, as they chatted over dinner, and in the hours between the child's arrival at home and bedtime. We had a very personal look at how our families behaved when they disagreed, fought, relaxed, played, and soothed each other.

The VLS also was the first study to employ a structured diary in studying divorce. In order to assess each adult's mood fluctuations and activities, I had them keep diaries. Three days a week at half-hour intervals, parents had to note where they were, who they were with, what they were doing, and how they were feeling. If a person was having sex, she had to note that in the diary; the same was true if she were out on a date, having a fight at work, sitting in a singles bar, arguing with her mother, or trying to soothe an upset child.

The diaries yielded a great deal of unique and very fine-grained detail. For example, I found that a woman's feelings of anger and helplessness usually lasted longer after a fight with a son than a daughter. I also found that casual sex produced extreme depression and feelings of being unloved in many women and sent a few to the edge. Though suicide attempts were rare in the VLS, the seven that did occur were all attempts by women, and all were triggered by casual sex.

The children in the study—who were age four at the start of the VLS—received even more intense scrutiny. They were observed alone and with parents, peers, and siblings. We observed them at home, in school, on the playground, and also at the Hetherington Laboratory at the University of Virginia. Parents, teachers, and study observers were asked to assess each "target child." As the child grew older, the list of assessors grew to include peers, brothers and sisters, and the child himself, who was periodically asked to make self-assessments.

One of the most important aspects of the VLS was the use of a non-divorced comparison group. With its help, we were able to distinguish between the normal changes all families and family members undergo and changes that were linked directly to the impact of divorce and remarriage.

Initially, the Virginia Longitudinal Study of Divorce, which was launched in 1972, was intended to study how seventy-two preschool children and their families adapted to divorce at two months, one year, and two years. To provide a yardstick of comparison, seventy-two non-divorced families were also included in the study. The study's two-year time limit reflected then current thinking that most families had restabilized by two years after divorce.

But then something unexpected happened. The seventy-two men and women in my divorced group began to remarry and form stepfamilies, and the seventy-two couples in my married comparison group began to divorce. I seemed to be studying a moving target!

At first, I was frustrated. Didn't these folks have any respect for science? But then I realized I had been given a golden opportunity. Women's liberation and employment, no-fault divorce, the sexual revolution, self-actualization, the movements of the sixties and seventies, all were dramatically changing American mating habits. In the blink of an eye, the entire country seemed to jump from the paternal certainties of *Father Knows Best* to the postmodern chaos of *The Brady Bunch*.

Politicians, religious leaders, newspapers, magazines, and television documentaries decried the "breakdown of the nuclear family"; my fellow academics hailed the "emergence of the non-traditional family." But whatever phrase people chose, everyone agreed: America was in the midst of an unprecedented social change—one that would be played out for decades to come in the nation's living rooms, bedrooms, courtrooms, and legislatures.

But was the change positive or negative or a little bit of both? Would casualties of the divorce revolution begin to inflate the statistics on domestic violence, welfare, school dropouts, unmarried mothers, out-of-wedlock children, juvenile crime, and substance abuse? Or was the revolution simply a reasonable, even a healthy adjustment to a world where female needs were considered the equal of male needs, and where longer life spans made monogamy seem more burdensome than it had when people died at younger ages? As society changes, shouldn't social institutions such as marriage and family also change in response?

I decided my preschooler study would be a good vehicle to explore these questions. I already had a large body of data on divorce and I had a study sample that was coupling and uncoupling and recoupling as energetically as any group in the country. However, if I wanted to use the study as a vehicle to explore not merely divorce but postnuclear family pathways, I would have to expand the time frame and enlarge the number of participants. At six years after divorce, I raised the number of families from 144 to 180—equally balanced between divorced, non-divorced, and stepfamilies, with two children in each family. The original target child and the sibling closest in age were studied throughout the remainder of the study. At eleven years after divorce, when VLS target children were fifteen, I increased the sample to 300 families and 600 children; and at twenty years, when the children were twenty-four, to 450 families and 900 children. Whenever one of the offspring cohabited for more than six months, married, or had a child, an additional full wave of assessment was done of the new family. Thus, we are currently continuing to study our families. It should be noted that at the end of the VLS, 122 of my original 144 families were still participating, a remarkable retention rate for a two-decade-long study.

However, in order to complete my picture of postnuclear family life, I also had to draw on data from two other longitudinal studies done concurrently with the VLS. Indeed, a VLS finding inspired one of them. I noticed that early adolescents had more difficulty adapting to a parent's remarriage than younger children and older adolescents. So in the early 1990s, in conjunction with Glen Clingempeel, a clinical psychologist, I organized the 202-family Philadelphia Divorce and Remarriage (D&R) Study to explore why. The second study, the Nonshared Environment Study (NSES), done in collaboration with David Reiss, a psychiatrist, and Robert Plomin, a behavior geneticist, involved 720 families and 1,440 children. Designed to examine how heredity and environment contribute to differences in development among adolescent siblings in the same household, the NSES, which intensively examined more different kinds of stepfamilies than any previous research project, gave me an opportunity to explore a second question: How do different types of stepfamilies affect the well-being of remarried parents and their children? (More details on these studies are presented in the Appendix.)

While I have drawn heavily on all three studies, particularly the VLS, in a very real sense the new story For Better or For Worse tells about divorce and about the new life experience that has grown out of it is based on a superstudy of the nearly fourteen hundred families who participated in the Virginia Longitudinal, NSE, and D&R studies.

My approach to the study of divorce was that of scholar. But I knew from the outset that my work would have important practical implications—how could I not, when nearly every day of my research I was being asked: "What should I do? What does this mean? Should I stay or go?"

For Better or For Worse is many things—the summation of a life's work, a portrait of how America lives and loves now, and a practical guide to a new kind of life experience. But most of all, it is a response to my study participants' cries for help.

My work has given me a very unusual opportunity. For the last thirty years, I've had a chance to watch the marital and relationship mores of a society change, and I want to pass on what I have seen and learned to the millions of men and women who embark on the uncertain adventure of divorce each year. Though For Better or For Worse might be seen as a book about why marriages fail, even more it is a book about options and opportunities, about the choices to be made that can lead to fulfillment or to dissatisfaction and despair.

Part One

The Experience of Divorce:
Children and Adults in
the First Six Years

2

The His and Her Marriage;
the His and Her Divorce

*A*fter a divorce, people often imagine that if only they could go back
and make a tiny adjustment here or there in the past—not answering a particular phone call, say, or displaying an ounce more resolve in a
weak moment—life would have turned out differently for them. And
sometimes they're right. But I don't think any of the "if-onlys" Liddy
Pennybaker mentioned at our first meeting would have made a difference; there was still the overwhelming fact of who James and Liddy
were when they met for the first time.

James and Liddy agreed about very little at the end of their marriage, which like the end of so many marriages was bitter. But the Pennybakers still did agree on one thing: how they fell in love. Six years
later, James and Liddy could both recall the details of their first meeting
at a fraternity party. "I was talking to a friend and in walks my roommate
with the most beautiful woman I'd ever seen," James said at his intake
interview. "Tall, elegant, with legs that seemed to go on forever. But it

was the blond hair down to her waist that got me. Liddy was like a princess in a fairy tale. I knew I had to have her."

Liddy remembers pretending not to notice James staring at her when she walked into the party. "I knew who he was," she told me later. "I had seen James playing soccer, and I knew he was a big man on campus, and he was ridiculously good-looking. But he was very drunk, and he kept following me around saying, 'Rapunzel, Rapunzel, let down your golden hair.' At first I was annoyed. I tried to get rid of him. But he was persistent and very funny. What really broke the ice was when he quoted from a poem my dad and I had always loved,

> *Only God, my dear,*
> *Could love you for yourself alone*
> *And not your yellow hair.*

"How many soccer players quote poetry? The next morning, James was sitting in my doorway with a hangover and an armload of flowers. We walked and talked all day. I didn't want to get rid of him anymore."

However, a year and a half later, when James proposed, Liddy hesitated. Which James would she be marrying, she wondered: the sensitive young man who loved poetry and brought her flowers, or the swaggering, spoiled fraternity boy she had met on their first night? The two figures seemed to share joint custody of James. What Liddy thought of as the good James was thoughtful, witty, sweet, and, like her father, respectful in an old-fashioned southern way. The bad James was arrogant and controlling. This James also seemed to regard being James Pennybaker's girlfriend as a kind of public office, and he was not shy about passing on tips about the way the occupant of the office should dress, wear her hair, speak, and conduct herself. "I had to be perfect each time we went out," Liddy told me. "I felt like a show horse, but it didn't matter. James was so proud of me."

The first time James asked Liddy to marry him, it was not just the dark side of James that concerned her but also the differences in their backgrounds. "I don't know if we have enough in common to get married, Jimmy."

"The differences are only superficial and that's part of our strength, Liddy," James told her. "Opposites attract."

Liddy wasn't sure about the superficial part but she was about the difference part. Liddy was raised in the Shenandoah Valley, the daughter and granddaughter of Baptist ministers. The dominant emotional and intellectual force in her life had been her father. The Reverend Michael Witter encouraged Liddy's intellectual pursuits in a way unusual for the time in the mid-1960s in a small southern town; but there was a strict text to this paternal encouragement. Liddy's straight-A average through high school and college never expanded her father's expectations beyond the conventional. Liddy, he hoped, would become a community leader, perhaps a doctor or a lawyer's wife, but the Reverend Witter never imagined his daughter becoming a doctor or lawyer herself.

Liddy's style, intellectual and drolly humorous, made her religiosity—her sense of herself as a "Christian woman"—unexpected, and she was acutely aware and a little defensive about that. "I don't understand why people find it so amazing that someone like me would be a practicing Christian," she said to me one day. "Does every preacher's daughter have to look like she grew up in Dogpatch?"

James was a Virginian too, but his Virginia was the rarefied Virginia of old money and southern gentry, of hunts and country estates. The people James grew up with owned horses, lived on trust funds, attended fashionable prep schools, and had several residences, often including a large apartment in New York City like the one James's mother, Grace, lived in.

Grace—and James's eagerness to please her—was another reason why Liddy hesitated when James proposed. Liddy could never figure out whether the imperious, stylish Grace deliberately tried to make her feel like a member of *The Beverly Hillbillies* or was just too preoccupied with her own entourage of good-looking artistic young men to notice the reticent Liddy. Whatever the case, on her third visit, Grace was still calling Liddy "Lucy."

During our first meeting, I asked Liddy if her father's sudden death had had anything to do with her decision to marry James after refusing him twice.

"Yes," Liddy said. "But I don't think it's fair to blame James for pouncing on me in a vulnerable moment. After Daddy died, I needed to be taken care of. I had just lost the most important person in my life."

After the marriage, James and Liddy settled in Richmond, and James joined one of the city's most prestigious architectural firms. Following the birth of their first child, Bethany, the Pennybakers moved into a spacious 1880s house in the Fan district, one of the old, elegant, fashionable areas in Richmond. James and Liddy agreed that these early years were the happiest in their married life. They also agreed that when Adam arrived eighteen months later, the marriage began to sour. After that, their stories of what contributed to the deterioration of their relationship began to diverge.

"After Adam's birth things just fell apart," James told me. "Liddy had been sexually inexperienced before we married but became a wonderful, passionate lover. We just couldn't get enough of each other. But later she became so obsessed with the children that we never seemed to have any privacy, and she was usually too tired to make love or go out and have a good time together. When we did have sex, it was joyless. I love my children, but I want to have a relationship with my wife, too."

James went on, "Liddy gained weight after Bethany's birth, but after Adam she went from being a real beauty to an overweight frump and didn't care much about her clothes. She even cut off her long gorgeous hair, and got a short style she said was more practical. It made her look like a concentration camp commandant.

"I know it sounds self-serving," James continued, "but my affairs were as much Liddy's fault as mine. It was as if she wanted to drive me away. I have normal needs to feel loved and wanted and to have a wife I'm proud of. Liddy got so absorbed in her Mother Earth routine she forgot I existed. I didn't care about the other women. I didn't want anyone else, I just really wanted my old Liddy back."

Liddy described the end of the Pennybaker marriage differently. "We just gradually grew apart," she said. "Jimmy loved the children, I'll give him that. But he didn't want to be around them as much as I did and he definitely wasn't interested in doing the dirty work. He never got up with them at night or changed a diaper. He wanted to go out all the time like we used to before the kids; he said he had to socialize for business. But Jimmy loves to party; he doesn't feel alive unless he's got an adoring crowd around him. After awhile, it was just easier to let him do what he wanted to do. At least when he was out we didn't fight, and I didn't have to listen to snide little remarks about my weight."

Liddy said she probably could have continued living a parallel life indefinitely had James not started to drink heavily and had there not been a charge from the Greenbrier Hotel on their American Express bill from a weekend when James was supposed to be at a business meeting in Chicago.

"In the last few years of the marriage, I suspected that there were lady friends, but I just ignored it or tolerated it or maybe I didn't care enough," Liddy declared. "But this was just too much. How could Jimmy take someone to the Greenbrier? We were married there! And he wanted me to know what he'd done. He wanted to rub my face in it. Otherwise he wouldn't have put the hotel bill on the American Express card."

The James and Liddy Pennybaker I met in the mid-1970s were anxiously riding the cutting edge of the most significant change in American social history. Baby boomer couples like the Pennybakers were rewriting the traditional rules of marriage and family life, including the notion that a marriage must be preserved no matter how bad or how unhappy it makes the two people trapped inside it.

Over the coming decades, changing attitudes about gender, fidelity, morals, and the right to personal happiness would radically alter patterns of mating, of sexual behavior, of parenting and family life, until the America of 1950 began to seem as remote from the American milieu of today as some ancient kingdom.

In the 1970s, when I began my investigation of divorce, you didn't need an advanced degree to see that many of these new trends were going to turn family relations upside down. But as I talked to couples like the Pennybakers, I recognized that these changes were being experienced differently by men and women.

Other social scientists had commented that there are "his" and "her" marriages. Our work shows that differences in life experiences, resources, perceptions, and coping styles also create a "his" and "her" divorce, and for the same reasons.

Men and women weigh emotion and communication, sex and fidelity, work and money differently because they are socialized differently. Differences in upbringing also give men and women different ideas about what is tolerable and intolerable in a marriage, and about what you have to give to others and what you have a right to expect in return.

I realized that if I wanted to understand the country's new mating patterns, I would first have to understand how these gender differences shape male and female perspectives on love, on marriage, and on divorce.

Men and Women in Love and Marriage

Gender differences in intimate behavior become apparent as soon as men and women begin to play the mating game. Women approach love as informed consumers; metaphorically speaking, they kick the tires, look under the hood, run the motor, check the mileage. Women love love; but being practical-minded, not enough to ignore potential defects. Good looks and romantic love matter to a woman; but in considering potential suitors, a woman also looks at the practical, such as a suitor's economic prospects, emotional stability, trustworthiness, and what kind of father he will be.

Despite a reputation for practicality, males come off as hopeless romantics. They are much more prone to fall head-over-heels in love, as James Pennybaker did, and also more prone to idealize the object of their affection. If the bodywork is good and the grille pretty, often a man will buy on the spot, no questions asked.

Gender differences, important in mating, are even more important in a marriage. One unexpected advantage of studying families over time and of having a married comparison group was that when a couple divorced—as many did—we had detailed records of a family's relationships before and after the divorce. Out of this data emerged two important insights.

First, the postnuclear path begins in the marriage, because what happens in a marriage often influences what happens after it. For example, the emotional climate of a marriage influences the emotional climate of a divorce, and the role men and women play in a marriage, the habits they develop, affect their ability to adjust to postdivorce life. Second, although on the average there are certain common patterns of changes in the marital relationship over time, some ways of interacting and kinds of marriages carry a higher divorce risk than others. For most couples in the first four years of marriage, as romantic love fades, marital satisfaction declines, then levels out, and then declines again in the seventh and eighth years as the seven-year itch arises. It never fully recovers again until middle age, when for many couples there is a surge in marital happiness as the children leave. However, within this general cycle of marital satisfaction and discontent, some marriages are more likely to survive and some to break up.

Married couples build an emotional marital bank account. Couples who make more withdrawals than deposits are at greater risk for divorce. With every exchange of mutual support and goodwill, a couple adds to their bank balance; with every display of contempt, hostile criticism, and disengagement, they draw down on the account. What looks like an impulsive decision to divorce is often the result of years of bank withdrawals in the form of accumulated resentment, dissatisfaction, and boredom. However, men and women vary in how they value and weigh different kinds of emotional deposits and withdrawals, and in how these contribute to marital happiness or breakup. We identified five types of marriages based on the way couples express emotions, solve problems, communicate, and take on family tasks. In some of these marriages, men and women play very different roles. The first three types carry a high risk of failure, while the last two often endure because they satisfy the needs of both partners.

One:
The Pursuer-Distancer Marriage

The Pursuer-Distancer marriage, the most common type, is also the most divorce-prone, primarily because it unites two conflicting but widespread male and female styles. In 80 percent of Pursuer-Distancer marriages, the Pursuer role fell to the woman. Brought up to value communication and intimacy, she was usually eager to confront and discuss problems and feelings. The man, brought up to value stoicism, emotional reticence, and control, preferred to avoid confrontation and argument and played the Distancer role.

"Let's talk about our problems," a Pursuer wife would say. "How can we resolve our differences if we don't discuss them?"

"What problems?" a Distancer husband would reply. "We don't have any problems."

If the wife persisted, the husband often would resort to a classic Distancer strategy—withdrawal. He hid behind a newspaper, turned on the television set, played with the dog, or looked gloomily into his beer. He stonewalled.

Dr. John Gottman of the University of Washington, a distinguished observer of marital relations, has suggested that the tendency of women to pursue and men to withdraw reflects a very basic physiological gender difference. In disagreements, men get aroused more quickly than women, as reflected by a sharp rise in blood pressure and heart rate. Men feel flooded, overwhelmed by these physiological changes, and afraid of losing control. Withdrawal may be a male safety valve for decreasing intense and distressing conflict-inspired arousal.

The Pursuer-Distancer combination can be thought of as a mismatch. If both husband and wife enjoy exploring their problems, or if both prefer avoiding confrontations, they are at considerably less risk for divorce than are Pursuer-Distancer combinations.

The principal reason Pursuer-Distancer marriages had the highest failure rate in the study is that, in the long run, the male-female tug-of-war over communication and intimacy eats up so much goodwill that the marital bank account goes into overdraft. At a certain point, the Distancer man tires of his wife's constant carping or gets angered by it. More commonly, the Pursuer wife wearies of the pursuit and becomes contemptuous or withdraws. Although Distancer men may want to be relieved of a wife's nagging, they are dismayed when it is replaced by contemptuous disengagement. Dr. Gottman has remarked on the frightened expression they get when they first begin to encounter their wives' cold contempt. Pursuing and distancing strategies are persistent and will be used again in a second marriage if the same kind of marital mismatch occurs.

Connie and Simon Russell had a classic Pursuer-Distancer marriage. Connie was a wildly energetic sensation-seeker, who would try anything—hang gliding, scuba diving, whitewater canoeing. She was working to get her pilot's license when she met Simon at the party of a mutual friend.

Later, Simon told me: "Connie was like a little tornado in the room. Moving around talking to different people and laughing this great bawdy laugh. Men were around her like bees around honey. I had moved onto the deck to have a cigarette when she sat down next to me. She seemed more subdued and more approachable then."

Though she was twenty years younger, Connie had a more complicated romantic history than Simon. When they met, she already had had two cohabiting relationships and a series of other short affairs, while Simon had resigned himself—not altogether reluctantly—to permanent bachelorhood. What others might find a bit stodgy in Simon, Connie now found attractive: his steadiness, his self-deprecating sense of humor, his lucrative position as a partner in an accounting firm. Simon seemed like an island in the turbulent seas of single life.

However, Connie began to grow unhappy within months of the marriage, and her unhappiness intensified as the years passed. Although she tried to play the role of supportive wife and mother to their children, Michael and Celia, who were born in the first three years of the marriage, Connie began to feel she was living in a prison and outside the walls there was an exciting world she wanted to rejoin.

As Simon started to revert to his solitary ways—reading, listening to classical music, studying the chess column, hybridizing orchids in his greenhouse and watching interminable nature programs on TV, Connie frantically searched for ways to establish common ground. She really wanted to make the marriage work. She read about orchids, tried to learn how to play chess, suggested things they might do to make their life more interesting, and prodded Simon to talk about their problems.

However, since Simon had never been happier, he not only dismissed Connie's complaints, he couldn't understand them. What was all the fuss about? He loved Connie, didn't he? And he loved Michael and Celia even more. With them Simon found himself experiencing a level of emotion he had not thought he was capable of.

Connie's decision to leave the marriage came in the middle of one of Simon's nature programs. "The two of us were watching a pair of cockroaches mating," Connie said. "I thought, I've watched lions mating, elephants mating, jackals mating, snakes mating, but cockroaches mating is too damned much. Am I going to spend the rest of my life watching animals screwing? The next morning I cleaned out our bank account, packed up the kids, wrote a note, and left while Simon was at work."

Two:
The Disengaged Marriage

The high failure rate of Disengaged marriages—second only to Pursuer-Distancer marriages—had less to do with gender or any other kind of differences than with similarities. Disengaged marriages usually unite two relatively self-sufficient individuals who fear or don't need intimacy to achieve a sense of well-being. Some Disengaged marriages are marriages of convenience; the couple doesn't want intimacy or companionship, but they do want children or the security, status, and services a marriage can provide. Others are based on a romantic or sexual attraction, but once the attraction fades, there is little to hold the couple together. Disengaged husbands and wives lack the mutual interests, shared values, and common family backgrounds that are building blocks of an enduring and mutually satisfying marriage.

The Pennybakers grew into a Disengaged couple. James and Liddy, like many other study couples, came from different worlds; but unlike couples who build successful marriages, the Pennybakers never developed a group of mutual interests to bridge their differences. Liddy complained about James's long work hours and unwillingness to make time for the family, James about Liddy's disinterest in everything but the children and her church work.

The principal reasons why Disengaged marriages suffered the second highest divorce rate are, first, a Disengaged husband and wife often do not need each other for the lives they are leading. They could lead them just as well single. The other weakness of a Disengaged marriage is a lack of satisfaction. The marital bank account does not contain much mutual affection and support. Most Disengaged couples manage to muddle along for awhile; but in their late thirties or early forties, one of them begins to wonder: Is this as good as it gets? Disengaged marriages usually end with a whimper rather than a bang; the man and woman just drift apart.

Some Disengaged men and women can find happiness in a new marriage, if they discover a partner who shares their interests and values. Others, who have serious personality problems or a need for distance, are likely to carry over their disengagement into a new marriage or to avoid marriage entirely. The men and women in the latter group sometimes become Competent Loners.

Three:
The Operatic Marriage

I was first introduced to the Operatic marriage by the parents of my best childhood friend, Isabella Amato. One afternoon, Isabella and I were sitting in her living room doing homework when shouting erupted in the kitchen.

Isabella rolled her eyes and explained that her parents were having a fight about the new kitchen cabinets her father had spent the last two months building.

"Mom hates the knobs Dad put on them," Isabella explained. "She thinks they're chintzy-looking."

Suddenly, there was more shouting. The two of us leaped off the couch and dashed into the kitchen. When we arrived, Carlo Amato was searching frantically through a counter drawer next to the sink. His wife, Maria, was standing beside him, red-faced with rage.

"I hate those knobs," she screamed, pointing to a row of shiny pine cabinets above the sink. "They're ugly, Carlo. Ugly. Ugly!"

"I'll show you ugly!" Mr. Amato grabbed a hammer from the drawer and began smashing the shiny new cabinet doors. When he finished, he turned to his wife and smiled fiercely. "See, Maria! Ugly!"

That night I told my parents I was sure that the Amatos were going to get a divorce. But two weeks later I changed my mind. Coming home from school one afternoon, Isabella and I caught Carlo and Maria kissing passionately in front of the freshly repaired kitchen cabinets, which I noticed also had a new set of knobs.

While there are gender differences in Operatic marriages, a commonality overshadows them. Sensation-seeking Operatic men and women are emotionally volatile. A harmonious, placid environment bores Operatics, who take everything to extremes, including fighting and making love. For Operatics, quarreling often is a trigger for sex. Indeed, passionate lovemaking follows furious fighting so routinely that the couple begins to lose the ability to distinguish between arousal produced by sex and arousal produced by anger; but their sex life is great. Operatics had the highest level of sexual satisfaction in our studies.

At first the fighting-sex cycle is almost a game, but a danger lies in wait for these couples. Angry people often say hurtful, sometimes unforgivable things; moreover, anger can easily erupt into violence. Operatic marriages, which had the third highest divorce rate in the study, usually ended when one partner, generally the man, decided that the sex was no longer exciting enough to compensate for the constant conflict. But clean breaks were fairly uncommon. Often Operatics would reconcile, break up, reconcile, and break up again. Lingering attachments were common, and new, less tumultuous relationships often seemed bland and dull.

Four:
The Cohesive/Individuated Marriage

Today, when professionals talk about the "good marriage," they usually mean a Cohesive/Individuated marriage, which has been the cultural ideal for a generation now because it embodies so many baby boomer values. This marriage could almost be described as an expression of one very primary boomer value, gender equity.

Although characterized by an almost old-fashioned sense of intimacy, the Cohesive marriage is often very good at accommodating gender differences. The couples share responsibilities in the home and grant each other a great deal of autonomy within the larger marital "we." Despite often engrossing careers and some different friends and interests, however, the happiest times for Cohesive couples are times spent together. The marriage functions like a refuge the husband and wife return to at the end of the day for renewal, support, affection, and companionship.

Sturdily built, Cohesive marriages had the second lowest divorce rate in the study. But on occasion, the delicate balance between autonomy and togetherness—the twin foundations of Cohesive marriage—collapses. Usually, this happens because one partner begins to put more emphasis on "me" than "we," and the resulting imbalance leads to unhappiness and divorce.

Women from Cohesive marriages often do well after divorce, in no small part because a Cohesive marriage fosters qualities like autonomy, individuality, achievement, and self-expression, which can promote success in postdivorce life. Women from this category were overrepresented in the Enhanced group.

Five:
The Traditional Marriage

The norm thirty years ago, the Traditional marriage has even more marked gender differences than the Pursuer-Distancer marriage, but that does not mean it no longer works. The Traditional marriage, which had the lowest divorce rate in our studies, still works very well if a couple shares a traditional interpretation of gender roles. The old-fashioned male breadwinner/female homemaker roles have to be a source of satisfaction to both partners, and each partner must perform his or her role competently.

The Achilles heel of Traditional marriage is change. When one or the other partner begins to behave untraditionally, trouble follows. The experience of a wife in a married comparison group provides a case in point. When her children began school full time, the woman decided to take interior design courses at a local community college. Maybe with an associate degree in design, she could get a part-time job at a department store or decorating firm.

At first her husband liked the idea. "You need to get out of the house," he told her. But by the end of the first semester, he was complaining about her never being around when he needed her.

"I might have been able to talk Hank into letting me stay in school," the woman told me later. "But I couldn't talk him into making dinner for the kids three nights a week."

When attitudes and values change over the course of a successful Traditional marriage, the change usually is in the direction of the husband's values. If change occurs in the opposite direction, when a woman begins to move away from her husband's social and political values or his ideas on such things as women working, child rearing, or the authority of men, the most frequent result is an unhappy, dissatisfied husband.

Traditionalists are reluctant to divorce; they will put up with many irritations in order to maintain the integrity of the family. When divorce does occur, often each member seeks out another Traditional relationship. However, divorce provided a number of women from Traditional marriages with a first opportunity to exercise autonomy and to discover special competencies and talents—and many seized that opportunity with relish. At the end of the VLS, there was a substantial number of women from Traditional marriages among the Enhanced.

Men and Women Divorcing

All marriages have good and bad periods and all marriages encounter stress and have problems to solve. Generally, satisfying marriages weather the down periods well, but unsatisfying marriages often do not; they can be destroyed by even a minor stress. It is not a one-time event, such as an affair, quarrel, job loss, episode of physical violence, or TV program of insects mating that generally leads to divorce. Snap decisions like Connie Russell's decision to leave Simon are rarely as snap as they appear.

Even conflict within a marriage is not a good predictor of divorce. For many couples, arguing may be a way of life. The most intense conflict rarely appears immediately before a separation. For many couples, the fighting is long over and a period of distancing and sadness occurs as affection, respect, and the marriage unravel. As in Liddy Pennybaker's case, the emotional divorce often long precedes the legal divorce.

Divorce is based on cumulative grievances. Men and women not only marry for different reasons but also give up on a marriage for different reasons. A few of the most common follow.

Relationship Problems

Although some of their complaints were similar, men and women often weighed marital problems differently. For example, what half of women described as big problems—lack of communication and affection—were seldom emphasized by men. Different definitions of intimacy contributed to this common gender gap. When women ask for affection, they want an "I love you," a tender embrace or kiss, a response to a feeling, or a compliment on their appearance or activities.

Men define affection differently, as one of our marital exchanges illustrates.

Wife (querulous):	"You know, I'm having a terrible time in my new job. When I come home, all I want is a hug or a cuddle to show you love me, to help me get through."
Husband (casual):	"But you know I love you."
Wife (imploring):	"How do I know you love me?"
Husband (befuddled):	"Well, I come home every night after work, don't I?"
Wife (frustrated):	"Great! Just about two hundred million men in the country do that!"

Husband (desperate):   "Well, I washed your car. Why would I wash your car if I didn't love you?"

Women focus on tenderness, men on providing or on just being there and being married as signs of love. According to some women, the only feeling in their husband's emotional vocabulary was anger. Women, however, suffer no such limitations. Like the Inuit who has an inexhaustible vocabulary to describe snow, the modern woman has an inexhaustible vocabulary to describe her emotional states. This facility, too, can create problems.

"My wife's never met an emotion she didn't like," said one frustrated man. "But try to get an actual fact out of her! I can be arguing with her for ten minutes and still not know why she's upset. I'll know how she feels about the thing that's upsetting her, I'll know how it makes her mother feel about it and her friends and anyone else she can think of. But I won't know what the thing itself is."

About a third of the women in our studies also reported a lack of shared interests and an unfair division of domestic labor as major sources of marital dissatisfaction. The birth of a child often aggravated resentment of inequality in household tasks, particularly if the woman worked and had to assume the main responsibility for the "second shift" of child care and housework.

A quarter of our wives also cited that alcoholism, physical abuse, or extramarital sex contributed to the divorce. But serious as these problems were, surprisingly, they were not always sufficient to end a marriage. If a wife felt loved, she often stayed. However, most women did draw the line at an emotional commitment by their husband to another woman that they perceived as a threat to their own or their children's security. They would forgive an occasional one-night stand or drunken encounter but not a serious relationship.

Among men, spousal faultfinding, nagging, and whining often contributed to marital disillusionment. "There's no silver lining my ex couldn't find a cloud in," complained one recently divorced man. "Becky is the Princess of Darkness. She completely ruined the new house for me, wouldn't even give me a half minute to enjoy my little triumph—buying a three-hundred-thousand-dollar house. On our first night in the house when we were having a celebratory drink, Becky started. She couldn't stand the colors in the upstairs bathroom. Why hadn't I noticed the boiler needed to be replaced? When would we be able to afford a pool? Should we call the Environmental Protection Agency to see if the stream out back meant we were living on a wetland?"

Many men also blamed their marital disillusionment on the wife's immaturity or irresponsibility. And some men, like women, complained about spousal alcoholism and infidelity. However, sexual betrayal often produced a violent and unforgiving response in men. Even years later, if a once unfaithful wife became pregnant, often she would find herself challenged about the paternity of the child.

Income

Money is a frequent source of conflict in marital breakups. About a third of the men and women in my work listed financial problems as a factor in the decision to divorce; but again, we heard different stories from men and women.

Many wives grew disillusioned when a man failed to improve the family's economic situation. Their husband's inability to hold or find a job or his moping around the house and getting underfoot when he was unemployed were often factors in a woman's decision to divorce. Women worried about the economic impact of paternal unemployment on the children. Unemployed or low-paid men, who felt inadequate to begin with, often complained that spousal nagging and lack of sympathy made them feel even more incompetent.

"God knows, I tried to support us," said one man, "but without a high school degree, the best I could do was a nightwatchman's job. For a couple of years, I worked days at a fast food restaurant, too. But even with two jobs, I couldn't keep us afloat; we got evicted from two apartments. After the first eviction, my wife said, 'You're a loser, Bob.' After the second, I think my kids started thinking of me that way, too."

Unemployment, never easy on a marriage, had a particularly negative effect in homes where the woman worked. Typically, if male unemployment persisted, the working wife would gradually assume control over decisions about finances and the day-to-day routines of married life. When an unemployed husband and a working wife were discussing a marital problem, the woman usually dominated. She would talk more than her husband, advance more suggestions about solving family issues and problems, and put forward her suggestions more forcefully.

As power shifted, usually marital unhappiness rose—and not just among men; many working wives also grew increasingly discontented.

In time, financial problems frequently also became sexual problems. In the first stages of unemployment, men often would use sex as a kind of morale builder. "Look, I know how this sounds, but at least sex gives me a way to satisfy my wife, to show her I'm still a man," said one husband, who like many other recently unemployed men became more sexually aggressive. However, with the passage of time, sexual advances became a high-risk strategy for a man with a fragile ego. In most cases, excuses like "I have a headache" or "I'm too tired" from an increasingly angry, disinterested, preoccupied, or tired working wife, eventually brought the advances to an end. But not always.

Physical violence was twice as high in families with an unemployed husband and working wife than in families in which both partners or only the husband was employed. And while the violence was sometimes associated with sexual rebuffs, often it was triggered by more general feelings of loss of status and self-esteem. Feeling insecure and angry, the man would lash out at his wife and sometimes even his children at the slightest hint of disrespect.

After one particularly discouraging job interview, Harry Jordan returned home to find Ellie and the children already eating and all the chairs around the kitchen table occupied. The family was laughing, engrossed in eldest son Francis's funny description of the romance between the Jordans' spaniel and the very large St. Bernard who lived next door.

"What am I supposed to do?" an agitated Harry asked. "Eat dinner on the floor?"

"There are chairs in the dining room, Dad," Francis said.

"Good," Harry said, pushing the boy out of his chair. "Get one for yourself."

"You're a fool, Harry," Ellie shouted, as she pulled Francis from the floor. "You're a poor excuse for a man."

Harry picked up the chair, threw it at her, then stormed out to the crying and screams of his younger children.

Sexual Problems

Sexual difficulties also contributed to divorce. But among men, where sexual and marital satisfaction often went hand in hand, the most common sexual complaint was about frequency; there wasn't enough sex in the marriage. However, when women complained about sex, the complaint was usually about quality; the sex wasn't very good. It lacked tenderness and romance or it was perfunctory. Among women, the correlation between sex and marital satisfaction was lower than for men, especially after the birth of a child. Sex just wasn't as central to their feelings about the relationship. One woman said, "I do a lot of pretending. But you know, sex is not really that important. Tim is so sweet and loving. I've never even thought of looking at another man."

Race, like gender, also affects attitudes to marital sex. Among African-American husbands, for example, wifely support, low conflict, and a companionate relationship correlate more strongly with marital happiness and stability than sexual satisfaction.

Violence

Physical violence—either directed at themselves or at their children—contributed to some wives' decision to divorce. At least one incident of physical violence occurred in a third of our marriages that ended in divorce. The comparable figure for the non-divorced group was 15 percent, less than half.

The violence was not limited to men. Predivorce, women were almost as violent; they threw objects, scratched, hit, and kicked. But, of course, a 115- or 120-pound woman's blows are not as destructive as a 170- or 200-pound male's. Men used some of the same techniques as women, but angry men were more likely to punch, twist limbs, slam a spouse against a wall, or throw her across a room.

According to recent national surveys, in the separation period and in the months immediately after a divorce, spousal homicide rates jump by a factor of eight. Fortunately, as far as we know, no marital homicides occurred in our studies.

One reliable predictor of male violence is being walked out on; men who are left are more dangerous than men who leave. Another predictor is a history of verbal abuse. Men who are able to confine their aggressiveness to words during the marriage sometimes lose that ability afterward. However, the pressures of divorce can make even a man with no history of abuse suddenly snap and lash out.

Janet Coleman learned the hard way that violence can become a way of life. Richard, Janet's husband, was very affectionate, but also very jealous. During their courtship, Richard had sometimes raged at Janet for imaginary transgressions, which in his highly suspicious mind included having lunch with a platonic male friend, talking or dancing with other men at a party, or being driven home by a male coworker.

Three months into the marriage, Richard began to urge Janet to quit her job and become a full-time wife. "I want you to stay home," Richard said when Janet told him that she was pregnant. "I want you to take it easy. I'm afraid you might stress yourself. I love you so much, Jan; I don't want to risk anything bad happening to you."

The next time Richard told Janet he loved her was after he punched her in the Colemans' driveway. Janet was getting out of the car after a party when Richard accused her (falsely) of flirting with another guest and hit her hard on both sides of the face. The second punch split Janet's lip; bleeding profusely, she fled into the house and locked herself in the bedroom.

Janet was appalled by Richard's violence, but the next morning he was tearfully apologetic again, uttering the persistent refrain, "It's because I love you so much." When he came home from work, he brought her a bottle of her favorite wine and long-stemmed roses, and

Janet forgave him. The first in a long cycle of violence, apology, and forgiveness.

Despite the tearful apologies and the presents, Richard's violence became more frequent and increasingly brutal. He hit Janet when he didn't like a meal or when he found a button missing on his shirt. He hit her when she wanted to visit her mother or when she wanted to go out with friends. He hit her when they were alone and when their two children, David and Leah, were there. David and Leah were terrified, and the atmosphere in the house now became especially tense on evenings when Richard was late for dinner. Janet and the children knew the delay meant he had stopped off for a few drinks, and they also knew that Richard with a few drinks in him was even more prone to dangerous eruptions.

"The crazy thing is that after awhile the hitting began to seem almost normal," Janet said the day she showed me an old photo of herself. "Do you believe I allowed myself to sink to this state?" The woman in the picture looked fifteen years older and had the marbled, puffy face of a veteran prizefighter. "Richard was a classic abuser," Janet said, as she returned the photo to her billfold. "He isolated me; first from my friends, then my family. After awhile, I had no one to turn to."

The beginning of the end of the Colemans' five-year marriage occurred in a supermarket parking lot on a rainy March morning. Janet was walking toward her car when she ran into a former boss, Marcia Link, who was now living in northern Virginia. Marcia started to make a joke about Janet's sunglasses but stopped when she noticed a bruise on Janet's cheek. "Are you all right?" she asked.

Janet said she had an eye infection, but burst into tears. Over the next few months, Marcia made several efforts to persuade Janet to leave the marriage, but Janet refused. "I was sure if Richard came home and found me gone, he'd track me down and kill me," Janet said the day she showed me the photo. "And I was right, wasn't I?"

One evening, a few months after Janet moved into the new apartment Marcia had found her in Alexandria, she heard a knock on the door. It was alarming. Janet was alone—the kids were visiting Marcia's family—and it was after nine. The knock became louder and more insistent.

"Who is it?" Janet asked.

The muffled reply was hard to hear. Janet walked over to the window and looked out; there was a familiar black Chevrolet pickup parked on the street.

"Richard, go away, please."

There was a tremendous thudding on the door, which suddenly flew off its hinges.

"I'm going to call the police, Richard. *Go away!*" Janet was screaming now.

"I'm going to kill you, bitch!" Richard began to hit. Later that evening, a janitor found Janet lying on the floor, unconscious in a pool of blood.

Men and Women and the Decision to Divorce

Even the decision to divorce is affected by gender differences. Women usually initiate a divorce; and they approach the decision more deliberately and methodically than men. There is usually a long history of dissatisfaction and of thinking about leaving before a woman actually says she is going to leave. Maybe because they are less emotionally attuned, men seem to have a greater tolerance for bad marriages. Often in interviews, men would say, "I wasn't really happy. But I would have stuck it out if my wife had." Many men also were surprised by the request for a divorce. A quarter of men said that they had no idea their wife was thinking about leaving the marriage.

"I knew we had problems; I wasn't that clueless," said one man. "But Cindy and I had stopped fighting. We weren't talking much, either. But I figured that was progress. I mean, not talking is better than fighting all the time, isn't it?"

Like many other "left" men, this man remained unsure about why he had been left. "Cindy would say she was unhappy a lot. But I didn't know what 'unhappy' meant. I was unhappy, too; everyone's unhappy sometimes."

Children were the principal reason why men stayed in unsatisfying marriages. Many men said they were afraid of losing their children—

emotionally as well as physically—in a divorce. Women usually stayed for financial reasons; many said they hesitated about divorce because they didn't know how they would support themselves and their children. Women with sons also worried about losing a masculine role model for their boys and the difficulty of raising a male child alone. This fear proved well founded. Depression was higher in divorced women with sons, principally because boys are harder to raise alone. We found that these fears, plus perhaps a greater emotional investment in sons, led marriages with sons to be less likely to break up than those only with daughters—a finding confirmed by national surveys. When the end of the marriage comes, it often rapidly gains power after the first tentative suggestions for separation are made.

In the year before the bill from the Greenbrier, the Pennybakers had talked about their problems, but now their conversations took on a more practical tone—the size of Liddy's financial support, how to tell the children, when James would move out. James begged Liddy to relent, to consider a trial separation, but she refused. She had taken a long time to reach her decision and she was determined to stick by it.

People often remember odd incidental details about the end of a marriage. Liddy remembered that she almost broke her promise to herself not to be provocative when James walked into the kitchen wearing an irritatingly cheerful bow tie that morning. James remembered how much trouble he had packing; it was a task Liddy used to do for him.

James said, "I think we'll both be sorry," as he put a check on the kitchen table. His eyes filled with tears.

Liddy turned away. "Please go."

James stood in the rain by his car for one last look at his home where the people he cared for the most would be, but he no longer belonged.

Points to Remember

- Romantic love is a temporary glue. Marriages that last are marriages built on a fund of respect, liking, support, and mutual interests.

- As the years pass, the husband and wife come to see themselves less as man and woman, and more and more as partners and co-owners of a deeply cherished joint enterprise—one made up of family, children, friends, a shared life.
- A mutually supportive marital relationship builds an affective bank account of attachment and goodwill that helps couples weather difficult times in a marriage.
- A shared marital ideology is an important element in the success of a marriage. Even low-risk marriages like the Cohesive and Traditional marriages become divorce-prone when one partner adopts a new ideology.
- No one type of marriage is all good or all bad. However, Pursuer-Distancer, Disengaged, and Operatic marriages carry a high risk of failure, whereas Cohesive/Individuated and Traditional marriages are more stable.
- Money also is a frequent source of rancor in marital breakups.
- Men and women respond differently in all intimate relations and in divorce. Women want affection and open communication in marriage. Men want support, sexual satisfaction, and lack of conflict and criticism.
- When a man is unable to provide adequate financial support to his family, it erodes his status and power in the family, and contributes to spouse and child abuse and marital instability.
- Women are more likely to be the ones who leave a marriage and to have planned longer for the separation.
- The breakdown of marriage is usually associated with an accumulation of dissatisfaction and grievances over time rather than a single recent stressor.
- Postdivorce life begins within the marriage. This point has several meanings. One is that the marital relationship often spills over into the divorce. Stormy Operatic marriages often become stormy Operatic divorces, while loosely connected Disengaged couples often slip quietly away from one another.

3

Leaving and Letting Go:
Changes and New Chances
in the First Two Years After Divorce

"*I* remember reading a story that began, 'When I was six years old, I thought my father was nine feet tall.' That's how I felt about Daddy. On Sunday mornings sitting in church listening to him preach, I used to think I was hearing the voice of God. I was completely smitten by him. I still am."

Liddy Pennybaker said her childhood feelings about her mother were more ambivalent. "Our relationship wasn't terrible," she said at the one-year postdivorce interview, "but we weren't particularly close either. I resented Mother's sternness and pickiness and conventionality, and on some level, I suppose she resented my relationship with Daddy. I could never understand how a man as exciting as Daddy could marry someone as ordinary as Mother."

Liddy said that after her father died, she made an effort to patch up things with her mother. "When Mother moved to Richmond to live, I visited once a week; but we always ended up squabbling, so once a week became every two or three weeks, then once a month. Mother was resentful about it; she said I was depriving her of her grandchildren. Well, lucky her. Now she's going to get as much of her grandchildren as she wants."

Liddy was exaggerating, but only a bit. Between her job as a sales-clerk at a fashionable woman's store in Richmond and James's child support, she was barely able to make ends meet. Liddy had devised a plan to lift herself and the children out of poverty: she would return to school for an MBA. But to do that she would need help from her mother.

"Mom's the Catch-22 in my plan," Liddy said. "I can't do what I need to do without her help. But, oh"—she stopped and shook her head—"Daddy's little girl comes running home with her tail between her legs. Oh, this is the most fun Mother's had in years."

During the first two years after a divorce, a time commonly called the "crisis period," change—often dramatic change—becomes a way of life. Men, women, and children change roles, residences, economic classes, sexual habits, clothing, hairstyles, personal behavior, and careers.

Some of the changes are troubling, as when an esteemed geography professor suddenly begins ordering birds from the trees, or a young banker eavesdrops on his former wife and her lover. Other changes can be touching and humorous. A middle-aged surgeon suddenly discovers an unexpected taste for gold chains, motorcycles, and a ponytail. Still other changes are painful, as when, to build a better life for herself and her children, a young mother swallows her pride and moves in with her mother.

Many of these transformations are rooted in a phenomenon I call "the window of change." In the early postdivorce years, the stable self, the self which regulates behavior, breaks down, because its foundations—stable social roles (wife, mother, husband, father) and stable relationships (parent-child, husband-wife, friendships)—break down.

The dark side of the breakdown is a loss of self-control. With the policeman off duty, people begin to do strange, out-of-character things—or what are called "not-me behaviors"—like talking to birds. The bright side of the breakdown is an unusual openness toward change. With no internal mechanism to judge, scold, point fingers, or embarrass, people become more willing to embrace the new, to try things that, in other circumstances, they wouldn't dream of trying.

The postdivorce pathways I described in the first chapter often begin in the window of change, which usually is most wide open in the first few years after divorce. Although the window is never entirely closed, if no steps toward positive change are taken in the early years, they are less likely to be made later. And sometimes the newly divorced are more preoccupied with immediate stresses than with long-term, big-picture thinking. Just getting to tomorrow is hard enough.

Nonetheless, every time a divorced person makes a choice—about how to earn a living, about where to live and who to live with, about what kind of day care center or school to send her child to, about when to start dating and who to sleep with and how often to sleep with them—she is making a choice about the window of change and whether or not to embrace it. And as these choices mount, they begin to fold into one another until they form a pattern, a pathway. Without realizing it, the individual is on the road to becoming Defeated or Enhanced or Good Enough.

A happy second marriage or stepfamily can alter a path later. But switching paths midway through postnuclear family life is more difficult; once on a particular path, the steps tend to have a certain progression. One thing leads to the next—sometimes in surprising ways. For instance, our data show that a postdivorce choice about education can influence where a woman will build her new social life, which in turn can influence who she marries next time.

Challenges of the Early Postdivorce Period

In the public lectures I give on family transitions, I often describe the challenges of the early postdivorce period as the raw material of personal change. The reason: How these stresses are managed helps to determine whether a person's postdivorce future is better and happier, the same, or worse than her predivorce past.

Some of the most significant stresses faced after a divorce involve practical problems of living, some involve coping with emotional and personal change, and some involve changes in old relationships and building satisfying new relationships.

Domestic Chaos

Divorce destroys the reassuring rhythms and structures of family life, especially those that give a child's life order and predictability. When one adult is suddenly doing the work of two, household disorganization and overload often ensue. Pickup meals, irregular dining hours, erratic bed-, play-, and reading times all increase during the first year after a divorce. The children of newly divorced mothers are also more likely to be late for school and less likely to have help with homework.

"I really want to do more with the kids," said one recently divorced mother, "but there's so much cleaning and picking up to do when I come home from work. I feel like I'm giving one hundred and fifty percent all the time, and if anything goes wrong—if one of the kids gets sick, the car breaks down, or school closes for a snow day—I have nothing to fall back on."

The 14 percent of men in our study who had custody of their children also felt overwhelmed by family demands. But custodial fathers often had buffers unavailable to custodial mothers, including money to hire domestic help and, probably even more important, a more forgiving view of the parental role. In households headed by the father, youngsters were more likely to be required to keep their room tidy, to help out with the dinner dishes and cooking or yardwork, because men were less vulnerable to paroxysms of guilt if they didn't do it all themselves.

Newly divorced men who lived alone led the most chaotic lives. They rarely prepared a meal, got enough sleep, or went to bed at a regular time. They also had more difficulty with routine tasks like shopping, laundry, cleaning, and cooking. "You shop, you clean, you bring your clothes to the cleaners. In theory, single life sounds simple," said one recently divorced man. "But in practice, it's hard; I don't know why, but it is."

One reason why newly divorced men often feel this way is a lack of domestic skills. Even today, many men rely on women—mothers, partners, or wives—to deal with the details of domestic life. Additionally, men often feel too scattered and restless to stay in a new apartment long enough to clean it or cook a meal. "I can't sit still," said another man. "Even when I'm exhausted, I go out. For awhile, it drove me crazy. It seemed nutty, running out to a bar or a party when I had barely recovered from last night's hangover. But then I realized what was going on. Before the divorce, I could be alone because I was never really alone. Even when Judy and the kids were out, we were somehow still together. Now, when I'm alone in that apartment, I'm alone-alone. I was thinking the other day, I'm thirty-three, and this is the first time in my life I've experienced real loneliness."

However, newly divorced males do have two advantages in dealing with domestic chaos. One is girlfriends, who unlike boyfriends, are often eager to help with household tasks or child care. The other is what we called "casserole ladies." These are the female neighbors, friends, or relatives who appeared at the door, hot dinner in hand, on nights when the man's children were over or he looked particularly beleaguered. Alas, in thirty years of divorce research, I did not encounter a single example of a "casserole man."

Among our divorced men, there was a small group—about 15 percent—who, surprisingly, proved an exception to the general rule about male domestic incompetence. Skilled at housekeeping, at cooking, at grocery shopping, members of this group shared three relatively uncommon characteristics. They liked cooking, shopping, and decorating; they had a predivorce history of domestic involvement, including helping with child care; and they enjoyed exercising sole control over their lives.

One member of this group, Simon Russell, had already reassembled his neat, orderly bachelor life at the two-month interview. But Simon was having less success reassembling his emotional life. "The way Connie ended it was terrible, ugly," Simon said at the interview. "To just walk out with no explanation but a three-line note and to empty out the bank account.

"That's what I get for thinking with my libido."

Simon was being unfair to himself. If anything had clouded his judgment, it was his heart, not his libido; Simon's feeling for the much younger Connie had a protective element. Seeing a young woman who seemed vulnerable and in trouble, he had reached out to help her; but because the young woman was also very pretty and very lively, the unexpected happened, and stolid forty-year-old Simon fell in love. Eventually, the love would pass, but not the concern; it endured long after the divorce.

Economic Hardship

Running two households costs more then running one, so financial suffering afflicts both sexes after divorce. But there is also no denying that women usually suffer more than men because their income declines more sharply. At one year after divorce, VLS single mothers and children were living on a little less than half the income of non-divorced families— $16,000 annually as opposed to $33,000 (in 1970s dollars). For the one fifth of study women who had to apply for public assistance like Janet Coleman, divorce produced not merely economic hardship but outright destitution.

After beating her unconscious, Janet's former husband, Richard, disappeared forever. Two months later, with no child support and no job, Janet was evicted from her apartment.

"The landlord made it pretty clear we could work something out if I'd sleep with him," Janet said at the one-year postdivorce interview. "But I could never be that desperate."

In many stories of divorce, at what seems a hopeless moment, a pivotal figure—a relative, a friend, a colleague, a lover—materializes to offer hope. In Janet's case, that figure was Beth Halligan, a social worker at the County Welfare Office. "I was at the end of the end of my rope the day I met Beth," Janet said. "She was a life saver. She got us food stamps and found me a new apartment and got the kids into a Head Start program, so I could look for a job."

In Janet's case, as in many other cases, lack of child support contributed to her fall into poverty. A quarter of VLS men provided no support whatsoever; 50 percent inconsistent support. Only a quarter of the study men met their financial obligations regularly and in the amount ordered by the court. Like Richard Coleman, some men just disappeared; others tried to be responsible but lacked the financial resources to support two households. Remarriage or making paternal visits difficult also could cause a man to stop or reduce his child support.

Because it combines two very high-voltage issues—money and children—child support can become an issue even when it is paid in full and on time. Many women who received regular payments complained that the support they received was not large enough to raise a family on. Men, particularly men who rarely saw or had little control over their children's lives, had the opposite complaint: why should they have to pay for a family they didn't have any more? Former wives who made no effort to become economically self-sufficient were a target of male anger. Additionally, many men complained that the need to support two households on one check and child support obligations deprived them of a comfortable life and the ability to remarry.

Our economic data also helped to shed light on a long policy debate. Everyone agrees that emotional, psychological, and social problems are more common in single-parent families. But why? Many social scientists and policy advocates argue that the problems are solely economic: single-parent families are usually poorer. Remove the economic stresses and the children in these families will begin to look like children in non-divorced families.

But in our studies, this didn't prove to be the case. Single-parent families who had economic parity with non-divorced families still had a higher rate of emotional and psychological problems. Developmental disorders also were more common among children in stepfamilies which had incomes close to those of non-divorced families.

Unquestionably, working two jobs, living in a poor neighborhood with high crime rates, inadequate schools—all the common byproducts of poverty—do greatly stress a parent and a child. But my findings suggest that there are other reasons why step- and single-parent families are more problem-prone. One is the lack of a supportive partner; raising a child is easier with two parents. Another is the often complicated family dynamics in step- and single-parent families.

Emotional Changes

Emotionally, the first postdivorce year is usually difficult. The newly divorced are depressed, anxious, angry, and frequently emotionally unstable as well. Many people find themselves alternating between peaks of ebullience when they think of the new freedom and opportunities that confront them and depression when they think how hard it will be to build a new and better life. Said one divorced woman, "I can do what I want and be what I want. But what do I want to do and who do I want to be?" Dramatic mood swings seemed to be keyed to an internal clock. Many recently divorced men and women reported feeling euphoric in the morning when the day was young, and despairing in the evening when, in another life, they would be home with their families.

The newly divorced also tended to have an acute sense of failure. "I failed my kids," "I failed my ex," "I failed myself," were complaints I heard frequently. People wondered what their failures, particularly their marital failures, meant. Were they incapable of building happy relationships? Did they lack the ability to succeed in any marriage? For some men, failure fed on failure. Sexual dysfunction rates were about 10 percent higher in divorced men.

During the first year after divorce, complaints about a new social awkwardness and a decline in the ability to function in day-to-day life became common. Worries about job performance occurred among some men. However, for others, work became a kind of refuge, a sanctuary where they could hide from themselves and from their pain.

Loneliness, depression, and anger were the most common first-year emotions. Women were buffered somewhat by children, relatives, and familiar surroundings, since initially at least many women remained in the family home. But dislocation, loneliness, and a sense of loss made the early divorce months very wintry for men. Nothing upset a man more than coming home to an empty apartment at the end of the day.

The man who said he felt "alone-alone" told me that during the first six months in his new apartment, he stayed home a total of four evenings, and two of those four evenings he only stayed home because he had the flu and was too sick to go out.

In the early period, "left" spouses were the most unhappy and resentful, but by the end of the second year, there were few differences between those left and "leavers." However, for most people, the end of the first year, not the second year, was the most painful period of the divorce cycle. After the initial euphoria of being free and hopes for greater happiness, doubts about the past and concerns about the future increased over the first year. But in the second year there was an upsurge in emotional well-being as people began to adapt to their new life situation.

Social Relationships

Social networks alter rapidly after divorce. Old married friends often find it difficult to sustain independent friendships with both sides of a divided couple. The shared interests with married couples are lost as the newly divorced grapple with the challenges and opportunities of single life. One unexpected study finding was that when a married couple did sustain a friendship beyond divorce, usually it was with the man. The reason?

To make visitation easier, sometimes a divorced man would seek out couples with same-aged children. And not uncommonly, the people the man recruited were old friends with children. While the children played, the adults would socialize. Men also enjoyed another advantage vis-à-vis old friends. Single men were viewed as a dinner party asset; but often old married female friends viewed a divorced woman warily. "Dotty should be worrying about Paul, not me," said one recently divorced woman who, like many others, felt that if there was a "trust" problem, it stemmed from husbands who hit on their wives' divorced friends after a few drinks. Divorced women seemed to be viewed as fair game by married men.

Stay-at-home mothers, often acutely lonely after a divorce, complained about feeling "imprisoned" and "walled in." One woman said, "Do you know what it's like to be trapped in a child's world where nothing moves over three feet tall? I feel like I'm developing a special relationship with Mister Rogers. He's the only man I see anymore."

Working mothers often had more worries. They had to cope with child care and with juggling job and domestic chores. But because they also had two things stay-at-home mothers often didn't have, adult company and self-esteem, psychologically they usually did better. Post-divorce working women felt considerably less depressed and isolated than stay-at-home mothers.

If divorced men enjoyed an advantage in dinner party invitations, divorced women enjoyed an advantage in finding and using sources of support. Women would talk about their problems with anyone, but during the first year, they leaned especially hard on mothers and sisters and female friends. And while the newly divorced were often fatiguing to listen to, talk helped them. Many women said talk was a good antidote to first-year pain; they also reported that friends and relatives helped them to get a new perspective on the divorce.

"I spent the first six months blaming James for everything," Liddy Pennybaker said at the two-year interview. "Then, once when I was in the middle of a tirade, my cousin Catlin pulled me up short. 'James was everything you say,' she told me; 'selfish, underhanded, a heavy drinker, all of it. But, honestly, Lid, after the kids came along, you entered your own personal zone. You didn't have time for anyone anymore; not just James, but your mother and me. James probably got to feeling pretty lonely.' "

Men were more inclined to "tough it out" than to "talk it out," not least because they had lost the one person a man is usually comfortable disclosing to, his wife. Men rarely complained about feeling "trapped" as women did, but they often said they felt "rootless," "shut out," and at "loose ends."

Women, who frequently turned inward in the first year, became socially active again in the second, dating and attending parties and social events with new single friends. However, the needs of the children put a fairly low ceiling on female socializing. Even at two years after divorce, married women were going out more often.

Age also was important in the social life of women. Women who were in their late thirties or older at the time of divorce had fewer dating opportunities than younger women or middle-aged men. At the twenty-year follow-up, they were much less likely to have remarried.

Socially, men hit the ground running. Male social activity rose rapidly and dramatically, reaching a peak at the end of the first postdivorce year, the heyday of the Libertine. However, as the novelty of single life wore off, men often found themselves tired of feeling tired and of waking up in strange beds with women they barely knew.

"For me, the absolute nadir was one Sunday afternoon," said one of our divorced men. "I'd just come home from a Saturday night date and I was exhausted, hungover and depressed. I went into the bedroom to lie down, then I remembered, I have a date tonight! Oh Jesus, I thought, in four hours I'm going to have to do this all over again. When you're seventeen and jumping up and down with hormones, you dream about being a stud. But when you're thirty-eight, believe me, it's more fun to sit home with someone you care about and watch the Yankees."

During the second year, levels of male and female social activity became more similar as the men's declined and the women's increased.

Sexual and Intimate Relationships

Men and women, who had different sexual patterns in the first two postdivorce years, shared one commonality. Men—and even more, women—who used sex to achieve intimacy often ended up feeling even lonelier.

Like the man I just quoted, many divorced men were surprised to discover that all the cultural messages they had heard since boyhood about masculinity were wrong; being a playboy is work, and unless you have a Hugh Hefner–like tolerance for waking up in strange situations with strange women, frequently disappointing.

However, in contrast to men, whose tolerance for casual sex didn't wear thin until the second year, in women, casual sex frequently produced loneliness, unhappiness, and low self-esteem from the early months onward. When a man didn't call back after a one-night stand, a woman would often feel a combination of self-disgust and despair. Casual sexual encounters made many women feel out of control, unattractive and unloved, and most of all depressed.

"I've been sleeping with three or four men a month," Connie Russell said at the one-year postdivorce interview. "I don't know why I do it. I feel like hell afterward, but I do it anyway. Unless somebody loves me, I don't feel alive."

Connie also was using alcohol to salve her loneliness. She would get drunk at a bar, meet a man, and take him home. At the twenty-year interview, Celia Russell, Connie's daughter, said, "There probably weren't as many men sneaking out the kitchen door mornings as I remember there being. But there were an awful lot. Michael used to say, 'Pretty soon we're going to have enough uncles to start our own baseball team.' " Celia's other vivid memory of childhood was of putting herself and Michael to bed because Connie had passed out on the living-room sofa.

About a month before the two-year interviews began, Connie's life reached a new low point. One evening after work, she drove over to her sister Lola's to pick up some hand-me-down clothes for Michael. Lola was out—at a bridal shower, said her husband, Daniel, who invited Connie in for a drink. "I'm still not sure how it happened," Connie told me at the interview, "but one drink led to another, and at some point, Daniel put his hand on my breast. The next thing I remember, the two of us were on the floor naked and Lola was standing over us. What kind of a monster am I, fucking my own sister's husband? She had always looked after me like a mother. Even if she could ever forgive me, I can never forgive myself."

The next morning after Michael and Celia left for nursery school, Connie washed a bottleful of Valium pills down with a fifth of vodka. "When I didn't show up for the pickup, the school called Simon," Connie said. "He found me passed out in the bathroom when he brought Celia and Michael home."

The intimacy Connie and many other divorced men and women seek in sex has three components. The couple value each other's well-being as much as their own; they have a strong desire to be with one another; and they find each other a source of security and support in times of stress. When these three elements were present, I usually found a strong, positive correlation between happiness, high self-worth, and frequency of sexual intercourse; when they were absent, a strong correlation between unhappiness, feelings of worthlessness, and frequency of sex. Sex with an intimate partner is enhancing; sex with a stranger is often personally destructive.

Some people may see this association as a validation of conventional morality: unmarried sex is wrong; ergo, people who indulge in it rightly suffer—by feeling unhappy. But I think the correlations have much more to do with the human need to feel loved and valued. An intimate relationship is, as the sociologist Christopher Lasch once said of the family, "a haven in a heartless world." It provides an anchor and protection against adversity. And while sex often enriches intimacy, it is only a part of intimacy—and not even the most important part. Life without sex is bearable for most people. Life without a person who loves and values you rarely is.

Casual sex has a negative effect because an unintimate intimate act only underscores loneliness. It is as if the individual were underscoring her loneliness with a Magic Marker. For both sexes, the best single predictor of happiness and well-being two years after a divorce was a new intimate relationship. Often as I watched depressed and lonely adults turning to psychotherapy for help, I thought, If only you could meet someone who loved and appreciated you, that would be the best therapy you could have.

Relations Between Ex-Spouses

In the early period after a divorce, the relationship between former spouses is highly charged and filled with anger and ambivalence. And these emotions often make themselves felt in the legal and emotional problems that accompany the breakup.

The Legal Divorce

Outstanding legal issues such as money, parenting, and visitation rights are major complicating factors in many divorces. And, of course, wherever there's a legal issue, there's a lawyer. Lawyers often protect and defend and advise. But their training in the adversarial process can stir up latent anger and resentment, turning a "friendly" or even a relatively neutral divorce into an ugly, destructive one.

Although a great deal of energy and money are expended on legal agreements, couples seldom honor them. In a large California survey,

Eleanor Maccoby and Robert Mnookin of Stanford University found that only about one third of couples kept to their initial legal agreements about money, custody, and visitation. Based on my experience, most people seem to regard a divorce agreement as a work in progress and informally negotiate these issues as individual circumstances change. Whenever mothers become employed, work schedules change, one parent remarries or wants to move to another part of the country, or children grow older, the choice of which parent a child resides with, as well as visitation schedules and support, may alter.

On the advice of a divorced friend, James Pennybaker hired a lawyer, whom the friend described as a barracuda. The lawyer buried James's financial assets in his company, made Liddy sell the family home, and made sure that James's monthly child support payments were modest. However, a year after the divorce, James decided he wanted to see the children, Bethany and Adam, more often than the once a week decreed by the court.

Liddy told James's lawyer to tell him to "drop dead." A week later, James sued for a reduction in child support.

"How can he do that?" Liddy asked, when her lawyer called to tell her about the suit.

"You're working now, Liddy. You weren't when you signed the agreement. Sorry, Lid, if you fight the extension of visitation, James will probably win on support."

Liddy reluctantly yielded.

A few days later, Liddy got an unsigned postcard in the mail: " . . . And you don't mess around with Jim," was all it said.

"I didn't know whether to laugh or cry when I read that," Liddy said.

I told her I didn't understand.

Liddy smiled. "The line comes from an old Jim Croce song Jimmy and I used to listen to:

> *You don't pull on Superman's cloak.*
> *You don't spit into the wind.*
> *You don't pull the mask off the Ol' Lone Ranger*
> *And you don't mess around with Jim.*

Liddy began to laugh. "The whole thing is so typically James. Endearing and infuriating at the same time."

The Emotional Divorce

Liddy's ambivalence is typical of many of our couples at a year after divorce. She was angry at Jim and had no illusions about a possible reconciliation, but she still had a soft spot for his sense of humor and some tender memories of the good years they had had together. In many couples, although a residue of resentment and hostility lingers after divorce, so too does a residue of attachment. At the one-year mark, at least one partner in three quarters of our divorced couples was having second thoughts. Former husbands and wives were telling us, if not each other, that maybe they should have worked harder at the marriage, and that the alternatives no longer looked very good.

The two-month data helped to quantify this lingering affection and dependency. About 15 percent of our couples reported having sex at least once since the divorce; and three fourths of the women and two thirds of the men said that in an emergency, they would call their former spouse first. Astonishingly, over 15 percent of VLS men were still doing odd domestic jobs for their former wives and 8 percent served as occasional baby-sitters.

The amount of time the newly divorced spend fighting over trivial subjects also may be a measure of lingering affection. A man or woman may goad an ex-partner just to get a reaction. Anger is often seen as preferable to indifference in someone who has formerly loved you. At least it's an intense emotion.

There's also another subtext to first-year fights. The man and woman are trying to wrench free of each other's gravitational pull. And, in time, the fighting usually works. By two years after divorce, both attachment and conflict had declined. Among the 20 percent who were still fighting, many were using conflict to maintain contact with a spouse they still cared for, but not all. Some ex-partners fought because they still resented each other. Resentment tended to be more sustained in women and attachment in men, who often had unrealistic fantasies of reconciliation.

Two nights before his second marriage, a slightly drunk James Pennybaker called Liddy. "It's still not too late for us," he said.

"It's been too late for us for a long time, Jimmy," Liddy said.

Two days later, Liddy received a package in the mail. When she opened it, she found the gift she had given James at the time of their wedding, a leather-bound copy of W. B. Yeats's *Collected Poems*. "I think of it as James's going-away present," Liddy sighed. "I don't know why, but I suddenly feel bad about everything."

Unlike James's persistent attachment, for most of the divorced, old passions have cooled by two years after divorce. One woman described being startled to find her ex-husband seated at the next table in a restaurant. It was the first time she had seen him in eighteen months. "At first I thought, this is awkward. Then I realized there was none of that crazy longing left and even the anger had just leaked away. He was just another balding, portly, pleasant-looking stranger."

There is one situation, however, which frequently seems to spark intense feelings. When a former spouse remarried, divorced men and women often reexperienced the same sense of loss, betrayal, anger, and anxiety they had felt when they divorced. Interestingly, the feelings occurred even in spouses who had remarried first. Spite also was a common response to an ex-partner's remarriage. However, women were bigger grudge carriers than men. Often, on remarriage, a man would find an old, and he thought settled, issue being reopened. Children also became targets of maternal anger. They would be accused of harboring divided loyalties or of preferring their father and his new wife to the children's "real" family.

Rivalry between first and second wives, often intense in the early years of remarriage, sometimes continued for decades. Typically, the new wife would accuse the former wife of maternal incompetence, of not caring for the children adequately or of failing to discipline them. A missing button, dirty fingernails, or poor table manners were often remarked on. Former wives on the other hand often accused their successors of trying to lure the children away or trying to replace the first wife in the children's affections. One other common effect of remarriage was a renegotiation of visitation, custody, and support issues.

Interestingly, female remarriage rarely aroused anything close to this kind of fuss. Half of the divorced men viewed a former wife's remarriage favorably and were reasonably civil to their ex-wife's new husband. Of course, there may have been a measure of self-interest in this male civility, since a first husband's financial obligations sometimes ended with the new marriage.

Vulnerability to Illness

The newly divorced have more physical and psychological problems, which usually peak in the early postdivorce years, then diminish. My work suggests that there are often predivorce roots to postdivorce problems like alcoholism, drug abuse, accidents, depression, and antisocial behavior. Indeed, these problems frequently contributed to the end of the marriage, though divorce usually made them worse. The one striking exception to the otherwise general rule about a postdivorce decline in health were women who had been in distant or hostile marriages. The women in this group often experienced an improvement in physical health as the depression they had experienced in their marriage lifted.

I found that during the first year, visits to the doctor tripled among women and almost doubled among men. There was an increase in colds, headaches, stomach and intestinal upsets, sleep disorders, pneumonia, mononucleosis, and hepatitis in our newly divorced adults. What makes the recently divorced so vulnerable to illness? Stress. Divorce-induced stress weakens the immune system, creating a greater vulnerability to infection and disease.

Work by Janet Kiecolt-Glaser and her colleagues at Ohio State University suggests that after a divorce the immune system follows the same two-year pattern of breakdown and regeneration as emotional stability. Dr. Kiecolt-Glaser's data show that immune system disruptions, most pronounced in the first year, abate in the second year after a divorce, as stress declines.

Dr. Kiecolt-Glaser's work and mine also dovetailed in another way. I found that lingering feelings for a former spouse can put a person at emotional risk after divorce. Dr. Kiecolt-Glaser's data suggest that lovelornness also constitutes a health hazard. She found that attachment to a former husband often prolongs a woman's vulnerability to immune system disruptions.

The Ohio State researchers' data also confirm my finding about the end of the first year being the most painful point in the entire divorce cycle. Immediately after divorce, many of the men in her study maintained relatively normal immune function, but Dr. Kiecolt-Glaser noticed that the closer the men got to the one-year mark, the more vulnerable their immune system became. In the second year, immune system function in the group who had left their marriages was indistinguishable from the men who had been left.

The bottom line of this research: disappointments in love can produce real physiological change—change that, in some cases, may be severe enough to produce physical illness.

Postdivorce vulnerability to physical and psychological distress is a hazard not only for adults but also for their children. These problems may sideline parents at the very moment when the children most need their support.

"Not-Me" Experiences and the Changing Concept of Self

As the social roles, relationships, and routines associated with marriage that contribute to a married individual's sense of identity are peeled away after a divorce, many complain of not knowing who they are. One divorced man said, "I lost my center when I lost my family. I don't know who I am or where I'm going. I don't recognize myself." Women who had identified with and lived through the status and achievements of their husbands had an especially difficult time. One non-working woman said, "I used to be Mrs. John Smith, the bank manager's wife. Now, I'm Mary Smith. Who is Mary Smith?"

Most divorced men and women find their concept of self changing. For some, it is a voyage of positive self-discovery; for others, it reveals hidden dependencies and personal vulnerabilities they never knew existed and didn't wish to know. The refrain, "I can't believe I did that; that's not really me," was frequent as divorced men and women found themselves behaving in ways that astonished them. Describing how he had pleaded with Liddy to stay in the marriage, James Pennybaker said, "I'm not like that, you know. I don't snivel or beg anyone for anything."

The flurries of self-improvement—like losing forty pounds—and social activity that often follow divorce are an attempt to rectify a damaged sense of self and to recapture some badly needed esteem. At one year, many men were in a frenzy of activity. As contacts with old friends declined, dating and casual social encounters at bars, clubs, cocktail lounges, and other social gatherings increased for both sexes. The newly divorced also engaged in programs of self-improvement. They experimented with recreational activities, intellectual pursuits, with new job opportunities, and their appearance. Many entered therapy; others took night school classes in architectural history, potting, languages, horticulture, modern dance, creative writing, karate, or Tai Chi. Courses designed to promote job opportunities and economic security were particularly popular among women. The one exception to the activity rule—and it was a significant one—was the large number of divorced mothers who found themselves boxed in between economic and child care concerns.

Innovations in appearance could go to two extremes. Some divorced men and women, particularly if they were depressed, became unkempt and disheveled; others became stylish and attractive. Weight gains and losses of fifteen pounds or more were common. Many also became involved in physical fitness activities, such as jogging, bicycling, swimming, and aerobics. Some men became obsessed with bodybuilding. Women often dyed or restyled their hair and some had plastic surgery—a nip or tuck here or there, a nose job, a skin peel or breast augmentation. Many of our divorced men and women strove for a more youthful, sexier appearance, and many attained it.

Walking down the street one day, Dick Leventhal saw a woman with an absolutely perfect figure ahead of him. Normally, after an admiring glance, Dick would have gone on his way; but being five months out of a ten-year marriage, his inhibitions were still off at the beach sunning themselves. He decided to follow the woman. Two blocks later, about to catch up with her, the mystery woman suddenly spun around and shouted, "You bastard, Dick, if you don't stop following me, I'm going to get a restraining order!"

Stunned, outraged, then just embarrassed, Dick turned and walked away. The screaming woman was his former wife, Cally, whose loss of forty pounds had rendered her unrecognizable. "That bitch," Dick said, when he told me about the encounter, "before the divorce, I was always after Cally to lose weight. She slimmed down just to spite me!"

Divorced men were also likely to experiment with their appearance. At one year after divorce, one of our divorced businessmen who had previously been a buttoned-down, gray-suit type pulled up in his new Corvette wearing black leather pants, boots, a studded belt, and open shirt revealing a leather-thonged medallion on a black hairy chest. Motorcycles and sports cars, beards and mustaches, hip clothing, all were common features in our newly divorced men.

This frenzy of self-improvement began to abate noticeably in the second year, and its long-term consequences varied by activity. Jogging, bicycling, and similar pursuits had the beneficial effect of keeping thoughts about the divorce at bay, and even improving health, but in the long run didn't lead anywhere. However, educational and job-relevant programs often did. They pointed many women onto paths that led to increased self-sufficiency and self-esteem.

Men and Women at Two Years After Divorce

One day in her second postdivorce year, Janet Coleman saw an ad in the paper for a floral arranger, something she had always dreamed of doing. And Janet had a knack for it. Weren't people always telling her how wonderful she was with flowers? She stood up to reach for the phone, then immediately sat down again. "Oh, don't be a fool," she told herself. "You have no professional experience; you haven't a chance." But Janet couldn't quite let go of the idea. After she finished the laundry, she went back into the kitchen and reread the ad. The job sounded really interesting. "Well, all the florist can say is no," she told herself. "And I really need a job."

Janet, who had never considered herself much of a saleswoman, surprised herself that day. "Well, if you're nothing else, you're determined, young lady," the florist told her. "Come in tomorrow. I'll give you a tryout."

The following year, the florist, a grandfatherly man named Gordon Cramer, promoted Janet to store manager. When Gordon retired five years later, Janet opened her own business, "Janet's Garden," catering to wealthy clients, hotels, and embassies. At the twenty-year follow-up, Janet had expanded into full-fledged nurseries. "Janet's Garden" had six garden centers, fifty employees, and fifteen trucks.

Most pathways out of divorce begin like Janet's with a combination of openness to change—a willingness to try something unthinkable in other circumstances, like applying for a job for which you have no qualifications—and raw, aching need. These elements, which rarely coalesce at other points in life, come together quite frequently in the crisis years.

Procrastination and second-guessing are luxuries the newly divorced can rarely afford. Urgent needs press in from every direction: to make money, to restore domestic order, to create a support system for the children. And having temporarily slipped the restraints of inhibition, options once unimaginable—like moving in with your mother—become very imaginable.

Although most dramatic in the crisis period following divorce, usually the process of change was gradual, incremental. The boost in self-confidence produced by an unexpected success would lead an individual to take on a larger challenge, and success at that challenge, a still larger one. The last thing on Janet Coleman's mind the day she called the florist was becoming a businesswoman; but success as a floral arranger and then a store manager convinced her that owning her own business was a very realistic goal.

Many postdivorce pathways begin with a self-discovery—the individual finds she can run a home or a business competently. And very often, like a stone tossed in a stream, the self-discovery has a rippling effect. It begins to influence the kind of people the individual meets, the opportunities that open up to her, the skills she develops, not only careerwise but personally, the way she dresses, looks, and acts, and often who she marries.

"You know, I almost don't recognize her anymore," Janet's old friend Marcia said as we met when I was leaving Janet's home after her eleven-year interview. "There's something different about her now."

"Janet's become a successful businesswoman," I said.

"It's not just that she's successful and dresses stylishly. It's more than that," Marcia said. "It's hard to put into words. I guess it's that Janet seems more important, a bigger person, her own person."

In the first two years Janet had taken the preliminary steps and exhibited styles of coping with challenge that placed her on a constructive path. Men and women grappling with the changes following divorce started down various life paths, and although the early steps were important, there were no inevitable destinations. They were still to encounter many crossroads where new problems and opportunities had to be dealt with and choices made.

Of the three broad groups to emerge at the two-year point, the largest and most successful was composed of men and women who had embraced the window of change. What might be called successful changers didn't just talk about "making a better life"; they worked and sacrificed to make life better, they returned to school, and if that necessitated moving in with a parent, they moved in, and if the parent was difficult, they learned how to get along with her. They explored and tested all the resources available to them. If it took a month to find day care they could trust, or a shared child care arrangement with another single parent, they spent a month looking.

For members of this group, which produced many future Enhancers and Competent Loners, managing stress effectively was a transforming experience. The mostly women in the group learned new things about themselves—I can excel in school or in a job, I can raise my child alone, I can even get along with my mother—and these discoveries provided the basis for a new identity; successful changers began to think of themselves as competent, effective human beings. Not everyone on this path at two years stayed on it later, but most did.

People in the middle group were more interested in coping with change than in using it as an instrument of personal growth. Startling self-discoveries were rare in this group, which produced many future Good Enoughs, but so were serious problems. Reasonably able stress managers, members of this group often emerged from divorce relatively free of permanent scars. However, the pathways chosen by this group were often circular in nature; five and ten years later, many members were living a new version of their old predivorce lives. The cast of characters had changed, but not the emotional dynamics.

The third broad group might be called the immobilized; its members were still grappling with the postdivorce problems that everyone in the first two groups had solved or was in the process of solving. At six years after divorce, many members of this group still remained emotionally and psychologically mired in the early postdivorce years. The immobilized often turned into the Defeated.

Why do some people succeed, while others fail, and still others just muddle through?

The answer lies in certain risk and protective factors, phenomena we'll examine in the next chapter.

Points to Remember

- Divorce is an opportunity for personal growth and a better life as well as a time of stress and confusion.
- Be prepared for problems in the first year. Things will probably get worse over the course of this first year, then improve radically.
- Doubts about the divorce don't mean you made a mistake. Almost everyone, including those who initiate a divorce, has doubts at one point or another during the first two years.
- Don't expect postdivorce reactions to be confined to the emotional and to practical problems of living. You probably will also find yourself doing and saying strange, even embarrassing things. Be kind to yourself. The early years are not a time to be judgmental. Besides, you have plenty of company.

- Women enjoy an emotional advantage after divorce and men a financial advantage. Women need to make every effort possible to improve their education and job skills. Most can't count on the ex-husband's contributions as their main source of income.
- Anger and lingering attachment to your ex-spouse are barriers to adjustment and well-being. Get over it and move on.
- Women are more likely to harbor resentments and men to have tender feelings and unrealistic fantasies of reconciliation following divorce.
- Reality rarely matches fantasy. A busy sex life with many attractive and interesting partners looks great on television, but the glamour of sex wears off pretty quickly. Casual sex often exacerbates rather than allays loneliness.
- The emotional distress after divorce leads to disruption in immune system functioning and increased illness.
- Talking to other divorced men and women can be helpful and enlightening. You can learn what to expect and also what not to feel guilty about. You learn that you are not alone in your problems and how others have solved similar difficulties.
- Receptivity to change is not the same thing as creating change. Real change, life-transforming change, requires persistence and a willingness to sacrifice, but from the perspective of ten or twenty years, the effort looks more than worthwhile.
- Take it one day at a time. Build on your successes. Goals are important, but no life path is ever perfectly straight. There are always unexpected twists and turns. Be prepared for defeats and setbacks and take advantage of unanticipated opportunities. Also be prepared for the serendipitous. In divorce, as in life, sometimes things just happen. Energy expended trying to control the uncontrollable is wasted energy.

4

The Balance of Happiness:
Why People Succeed or Fail After Divorce

*L*iddy Pennybaker, in spite of her apprehension about living with her mother, found that her life restabilized after the move. Things became less hectic and more ordered. Although she was going to school full time and working part time, she didn't have to deal with the daily struggles of housework, shopping, and laundry. Most important, she knew the children were well cared for and happy.

It hadn't always been easy. At first there were conflicts over minor issues—how to squeeze Liddy's austere Mission-style furniture into Ginny's Victorian parlor, whether the family should eat only organic foods, and which church they should attend. Liddy and Ginny also clashed over the children. The affectionate but permissive Liddy put few restrictions on Adam and Bethany. She let them finger-paint in the living room, eat candy before dinner, and leave a trail of toys throughout the house. Ginny, though loving, was less indulgent. Old-fashioned in her child rearing, Ginny expected children to be obedient and responsible. Under her gentle but firm hand, Adam and Bethany began picking up after themselves, stopped interrupting adult conversations, displayed greatly improved table manners, and were generally more cooperative and obedient.

"I know Mother doesn't mean it," Liddy said at her two-year interview, "but she makes me feel superfluous sometimes. The children run to her when they get hurt, and want her to read to them and tuck them in at night. They still love me, but I'm not the only game in town. I can't help but feel envious. I try to squeeze as much time in with the children as I can, but Mom's there all the time and they've developed happy little routines I can't share. On Wednesdays, they go to the library together and for an ice cream treat afterward. On birthdays, Mother bakes them a four-layer chocolate cake, with little charms and money hidden inside. It's a big production and has become a sort of birthday ritual."

Another ritual developed. Liddy noticed that most nights when she came home from work or classes, Ginny was still up with a waiting cup of coffee or cocoa. They would sit down together for half an hour and talk about what the children had done and Liddy's day, or reminisce about the past and plan for the future. Ginny's stories were often very funny. One night they laughed so hard they woke the children. Much to her surprise, Liddy and her mother were becoming friends.

The painful changes divorce produces also have a positive side. They can, as they did in Liddy's case, open the door to better relationships or a new career. Few events in life open the door to the new and unexpected as widely as divorce. For the women in my study as for women generally, the greatest mechanisms for self-discovery proved to be work and new intimate relationships. Many women discovered talents and skills they didn't know they possessed until they were suddenly thrust into the role of family breadwinner. Which is to say, for divorced women, change is often a serendipitous process set in motion by desperate need.

Some women, like Liddy, eventually became remarkably successful in all areas of their lives. Others, like Janet Coleman, had a more common pattern and were competent in some areas but did not cope well in others. Janet certainly was successful in her work, and she was a caring, concerned parent, but she continued to have troubled relationships with men. She either became involved with safe, bland men she eventually left, or domineering men who exploited or left her. Contempt and fear powered her relationships.

Les and June Wilson, Janet's parents, never quite forgave her for marrying Richard Coleman. The Wilsons, who now lived a neat, orderly, middle-class life, saw Richard as a "redneck" who was a symbol of the truck stop life they had spent a lifetime trying to escape. When Janet met Paul Devereaux, she saw their relationship as a way of vindicating her worth to her parents and herself. Paul was charming, well mannered, and effortlessly erudite. He seemed everything the Wilsons could ask for in a son-in-law or Janet in a fiancé. But Paul also turned out to be a sometime musician and sometime gambler, with chronic money problems.

"This is a little embarrassing," Paul said on their second date, when he asked Janet for two hundred dollars until the end of the month. Janet managed to squeeze out the money, which was never paid back. A few months later, Paul needed money again. Except this time he needed a couple of thousand dollars.

"You know I don't have that kind of money," Janet told him.

"What about Gordon?" Paul said. "He's got money and he's crazy about you. Ask him for a loan." Janet did, but she didn't tell Gordon the money was for Paul; she said David, her younger child, was sick and the medical bills were piling up. Janet hated herself for lying. Gordon had been kind to her when she needed it most. But she couldn't bring herself to say no to Paul, who never paid back that loan either.

As soon as "Janet's Garden" became profitable, Paul's financial needs expanded. At that point, Janet estimated that he owed her over five thousand dollars.

"Paul thinks of me as his little piggybank," Janet said to me one day. "Whenever he calls and says, 'Jan, honey,' I know what's coming next."

"Have you ever considered saying no?" I asked.

Janet sighed. "I love Paul, but it's even more complicated than that. I think in some crazy way it's tied to Richard. I said no to him and look what happened to me."

Janet's problems with Paul but not with men in general were solved to some extent when Paul met a rich widow on a trip to Las Vegas and moved to the West Coast, his debts still unpaid.

Why People Win or Lose After Divorce

Traditionally, the story of divorce has been the story of risk. Most family scholars have argued—and some continue to argue—that in order to predict where people will be five, ten, fifteen years after a divorce, you need to look at the risks in their lives. And indeed, risk plays an important role in every postdivorce story.

But if risk alone matters, why do newly divorced people who face the same level of domestic chaos and economic and social pressure end up in very different places five and ten years later?

Demographics, a frequent explanation for such outcomes, provided a partial answer. Being young, well educated, and perhaps affluent sometimes gave a person an edge but sometimes didn't. I saw many educated, financially secure men and women become undone by the failure of a marriage. Overwhelmed by despair and stress, they became involved in destructive relationships, ignored their children, or began drinking too much.

Conversely, many people from less auspicious backgrounds, people in economically deprived families and with only a high school education, became positively energized by divorce. Why were so many of these supposedly "demographic duds" able to flourish in such a difficult environment? Why did the challenges and stresses associated with divorce lead to remarkable attainments in some of our divorced men and women and to unhappiness and failure in others?

The answer lies in certain risk and protective factors, and how they operate. Stresses such as those accompanying divorce activate a set of risk factors that make individuals more vulnerable to negative outcomes after divorce or a set of protective factors that buffer them against adversity. Risk and protective factors represent more than just a series of individual buffers and vulnerabilities; taken together, they also determine resiliency or the capacity to be adaptable in the face of hardships and to rebound from setback and defeat.

Resiliency is what develops when risk and protective factors coalesce. Although it is not a simple matter of subtracting the number of protective factors from risk factors, in general when protective factors predominate in the mix, people have a greater capacity to rebound. Like the Energizer Bunny, they just keep going. When risk factors predominate, people become brittle and easy-to-break. The stresses of divorce not only knock them down but may keep them down.

While risk and protective factors are ever present, the familiar routines of everyday life mute their effect. People do not have to draw on their innermost emotional, intellectual, and psychological reserves to get up in the morning or drive down to the store for a carton of milk. So, until a crisis like divorce suddenly makes just getting through the day a tremendous challenge, most men and women don't know how deep their emotional and intellectual reserves go or what talents and skills lie hidden in them.

One way to think of risk and protective factors is as a kind of Pilgrim's Progress on the road from divorce. Along every life path is a series of hazards to be avoided and opportunities to be exploited. A person did not succumb to depression or to substance abuse; she did make the most of a new job or the influence of a new group of friends. Or vice versa. However, to understand how these factors come together to create a life path, it is first necessary to know something about them. And that is the subject of this chapter.

Everyone, including children, enters life after a divorce with a set of protective and risk factors that changes as they and their circumstances change. Here are the most important of these factors for adults coping with divorce and its aftermath, followed by an explanation of how they function.

Protective Factors

Social Maturity

Social maturity is a great asset after a divorce. To be mature means four things. It means being able to plan for the future; to exhibit self-control; to be flexible and adaptable in coping with problems; and to be socially responsible.

- *Planfulness.* Many newly divorced people I spoke to knew they would have to take some active steps to build a better life and make sacrifices to get there, but few arrived in my office with a master plan and a timetable. However, the planful had concrete rather than general goals and also a pretty good idea of what had to be done to achieve their goals.

    Liddy Pennybaker didn't just want "a good job" in five years; she wanted a good job in the financial services industry, which she knew would require an MBA. She also was willing to accept short-term pain—moving in with her mother—to achieve that goal.

    Liddy's willingness to delay gratification is another characteristic of people who plan, and though it sometimes makes their early years difficult, it has a protective effect in the long run, and not just economically. Because they know what they want, they are less likely to make the kind of rash decisions—like rushing into a new marriage or live-in relationship—that are easy to make when you are confused, emotionally unsettled, and newly divorced.

- *Self-regulation.* In the first year, stress and anxiety, depression and anger are common; but some people found ways to control these and the other difficult emotions associated with the failure of a marriage. They didn't let their emotions cloud their judgment, affect their parenting, or make them act in impulsive or self-defeating ways. For some of our divorced men and women, self-regulation was a well-established personality trait. Others had to struggle to control their emotions. Prominent in this second group were newly divorced mothers with distressed, demanding children. Said one young woman, "There are so many times now when I just want to scream, 'Stop it!' But the kids are already upset enough; my freaking out will only make things worse. I try to focus on their feelings, not my own."

• *Adaptability.* Right after the divorce, Liddy's anger made her unbending in many little ways. One was her punctiliousness about visiting days: James had to arrive exactly when he said he would and the children had to be back exactly when Liddy said she wanted them back. One evening when James violated Liddy's rules by bringing Adam and Bethany home an hour late, he and Liddy had a terrible row. It ended with Adam and Bethany in tears, James shouting, and Liddy furious.

That night, James called and suggested a truce. "We're killing the kids with fighting." Liddy was relieved. She knew she and James couldn't go on this way. However, the most important consequence of the truce was that it got the Pennybakers talking to each other again. And out of their conversations, a cooperative co-parenting relationship slowly evolved.

Rigidity, which destroys many marriages, also destroys many divorces. Mature individuals are adaptable and flexible. Unlike many married and divorced couples, they avoid turning solvable problems into unsolvable ones.

• *Social responsibility.* At first glance, social responsibility, the final component of social maturity, seems unconnected to the experience of divorce. How does being sensitive and responsive to other people's needs and helping others enable a person to endure the failure of a marriage?

According to our data, in two ways. First, people who give a lot to friends, coworkers, and the PTA—the essence of social responsibility—get a lot back when they need help. And secondly, people who feel bad about themselves after a divorce begin to feel good about themselves when they help a colleague solve a work problem or see a friend through a difficult relationship.

Autonomy

Nothing completely protects against the stresses of the early years, but autonomous people, that is, people who are comfortable being alone and making decisions by themselves, find the intense "singleness" of postdivorce life easier to adjust to. Although an important source of support, men and women who rely on friends and relatives to solve their problems often do not make much progress. The recently divorced are very needy, and friends get tired of being leaned on. One friend of Connie Russell's said, "It's been two years since the divorce and Connie's still whining. I've done everything I can to help her. I feel sucked dry. Connie's got to start solving her own problems."

Some of our most independent women found the relief from joint decision making one of the greatest boons of marital breakup. Marsha Klein, a very feisty, autonomous woman, said: "I don't have to negotiate about where to go on vacation or what kind of car to buy or argue about how to discipline the children. I just do my own thing. The freedom is wonderful!"

Internal Locus of Control

Can problems be solved through our own efforts, or are most of our difficulties beyond our control, somehow the result of malign fate? Are we at the mercy of events and the actions of others, or can we shape our destiny and improve our life situation?

People with an internal locus of control or sense of self-efficacy think their problems can be solved through their own striving and this belief often makes them proactive following divorce. Instead of passively reacting to events, problem solvers try to shape them. They go back to school, open new businesses, find good child care, and build social networks. People with an external locus of control, on the other hand, tend to feel helpless and to just endure. First, they try to outlast their problems; and if that fails, they passively try to learn to live with them.

Locus of control is not a fixed, unchanging trait. It is developed through life experiences and the responses of others. It can be both learned and altered. Infants with unresponsive parents often begin to think they have no control over their lives. But an unresponsive or abusive spouse like Richard Coleman can also foster a sense of helplessness. Janet Coleman's business success and her sense of being admired and valued by Gordon and Marcia, her children, and her clients pushed her score on the locus of control scale from the bottom 25 percent on entering the VLS to the top 25 percent in internal control at year six into the study. But even that improvement was not enough entirely to wash away the effects of five years with Richard Coleman. Although in most areas of her life she was an active and effective problem solver, with aggressive men, Janet continued to feel helpless. There was not only Paul Devereaux, there was also the bullying office manager Janet hired and was afraid to fire even when an audit showed he was stealing. According to David Coleman, who was running "Janet's Garden" when the study ended, if Janet's mentor Gordon Cramer had not stepped in and fired the office manager, the man could have ruined the business.

A feeling of powerlessness was common after a divorce. For some people, like Janet, self-efficacy gradually increased, but isolated areas of helplessness remained. For others, like Connie Russell, helplessness was pervasive and more long-lasting. At six years after divorce, she still relied on others to solve her problems. A persistent refrain in her interviews was "What's the use? Nothing I try works, anyhow." But the truth was she had made no moves to deal with her problems.

Religiosity

Religion per se does not protect people. The religious and the secular suffer equally when a marriage fails. But a religious lifestyle often does act as a buffer because it provides access to an unusually strong support network. The social isolation, loneliness, and lack of support frequently found after divorce occur less often for those with strong religious affiliations. People in religious networks know and help each other. They share a similar set of beliefs about right and wrong, good and bad, duty and responsibility. Their similarities draw them together.

Church attendance, Bible-reading classes, and church-related activities like dinners and bazaars provide not only an opportunity to socialize but structure, especially in the lives of single mothers. Religiously oriented mothers reported that dressing up and going to church on Sunday gave their families a much-needed sense of normalcy and stability.

Another benefit of involvement in a religious group is that it helps in raising children. Someone is always available for baby-sitting. Boys have plenty of male role models and the people who staff the day care facilities are usually conscientious, responsible, and eager to reinforce the values a religious-minded woman wants her child to absorb.

Liddy Pennybaker's religious involvement paradoxically both undermined her marriage and later served as a protective factor after divorce. James, an avowed atheist, had been openly and publicly contemptuous of Liddy's religious beliefs. He resented the time she spent in her church activities, and this contributed to Liddy's increasing alienation in the marriage.

However, Liddy's religiousness became an important aid to her after the divorce. When she moved into Ginny's house in a semigentrified area on Richmond's north side, she began to attend a church in the neighborhood with a racially diverse congregation. There she met Katie Jackson, a small, lively, voluble African American with a weakness for lost souls and the antennae to spot one anywhere within a hundred-mile radius. Sensing Liddy's shyness at her first prayer breakfast, Katie introduced her to other members of the congregation, invited her home to dinner, and began taking her to choir practice and church outings. As Liddy felt herself sinking deeper into the life of her new church, she experienced a sense of rootedness, security, and belonging she had not felt since she was a young girl in her father's congregation.

Work

Many adults said that work was one of the few safe harbors available to them after divorce. Some men, having lost their home and families, came to rely on the familiar setting and routines of work for a sense of continuity and stability. Although men often complained about being unable to work effectively, they also frequently threw themselves into work; staying late and coming in weekends provided an escape from loneliness and stress.

One man in our study, Anthony Coombs, complained: "If I stay home, I keep obsessing about Maggie and where I went wrong in the marriage. But once I'm behind my desk and working, I feel in control and competent. There I'm not a failure."

Even now, when an increasing number of women are employed, only two thirds of married women with young children work, and of those, over half work intermittently or part time, usually in service, clerical, or white-collar jobs. Only about one eighth of women with children were involved in a full-time career or profession at the time of divorce. It is not surprising then that for women, the principal protective effect of work was in self-discovery. Many women emerged from a five- or ten-year marriage with few professional skills and little stable work experience, but necessity pushed them into improving their situation. They raised their aspirations, went back to school, moved into more challenging jobs, and changed not just their economic status but also their self-image. They began to see themselves as effective, resourceful human beings, and they met new people at work—often more interesting people as their work status improved. It didn't take being a doctor or lawyer or professor or head of a corporation to protect women. Most kinds of work could be protective. The role of family breadwinner boosted a woman's battered self-esteem and work got her out of the house—no small thing after a divorce. For many women, a job at McDonald's was preferable to a solitary life at home.

Social Support

In making the decision to divorce and in the early steps of marital breakup, what I call transitional figures—people who facilitate the transition from marriage to divorce—are among the most powerful sources of social support. Part counselor, part comforter, and part consigliore, a transitional figure provides support and advice during the decision to divorce and the transition to single life later. They may also help with practical matters like finding a new apartment or day care center and social ones like finding new friends. Typically, parents, siblings, or close friends act as transitional figures; but not uncommonly, a lover will play the role.

Being a romantic transitional figure is a high-risk endeavor. Only about 15 percent of VLS participants who were romantically involved with another person married that person after the divorce. People who are able to provide solace in getting out of an unhappy marriage may not seem so desirable in a long-term relationship. Indeed, after the transition to single life, many transitional figures find themselves, like Denise Carlisle, discarded.

I never met Denise, but Eric Oltmanns, a VLS participant, talked about her so much I almost felt I knew her. At the two-month interview, Eric credited Denise, who worked in the office next to his, with helping him to see how selfish and immature his former wife, Judy, was. "I don't think I would have had the courage to ask for a divorce without Denise," Eric said. "She's the most wonderful person. She's my best pal. We do everything together: go to the movies, go out to dinner and parties. I don't know how I would have survived the last few months without her."

But Denise had not wanted the role to stay at best pal; she thought that the relationship would eventually grow into marriage. And when it didn't, she became angry. At the one-year interview, Eric reported that since he had begun dating other women, Denise had become distant. Eventually, their relationship returned to what it had been—a cool exchange of hellos in the hall.

All support systems are not transitory. Some, such as those with family and friends, may be enduring. However, as the stresses people encounter change over the course of life, the effectiveness of different relationships to act as buffers may alter. Friends and colleagues at work, parents, siblings, lovers, a therapist, fellow church members, or an Alcoholics Anonymous group may at different times serve as major sources of support and protection.

A New Intimate Relationship

The most powerful buffer against postdivorce stress—a new intimate relationship—often produces a decline in depression, health complaints, and visits to the doctor, and an increase in self-esteem. When someone loves and values you, you begin thinking that you are worth caring about.

Love really does heal, and sometimes more than just heal; sometimes, it saves. Lest that sound like hyperbole, let me tell you the rest of Connie Russell's story. After her suicide attempt, Connie's life deteriorated steadily. She lost custody of her children and her problems with alcohol worsened steadily.

Connie usually began drinking with a pickup in the morning and continued all day. On our visit six years after the divorce, she clearly had been drinking. Her hands shook, she was sometimes incoherent, and she complained of blackouts. Her conversation was punctuated by tears and wild laughter. Her apartment was a mess, littered with bottles, dirty dishes, empty TV dinner packages, and discarded clothing. The stench was overwhelming.

Connie's bottoming-out point was waking up in a motel room one morning, naked, with her wallet gone, no memory of how she got to the room, or why her arms and face were covered with bruises. A few days later, Connie attended her first Alcoholics Anonymous meeting. A year later, she married a man she met at the meeting, a police sergeant named Bob Keatly.

For Connie, marriage was less a happy ending than the beginning of a happy ending. In the early years of the marriage there were a half dozen relapses, many quarrels, and one separation from Bob. Connie's relations with Simon and the children also remained strained.

However, eventually the turmoil ended and Connie settled into something resembling a normal life. Bob's personality had a lot to do with her recovery; low-keyed and relaxed, he was an easy man to like. Indeed, Simon and the children, who admired the way he helped Connie, came to be extremely fond of him. At the twenty-year interview, Connie, still happily married, had been alcohol-free for a decade and her relationship with the adult Michael and Celia was congenial, if not especially close.

When I asked Connie about why she had changed, she said, "I don't really know. In some way, being loved by a man like Bob inspired me. I wanted to be the woman he thought I could be, the one I think he fell in love with."

The effects of a new, intimate relationship are so profound it is worth repeating my findings: after a divorce, nothing heals as completely as new love. True for women, this finding is even more true for men, who, being less socially adept and more emotionally isolated, often feel unsupported in the early years without a new partner.

Risk Factors

Antisocial Personality

The term *antisocial* is associated with social outcasts, with bikers and drug dealers and criminals, with people who engage in truly aberrant and dangerous behaviors. And antisocial personalities do behave destructively. They have little respect for authority, are violent, irresponsible, and amoral. But less extreme forms of antisocial behavior also can make people vulnerable to adverse outcomes following a divorce. People who constantly quarrel with friends, family, coworkers, and employers, or who are insensitive, unreliable, explosive, impulsive, and aggressive, or get into minor hassles with the law are also acting antisocially.

According to conventional wisdom, the antisocial are the products of a stressed, troubled, poverty-ridden childhood. But our work suggests that conventional wisdom oversimplifies a complex problem. Often the antisocial do live stressful lives, but the stress is usually self-generated. Irresponsibility, violence, and substance abuse make the marriages, friendships, and work situations of the antisocial unstable, and so does their own inability to negotiate or compromise, to see a problem from another's perspective, or to learn from mistakes.

Sam Dunn's history exemplifies the antisocial personality in action. By the time the VLS ended, Sam had left behind a trail of three broken marriages, six children, and innumerable affairs and short-term live-in relationships. In both his professional and his personal relationships,

Sam showed the lack of insight and responsibility and an inability to learn from experience that are characteristic of the antisocial. At the time of his final interview, he was involved in an acrimonious breakup with his law firm because of suspected financial improprieties and in the dissolution of his third marriage. It was not the first time he had been asked to leave a law firm because of questionable behavior, but it was the first time a wife had left him. Sam was outraged. He played the role of injured, aggrieved husband to the hilt, in spite of the fact that the same behavior had led to marital problems in all three of his marriages—repeated affairs, lying, explosive rages, and substance abuse. His soon-to-be third ex-wife, Marnie, said, "Sam is a chronic liar. He lies to me and to the children and to his friends and to his clients and the other lawyers at work. I sometimes think he lies to himself. He seems to think that saying something makes it true. He had been very contrite about having an affair with a young legal aide at the office and swore it would never happen again. A week later at a party, I found him humping the hostess in the back kitchen. He had the gall to say, 'Wait, Marnie, this isn't what it seems'! I didn't know whether to laugh or cry."

Impulsivity

Eileen Kane's last marital act was to throw a glass of wine in her husband, Stan's, face and storm out of a dinner party. At her intake interview, Eileen described herself as a reformed woman. "I'll never do anything that stupid again," she assured me.

A year later, Eileen's new boyfriend found *cheat* scribbled across the windshield of his new BMW in bright red lipstick. "Cheat . . . who with?" demanded the boyfriend, when he called Eileen. "Don't play dumb with me," Eileen snapped. "My friend Susan saw you and your secretary having lunch Wednesday."

"You idiot!" the boyfriend exploded. "Wednesday was Secretary's Day. You're supposed to take your secretary to lunch on Secretary's Day."

That afternoon, Eileen received a two-word e-mail from her boyfriend: "It's over."

Impulsive people act without considering consequences or alternate solutions. In other words, they often act on raw emotion, and after a divorce, this tendency creates risks. Because they say and do things without thinking, like Eileen, the impulsive frequently alienate new intimate companions as well as other potential sources of support, including friends and family. Impulsive behavior also can exacerbate the already difficult parent-child relationship. Children with impulsive parents often complained that depending on a parent's mood, the same behavior would elicit rage, amusement, or be totally ignored.

The tendency to act first and think later also makes the impulsive particularly vulnerable to esteem-damaging casual sexual encounters. And because choices are not thought through, they often make bad decisions. Many impulsive divorced women spent their late thirties and early forties regretting the dead-end jobs and unhappy second marriages they rushed into after a divorce.

Neuroticism

Neurotic behavior involves a cluster of anxious, obsessive, depressed behaviors. It creates postdivorce risk in several ways. A clever little study highlights one.

The experimenter wanted to see if depression—a key component of neuroticism—had a social cost. In other words, did it drive people away? To answer the question, the investigator had each study participant spend a short time in a waiting room with either a depressed or a non-depressed stranger.

Would the "blue" stranger become an object of sympathy? the experimenter wondered. Would his study participants be touched by the stranger's emotional pain? Would they reach out and try to help him?

No.

When offered a second chance to visit with the depressed stranger, the study participants took a pass. They said the stranger depressed them. He whined, he complained, he was boring. He made a terrible companion.

Besides driving away potential sources of support, neuroticism and depression also carry two other risks. They siphon off important energy needed to build a new life, and may ignite a cycle of worry and helplessness whose net result is to make stress seem so overwhelming that emotional paralysis results.

Many of the VLS participants who were still "stuck" at the two-year point were stuck because depressed or anxious men and women perceive their problems as being just too big to solve.

Attachment for a Former Spouse

In the film *New York Stories*, a quirk of fate transforms Woody Allen's mother into a gigantic, hectoring heavenly body. Every time poor Allen looks up in the sky, his Mars-sized mother reminds him to eat his vegetables and change his underwear in front of half the world. At one point or another, most of us, like Allen's character, have obsessed about a person. We wonder where they are and what they are doing. In imaginary conversations, we explain our feelings and motives, and often as well accuse the person of not loving or caring for us.

Sometimes, as in the Allen movie, the object of obsession is a parent, but more often it is a lover—a lover who has spurned us. Though we think about the person constantly, it doesn't automatically follow that we still love them. Some lingering attachments are based on the dependencies created by the dailiness of a marriage. "I wouldn't say we're in love," declared one married man; "it's more like my wife and I need each other and are friends."

However, most people who obsess after a divorce do so because, like Reynolds Boyce, they still feel attached to a former spouse by a complex blend of emotions that includes but is not limited to love.

Reynolds, who married his brother Everett's former girlfriend, never suspected that his wife's decision to marry him might have anything to do with Everett's decision to leave for California without her after college.

"What was even stupider," Reynolds said at his intake interview, "is that even after Everett moved home again, I didn't suspect anything. Then, one afternoon, I walked into a restaurant and there the two of them were, sitting in a corner booth, holding hands."

After the divorce, Reynolds exhibited the classic symptoms of lingering attachment. He obsessed about Katrina, he picked fights with her and Everett, he played on her maternal guilt. He told Katrina that their daughter, Mindy, hated her for betraying him, and he told Mindy that her mother was a "cheat" and a "slut." What makes lingering attachment a risk factor is its Velcro Effect. The person remains stuck in place; effort that could and should go toward making new friends or forming a new intimate relationship goes, instead, into obsessing about a former spouse. Six years after the divorce, Reynolds was still living in a one-bedroom apartment, still plotting ways to take revenge on Katrina, and still uninterested in other women.

However, in time, most people do get over an ex-spouse. And at six-year interviews, we noticed a change in men and women who were finally letting go. Their version of the divorce was becoming similar to their former spouse's version.

People make up scripts about why the divorce happened, and the role each partner played in it, to somehow make the divorce seem more understandable and manageable. But since time has a way of altering perspectives, divorce scripts are constantly being revised and updated. In the first version, usually people cast themselves in the role of noble, long-suffering victim; the divorce was all the other spouse's fault. How could she leave? I loved her so much. But three or four years later, an update of the script has the individual acting more as a co-conspirator than victim. Maybe his former wife was right; maybe he wasn't a particularly involved or caring husband and father.

This certainly was true in the changes in the Pennybakers' reports about what led to their mutual breakup. James initially blamed Liddy's religiosity, her obsession with the children, her sexual aloofness and deterioration in appearance, and his own loneliness for the divorce. Liddy had blamed James's egocentrism, social climbing, preoccupation with building his practice, contempt for her religion, lack of participation in child rearing, and infidelity.

By six years after the divorce, Liddy and James's stories had converged; and as was true in many divorced couples, as their stories became more similar, they fought less and cooperated more.

In the six-year interview, James said: "I guess I was too involved in getting to the top and didn't spend enough time with Liddy and the kids, although I loved them. I nagged Liddy about all sorts of things—her weight, her preoccupation with the children, her religion. I was really unkind about her religion. It meant a lot to her. I should never have gotten involved with another woman. I knew a woman like Liddy would never put up with it, but I felt shut out and lonely."

Liddy's story was: "I guess we drifted apart because we had different obsessions. I was obsessed with the children. Looking back, I see it was too intense. It was probably unhealthy. I never wanted to be away from them. Jimmy was obsessed with his career. If Jimmy had spent more time with the children and I had gone out with him more and entertained his colleagues more, things would have been better. But we're both stubborn and just dug in our heels. I was furious at him for his constant nagging about my weight and my religion. I know I shut him out, but I was just so resentful, I couldn't help it. It's strange the mean, petty things you can do to someone you love that finally drive you apart. I was hurt about other women in Jimmy's life, but they weren't the most important things in the divorce."

Cohabitation

Cohabitation is the fastest-growing form of relationship in America. Only a tenth of VLS parents lived together before marrying the first time, but fully a third had cohabitated before marrying a second time. The rate among recently divorced and married VLS couples is even higher. Almost half lived together before a first marriage and 60 percent before a second marriage.

Many of my colleagues believe America may be moving toward the Swedish model, where cohabitation is now as acceptable as marriage and children born in these unions bear no stigma. Some people applaud the change. They see cohabitation as a kind of trial marriage; a couple gets an opportunity to see how well they fit together before making a legal commitment. However, living together actually increases the divorce risk.

Why?

Cohabitation attracts the less traditional and the less traditional are less likely to feel bound by rules. Furthermore, living together does not involve much of a commitment; and when a couple decides not to live together any more, there are not many legal and social impediments to make them hesitate.

Cohabiting relationships, especially a series of cohabiting relationships, also can have adverse effects on children. Children are less accepting and have more problems when their parents cohabit than when they remarry. But in long-term cohabiting relationships, a child may have become attached to the parent's partner and be deeply distressed at a breakup.

Promiscuity

At the twenty-year interview, one of my long-term Libertines recalled sitting in a singles bar one night, staring into the mirror. She suddenly saw herself as "a laughable old trout with too much makeup and a too short skirt trying to compete with twenty-year-olds. I used to be the star of the place," the woman told me. "Now I'm forty-five, which means I'm the girl you take home at the end of the night if you've struck out with everyone else."

At the twenty-year follow-up, the Libertines category was much smaller than in the early years, but its remaining members were among the most depressed people in the study. These die-hard Libertines were worried about everything—losing their looks, youth, and sex appeal. The Libertine lifestyle was particularly risky for women, who often found themselves caught up in a cycle of promiscuity and substance abuse that went something like this:

Women with low self-esteem or problems with alcohol or drugs are especially vulnerable both to participating in casual sexual relations and in one-night stands, and to suffering afterward. The lack of caring in the sexual relationships, the waiting for phone calls that never came, led to feelings of worthlessness, helplessness, and depression. Many of these women ended in the Defeated category in the end of the VLS, while a few attempted to take their lives. The seven suicide attempts that occurred during the study all took place after casual sex and all were by women.

By the end of the study, sexual attitudes had changed. So I began to wonder if what was true in 1975 was still true in the 1990s. Maybe my findings on promiscuity were out of date? Many newer VLS participants seemed to agree with the woman who told me, "What's nice about having sex right away is that it eliminates all that first-date awkwardness in trying to make conversation."

However, reviewing the histories of couples who had divorced in the last decade, I found the same dissatisfaction with a prolonged period of casual sex and the same desire for a stable, intimate relationship. The only change was in guilt. People felt less guilty and were more open about casual sex in the 1990s than they were in the 1970s. Still, the characters in *Frasier*, who constantly yearn for intimacy and trip over themselves when they try to find it, are a better guide to divorced life in the 1990s than the breezy, bed-hopping characters in *Sex and the City*.

Socioeconomic Status

The two closely related demographic characteristics which define socioeconomic status, income and education level, often break apart after a divorce. We found that women with college degrees sometimes went on welfare or became economically dependent on their families again, or, as Liddy Pennybaker did, moved in with a parent. However, the better-educated adults in our study tended to be less depressed, more satisfied with their lives, and better parents both before and after divorce. This was not just because they were less likely to be poor than less educated men and women, but also because they were more likely to be working and working in gratifying jobs.

Not surprisingly, an abrupt drop in socioeconomic status often led to depression; but you don't have to be destitute to be depressed. Women who could no longer afford a private school or summer camp for their children, or to maintain a stylish wardrobe or busy social life, or who had to move to a smaller house or apartment also became depressed by a divorce-imposed reduction in living standards.

While marked declines in income often occur after a divorce, most people eventually right themselves. In our studies, even the subset of women who dropped below the poverty line moved in and out of extreme poverty. Few of our divorced women remained on public assistance for a continuous period of more than a year. The average sustained period that women remained in poverty was about seven months. Divorced women move out of poverty as they gain more skills, get a job, or remarry, and fall back into poverty with job loss or unexpected economic emergencies.

On average, VLS divorced women moved four times in the first six years, but poor women moved seven times. In the best of circumstances, residential instability is distressing and disorientating; but among poor women, it often produced a dangerous ripple effect. In search of cheaper rents, divorced women would move their families into progressively poorer neighborhoods with higher rates of crime and unemployment, with more inadequate day care facilities and schools, and more single mothers and children who had serious behavior problems.

The mothers who got caught in this downward spiral spent great amounts of time worrying about things other parents take for granted, such as their child's physical safety and whether the child was learning anything at school or being affected by all the crime and alcohol and drugs around him or her.

Family History

Many characteristics that put an individual at risk for having problems in intimate relationships are to some extent transferred across generations. Antisocial behavior, neuroticism, alcoholism, and aggression in parents all increase the risk of these behaviors occurring in their offspring, and these behaviors are major threats to marital stability in both generations. This is partially based on heredity and partly on learning experiences. Parents with these characteristics often have poor problem-solving skills, are unable to resolve their marital differences, and serve as poor role models for their sons and daughters.

Their children don't learn how to listen, compromise, deescalate anger, or soothe and support their partners. Thus, it is not surprising that the risk of divorce may be transferred across generations. Adult children of divorced parents have an increased marital failure rate, and the failure rate is highest of all among adult females. The reason? Women regulate the emotional temperature inside a marriage and carry the burden in marital problem solving.

How Risk and Protective Factors Work

As a general rule, people with many protective factors do well after a divorce and people with many risk factors do poorly; but numbers alone don't tell the story. Risk and protective factors are governed by certain rules. These rules are outlined below.

Using Available Resources

In order to enjoy the protection of a protective factor, you have to use it. This may sound self-evident, but judging from the experiences of VLS participants, often available buffering factors are ignored.

For example, one half of VLS women had access to health care and financial resources, better schools, and after-school programs—to the kind of resources that can help to ease a new single mother's life and her concerns about her child. However, only about one quarter sought information about and exploited these resources. The other three quarters settled for convenience or ignorance. They relied on information from families and friends. They chose the school or day care center that was nearest or cheapest or easiest to enroll a child in.

The result? The women in the second group not only were more stressed and spent more time worrying about their child's well-being; they also missed more work time because their support systems kept breaking down.

Appropriateness

To protect, a factor must also be appropriate to a person's goals and life situation. For example, for Liddy Pennybaker, a new intimate relationship offered less protection than a sometime critical transition figure—her mother—because marriage was not among Liddy's early postdivorce goals.

"Maybe later," the newly successful and self-confident Liddy said at the six-year interview, when I asked her about marriage. "I don't know if I'd agree with Gloria Steinem that 'a woman needs a man like a fish needs a bicycle,' but, it's close. For now, I like my life the way it is."

By contrast, a new intimate partner was the right fit—the only fit—for Connie Russell, whose need for unconditional love was an essential element in her ability to begin believing in herself again.

Awareness of Timing

Timing also affects how risk and protective factors operate. Is the factor available when the person wants it? Even the most perfect partner won't buffer someone unready for a new intimate relationship, and even the best support system won't be effective if a person is too depressed to use it.

If Liddy Pennybaker had not struggled for a year working part time and going to classes at night, she might have been unwilling to move in with her mother. Conversely, James Pennybaker's lingering feelings of attachment probably would not have posed as great a risk if Linda Crankshaw, who looked strikingly like Liddy, had not appeared on the scene soon after the Pennybaker divorce.

"I think I married Linda so fast because I was still on the rebound and she reminded me a lot of Liddy. But as the country song goes, 'She ain't pretty, she just looks that way,' " James said the day he told me he and Linda were getting a divorce. "She was no Liddy. It didn't take long to realize that I'd made a horrible mistake. Linda was great in bed, but that's all she was great at. She was a really shallow, empty, petty person, and after our marriage she seemed to chatter all the time about nothing—gossip, clothes, goings-on at the country club. It drove me crazy. Once, when I was working on a big project, I temporarily moved into a hotel near the office so I wouldn't have to drive back to the country when I worked late at night. I liked it so much I never went back."

Change

Most risk and protective factors are transitory. Lovers appear and disappear, transitional figures emerge or fade away; work becomes more or less interesting; people fall in and out of poverty, gain or lose self-confidence, learn the importance of planning or continue to act impulsively. As life changes, the factors available to a person also change; often a single alteration can abruptly and dramatically alter a person's life trajectory—sometimes for better, sometimes for worse.

Levels of Stress

The ability of protective factors to protect, while significant, is finite. Beyond a certain stress level, factors may lose the ability to buffer. This is illustrated by the experience of Carol Rosenthal.

Often, when an impulsive mother like Carol is paired with a difficult child—high-strung, anxious, hard to soothe—like her son Tom, the result is a destructive cycle of negative parent-child behavior. However, in the early postdivorce years, Carol was protected by a support system, which included her mother, who was very nurturant and lived nearby, and several single-mother friends, who were available for emergencies.

Carol's experience was not unusual: under conditions of relatively low stress, we found that a divorced mother with personality problems such as impulsivity can parent a difficult, cranky, oppositional child effectively if she has access to a good support system. But the needs in this system are so delicately balanced that additional stress can produce collapse.

What changed the equation for Carol were two factors: a new critical, demanding boss, and the end of a long romantic relationship.

The new stresses made Tom's irritability and resistant behavior, which before had been merely annoying to Carol, grating. The new stresses also made it harder for her to control her own impulsivity. Now, when Tom did something wrong, instead of patiently explaining why his behavior was wrong, Carol yelled, threatened, even slapped him, which only exacerbated Tom's anger, confusion, and disobedience.

"I have no island of peace and security, no safe haven," Carol told me one day. "I'm just hanging on by my fingernails."

Individuality

A parent can help to buffer a child by her planning or self-regulation and she can try to foster these qualities in her child; but she cannot directly pass on her ability to plan and locus of control to that child. These must be learned. Protective and risk factors are non-transferable; every family member has his or her own unique set.

The corollary to this rule is that every individual family member follows his or her own individual path through family life after a divorce. Though parental competence and well-being are important to a child, parents can and sometimes do win in families where children lose, and children sometimes can win in families where parents lose.

The Emergence of New Pathways

Risk and protective factors take time to create a distinctive life path. What we saw in the early postdivorce years were massive changes and rapidly altering risk and protective factors associated with malleable, often temporary, styles of coping with the stresses that go with divorce. By the six-year follow-up, many of our men, women, and children in the VLS had embarked on a series of distinctive pathways and patterns of adaptation that some were to continue for the duration of the study.

Points to Remember

- Postdivorce outcomes are not predestined. Risk and protective factors change over time, but choices made, and actions taken, alter future opportunities.
- Seek out resources and use them. Just remember, opportunity only knocks; someone has to get up and let it in.
- Plan and work for long-term goals; short-term sacrifice may lead to long-term satisfaction.
- Take the initiative in shaping your life. Other people can't solve your problems for you.
- Don't make hasty decisions. Pain—and the desire to alleviate it as quickly as possible—can and frequently does make people do foolish things after a divorce, things that put the future at risk.
- Overburdened support systems can break down. People are eager to help after a divorce, particularly parents and siblings. But people also have limits; when they are asked to give too much, they often stop giving altogether.
- Cohabiting is not a low-risk relationship. Breakups are higher in cohabiting than marital relationships, and the risk of divorce is higher when a couple has lived together before marriage.
- Work affirms women as much as men. The women who did best in postdivorce life often entered that life through a door marked "Work."
- A new intimate relationship has the greatest healing effect after a divorce.

5

Six Ways to Leave a Marriage: The Pathways Men and Women Take Out of Divorce

I don't know if it would be fair to describe the stylish Lucinda as a trophy wife, but, extraordinarily attractive, her role in the Fredericks' marriage seemed not too dissimilar from her husband's S-Class Mercedes or the Fredericks' fourteen-room home.

Men—first Lucinda's father, then her husband, Louis—had always done her planning and thinking; so, after the divorce, Lucinda had no idea how to build a life for herself and her son, Richard.

For awhile, Louis's half-million-dollar divorce settlement put a cushion between Lucinda and the risk factors in her life. But within a few years, the settlement was gone—spent on travel, clothing, cars, and bad investments. I think Lucinda was careless about money because, in the back of her mind, she always thought Louis would give her more if she needed it; he might not care about her any more, but he cared about their son, Dickie. However, Lucinda's theory failed to take into account the workings of the general economy. Just as she was about to ask for more financial help, Louis's once prosperous real estate business collapsed in a recession and Louis moved to Florida to try to build a new life.

"The one bright spot in all this is that things can't possibly get worse," Lucinda said the day she told me that she and Dickie were moving in with her mother. But they did get worse. Four months later, Lucinda's mother died suddenly of a heart attack. Four years after the divorce, Lucinda was depressed, on welfare, living in a low-income housing project with an increasingly troubled Dickie.

For most of our divorced men and women who were doing well six years after the divorce, such as Liddy Pennybaker, some degree of effort and planning was involved. For Lucinda, it was the sheer serendipity of meeting Charles Gordon, a senior partner in one of the biggest law firms in Richmond, Virginia, unless you wanted to count the effort she spent on charming him into marriage six months later.

She was exuberant at her six-year interview: "From a slum on the south side to a mansion on the James River in a year. Not bad, huh?" Lucinda resumed the life of shopping, parties, entertaining, dining out, and travel that she had led before her divorce. She had once again found her niche.

Moving Down Life Pathways

The differing stories of Liddy and Lucinda and the hundreds of other divorced men and women we studied over time helped us understand how postdivorce pathways are formed.

First, it became clear that marriage, divorce, single parenthood, remarriage, and stepparenting are not independent events but are transition points in a continuous but changing pathway of intimate relationships. In order to understand the long-term effects of divorce, you have to understand what happened before and after; you cannot seal off one experience from another.

At the six-year point, cohabitation, remarriage, and stepfamilies were becoming common in the VLS. People were moving through other major transition points. And as with Lucinda, these new transitions were acting on the experience of divorce to modify it. Sometimes, the modification was positive—a happy second marriage was beginning to heal old scars—sometimes, the effect was negative—an unhappy second marriage deepened emotional turmoil—but in all cases there was a connection: the postdivorce transition points were reshaping the effects of divorce.

Second, although life pathways can always be altered, in examining the six-year data, I was struck time and again by the domino effect of choices made after divorce. Going back to school, switching jobs, having a child, or selecting a certain kind of mate—a single decision made to deal with a specific problem often changed everything for an individual because it determined which opportunities did and did not open up later. In observing some of our men and women make a succession of poor choices, it was like watching a series of doors—doors to a better life—slam shut. With others such as Liddy Pennybaker, choices were building blocks to a better life. Her decision to live with her mother while she got her MBA led to a new career and financial independence. Her truce with James led to a mutually supportive co-parenting relationship, and eventually to a new and more fulfilling life for Liddy and the Pennybaker children.

Third, men and women often take different routes out of divorce. The "his" and "her" divorce proved to be alive and well at the six-year point in the VLS. Its influence was found in many pieces of data, including remarriage rates; six years after divorce, 75 percent of men and 50 percent of women were remarried.

However, these figures reflect the different goals of men and women as much as they reflect the greater ease men have in finding a new mate. Like Liddy Pennybaker, women who were still single at the six-year mark often were single out of choice. They wanted time to enjoy their new careers and new sense of independence. Many said they preferred being on their own to living with an uninvolved or emotionally distant husband or one with whom they shared few interests. One divorced mother had a bumper sticker that said: I USED TO LIVE ALONE BUT NOW I'M DIVORCED.

At the six-year point, except for the Defeated, most divorced women were reasonably happy. Depression had declined from very high levels in the first year after divorce; alcohol abuse and emotional and health problems also were down dramatically, particularly in comparison to women who remained in unhappy marriages. Parenting competence was on the upswing; with daughters it was often at predivorce levels. Now, most women talked about their enjoyment of their children instead of the stress and their apprehensions about raising children alone, as they had earlier.

In summing up their situation, the majority of divorced women, in spite of the financial problems encountered by some, said that on balance divorce had been a positive event in their lives. It had freed them from a dying relationship, created opportunities for self-discovery, and exposed them to the satisfactions of work—"I'd work even if I didn't have to," 85 percent of the divorced women declared, compared to only 65 percent of working married women. They liked being responsible for the good and bad things that happened to them and living life on their own terms. Said one single mother: "Finally, I'm the captain of my own ship. It may be a little garbage scow but it's all mine."

At six years after divorce, contentment was also the general rule for men—but for different reasons. Only about 10 percent of males had achieved any dramatic, life-altering change; but since men were more interested in remarriage than in personal growth, few felt concerned about ignoring the window of change. The group doing most poorly at six years were single, and their trajectory highlights one of the major differences between the "his" and "her" divorces.

Single divorced women were often divorce winners, while single men were frequently divorce losers. Marriage and children are associated with more responsible behavior and greater well-being in men. The high rates of anxiety, anger, depression, accidents, drug abuse, alcoholism, and health problems we found in men who were still single six years after divorce underscored how vulnerable men were when they lived alone, whereas remarried men were doing relatively well.

At year six, the ex-spouse relationship, which had played a major role in adjustment in the first two years, had faded dramatically in importance for both sexes. On looking back at her first marriage, one woman said: "It seems like a bad dream or something I read in a novel. It just doesn't seem important anymore."

The Six Most Common Pathways
Men and Women Take Out of Divorce

Although postdivorce adaptive styles can be changed any time as circumstances alter, by six years after divorce, many of our men and women had started down a road they were to follow for the rest of the study. Some of these adaptive patterns are more common in the early period and some later. Some are more characteristic of men and some of women.

The Enhancers

Over time, members of the largely female group we called Enhancers grew more competent, well adjusted, and self-fulfilled. Enhancers, who accounted for a fifth of the VLS participants, were classic divorce winners.

Some future members of the group came to divorce with the advantage of protective personal characteristics. They were slightly better educated, more self-confident, physically attractive, or autonomous or achievement-oriented. But the group also contained a large number of women who looked very ordinary until the stress of divorce and the challenge of being a single parent activated latent competencies or forced them to seek out additional resources. The most notable thing about Enhancers was not where they started but their remarkable growth by the time the study ended.

The experience of Mary McKay illustrates this point. Mary had a shy, reticent personality that contrasted with her rather flamboyant appearance. She was statuesque, had the Duchess of York's flaming red hair, and dressed in a rather artsy style, with filmy flowing skirts, high-heeled sandals, and dangling earrings. She was thirty-four when she entered the study and just out of a fairly traditional marriage to a lawyer, who was using all his legal wiles to hide his assets. Mary's assets were like those of many future Enhancers: modest. She had a college degree in art, an ardent interest in and talent for cooking, and a wide circle of acquaintances among Charlottesville's well-to-do.

For awhile after the divorce, Mary thought about teaching art. But after a few phone calls, she discovered that art teachers were not in high demand in Virginia. Mary's other thought—common among VLS women who had a special interest or skills like Mary and Janet Coleman—was to turn a hobby into a business. Maybe she could start a gourmet catering service? Weren't her old friends and acquaintances always complaining about how hard it was to find a good caterer?

For awhile, Mary hesitated.

"To start begging friends for work," she said, when she told me about the idea for a catering service. "I don't know if I'm ready to become the hired help yet."

But as Mary's bills mounted, pride seemed less important than survival. One morning, she picked up the phone, took a very deep breath, and started calling friends for work.

Six years later, that first phone call and one desperate humiliated woman had grown into a thriving catering service with eight employees. Mary's biggest success, though, was personal, not professional. She had become more self-assured and confident, as you might expect; but she was also different in another way, too—a way that Janet Coleman's friend Marcia had tried to articulate when she said that Janet seemed more "important."

Years of responsibility—for a business and for a family—had given Mary a quiet gravitas, a weightiness of character that would have impressed, and I suspect intimidated, the frightened and confused young woman who had entered the study earlier.

However, to be considered Enhanced in our study required more than success in one area such as work. Many people who were successful vocationally and economically became so absorbed in their work that they made little effort to build a better life with their families and friends. Real Enhancers were successful in multiple areas of life and showed a remarkable ability not just to bounce back from setbacks and defeats but to create something meaningful out of them.

At the six-year interview, Vivien Andrews, a successful musician, had a daughter who had just been diagnosed with osteosarcoma, a form of bone cancer. "Sarah used to call me 'Magic Mommy' because I could fix things," Vivien said when she told me about the diagnosis. "But I can't fix this. I don't know if anyone can fix this."

Over the next eighteen months, bad went to worse. The girl's leg had to be amputated—the tumor was enmeshed in the surrounding blood vessels—and when an infection developed, more surgery was required. In between, a bad reaction to chemotherapy almost induced cardiac arrest. I can think of any number of justifiable maternal reactions to this situation, including self-pity and rage. But Vivien resisted both emotions; she remained strong for her daughter, and as time passed, strong for everyone else on the pediatric oncology ward. When she discovered the ward lacked a parents' support group, she organized one, and when she discovered the children had no regular entertainment, she convinced some of her musician friends to make weekly visits.

At the eleven-year interview, a remarkably poised and competent adolescent Sarah Andrews told me, "I wouldn't be here now without Mom. She saved my life. Literally."

Like Vivien Andrews and Liddy Pennybaker, who was a stock analyst at the six-year point, in addition to being professionally successful, most Enhancers were concerned and caring parents, had close supportive relations with friends and family, and were involved in community activities.

Romantically, Enhancers also were the principal beneficiaries of the "ripple" effect of work on a woman's life. As they moved up occupationally, members of the group began to move in new circles—law firms, universities, hospitals, and businesses—which exposed them to a new and more successful kind of man. The second time around, Enhancers usually married up. And their second marriages were usually more successful.

The Enhancers' path can be read as a story of opportunities seized and of hazards avoided or overcome, of adaptability and resiliency, and of an improved life situation attained both through striving and through caring relationships with others.

The Good Enoughs

Consistently the largest group in the VLS, Good Enoughs were the average man and woman coping with divorce. The group's members had some vulnerabilities and some strengths, some success and some problems.

Since they represented the average, Good Enoughs fell in the middle in most indices. They tried to look ahead and had some sense of personal effectiveness; when they encountered a problem, they attempted to solve it. People in the group attended night classes, made new friends, created active social lives, and sought out higher-paying jobs; but Good Enoughs were less proactive, less able to plan systematically, and above all, less persistent than Enhancers. At a certain point, Good Enoughs would run out of steam; they would quit school or begin putting on weight or stop trying to meet a different kind of man. Unlike Enhancers, Good Enough women usually married men who educationally and economically looked like their first husbands and often moved into second marriages that were not a great improvement over the first one.

Good Enoughs were frequently competent mothers; their children did nearly as well as the children of Enhancer mothers. Women in this group also dealt fairly effectively with the normal tensions and challenges of postdivorce life. But being less resilient than Enhancers, they were more likely to be knocked off balance when a new risk factor emerged or an important protective factor disappeared. Some, like Janet Coleman, had a persistent vulnerability that made them unsuccessful in one important area of their life or kept them dealing with the same problems.

At the six-year interview, Janet Coleman was still having romantic difficulties, though Paul Devereaux was out of the picture. After Paul's departure, Janet decided her problem was that she was attracted to the wrong kind of man. She liked assertive, good-looking men, but assertive, good-looking men intimidated her, so she got taken advantage of.

Todd Carlson, Janet's current boyfriend, was supposed to represent a solution to this problem. Todd was everything "bad boys" Richard Coleman and Paul Devereaux were not: quiet, unassuming, gentle, affable. On top of that, he was crazy about Janet.

"That must be a refreshing change," I said, when Janet told me how wonderfully Todd treated her.

Janet sighed. "I know how this is going to sound. But to tell you the truth, Todd is a monumental bore. Sometimes I wonder what's wrong with me. I'm attracted to men who frighten me and bored by the ones who are attracted to me. I keep telling myself I should try harder with Todd. But I don't want to spend the rest of my life with a man who doesn't know how to make me laugh."

Because risks and protective factors can change, sometimes a member of the Good Enough group, like Lucinda Fredericks when she faced financial ruin and the death of her mother, became Defeated. At other times the emergence of a new protective factor, as in Connie Russell's marriage to Bob Keatly, could lift a person from being Defeated to eventually being classified as Good Enough.

At the end of the VLS, the average Good Enough's postdivorce life looked a lot like their old predivorce life. They were muddling through, doing all right at work and at home, but they expressed a certain ill-defined restlessness and yearning for something better in life.

The Seekers

The people in the Seeker group were eager to find a new mate as quickly as possible. At one year postdivorce, 40 percent of men and 38 percent of women had been classified as Seekers. But as people found new partners or remarried, or became more secure or satisfied in their single life, this category shrunk and came to be predominated by men.

A male Seeker is the average man *in extremis*. To him, the true mystery of the universe is not the origin of the Big Bang but how to iron a pair of pants so the crease in each leg matches. Seeker men don't know how to take care of themselves and usually have little desire to learn. The men in this group also require a great deal of affirmation. They need someone to laugh at their jokes, to praise them and tell them how wonderful they are. Without a wife to supply validation, a Seeker male often begins doubting himself. Alone, Seekers succumb to anxiety, depression, and sometimes sexual problems. After divorce, a number of men in the group became vulnerable to erectile dysfunction for the first time.

Sufficiently self-aware to recognize their limitations in single life, Seekers are less cautious and selective about choosing a mate than other people. They pursue fix-ups relentlessly. The Seekers in my study badgered everyone—family, friends, colleagues at work—to help them meet new partners.

Charles Fitch, one participant, even had his mother canvass her friends for potential dates. In many ways, Charles was a classic Seeker—earnest, dependent, and somewhat immature. "The thing that used to drive me absolutely crazy about Charlie was the baby talk," his former wife, Judy, told me one day. "Whenever we made love, Charlie would drop into baby talk. For some strange reason he found it a turn-on."

Like most Seekers, Charles remarried quickly—within two years. His second marriage highlights another Seeker trait. Men in the group are not very interested in real emotional sharing or in personal change. They want a woman who will be supportive and undemanding, someone who will look after them, not ask annoying questions about feelings, who will let them watch television in peace and won't expect much in return. Consequently, Seekers often go from one Pursuer-Distancer marriage to another. Charles's second wife, Miriam, complained about the same things Judy Fitch used to complain about—his inability to talk about feelings, his lack of shared activities, and also his baby talk in intimate moments.

Predicting a Seeker's postdivorce style of parenting was difficult. But often it was associated with his former wife's gatekeeping behavior. Seekers who were encouraged to visit usually continued to see their children, but constantly changing pickup times and contentiousness could drive a man away. Upon remarriage, most Seekers neglected their children from the first marriage.

The Libertines

Predominantly male, too, this group also contained a fair number of women. Libertines sometimes came out of sensation-seeking Operatic marriages and often dressed in a hip, youthful fashion; they also spent more time in singles bars and had more casual sex than other men and women in the study. However, their wild life often had an obligatory quality.

Many members of the group had led fairly conventional middle-class lives until the divorce, and free now, they jumped at the opportunity to play the roles of the lover and bon vivant—at least for awhile. Unencumbered by children, men proved particularly enthusiastic Libertines; but their frenetic play had an element of avoidance in it. Three gins and a twenty-year-old was a favorite male antidote to depressing thoughts about angry ex-wives, sad, confused children, and empty apartments. However, beneath the racy exteriors, many Libertines were unhappy. They missed their families and felt guilty about their failed marriages.

At the end of the first year, Libertines often grew disillusioned with singles bars, casual sex encounters, alcohol, and drugs, and began to long for a stable relationship. Not only were most members of the group in committed relationships six years after divorce; most had reverted to their married, conservatively dressed selves.

It was noticeable that the incidence of affairs among remarried Libertines was no higher than among remarried Seekers. This may simply be a reflection of age, of course. At the time of remarriage, many men in the groups were in their forties. But it also may be that the adoption of a hedonistic lifestyle was a temporary aberration. Most Libertines were basically conventional, middle-class people, who reverted to their old selves when they remarried.

The Competent Loners

Though this group was small, only 10 percent of my study sample, I suspect its members may be a harbinger of things to come, since divorce, cohabitation, and the delay of marriage have dramatically increased the number of unmarried adults in the population.

What is a Competent Loner?

Well-adjusted, self-sufficient, and socially skilled, a Loner often has a gratifying career, an active social life, and a wide range of hobbies and interests. Competent Loners have everything they need to make their life a happy and fulfilling one.

Like Enhancers, whom they resemble in many ways, Loners are divorce winners; but unlike Enhancers, who often remarry, Competent Loners have little interest in sharing their lives with anyone. If someone remarkable appears, a Competent Loner may make an exception. But members of the group do not need a partner to feel complete.

"Never again," Simon Russell said, when I asked him about remarriage. "Even if there's reincarnation, no more marriages. I like the serenity and control in my single life." Except for the children, who greatly enriched his life, Simon was in many ways back where he started before his marriage to Connie.

Male Competent Loners like Simon were particularly interesting. They maintained orderly lives, had comfortable homes, cleaned, and cooked; remembered to pick up the laundry or else hired someone to pick it up for them. Most men in the group were also quite socially skilled. Where the average divorced man relies on the kindness of others for a social life—friends and friends of friends—Competent Loners are proactive. Many men in the group built and maintained very full social lives, among them Simon, who emerged as something of a social force after his divorce. Simon served on the board of a local avant-garde theater company; a few weeks before his six-year interview, one of the local papers carried a report about his appointment to the board of a regional book festival.

Simon also formed a relationship with a calm, capable woman, Louise Harris, a widow who volunteered at the theater and was the antithesis of the turbulent, impulsive Connie. They shared interests in orchids, sailing, and the theater—but neither of them was interested in plunging into marriage.

The Defeated

Some of the Defeated already had problems before the divorce which worsened after the breakup, when they found the added stress of a failed marriage was more than they could handle. Others had difficulty coping because divorce cost them a spouse who had supported them, or in the case of a drinking problem restrained them; still others, like Lucinda Fredericks, found the stresses of divorce activated vulnerabilities that hadn't been salient in their previous lives.

Lack of education or deficient job skills may not be important as risk factors when a spouse is wealthy and working. But as Lucinda discovered, they become critical when a divorced woman has to be self-sufficient.

For most people, defeat was temporary. Some of our participants, such as Janet Coleman, who had been Defeated and helpless in an abusive marriage, through the support of friends and their own initiative built a better life. Lucinda Fredericks, through the sweet serendipity of meeting a wealthy man, stopped wallowing in self-pity and moved on to a personally satisfying life. However, 10 percent of VLS participants who were still Defeated at the end of the study remained mired in despair, immobilized by depression or lethargy. They began to drift through life without purpose or happiness—the way Walter Clayton did after his second wife, Sophia, left him.

A professor at a community college in a small college town, Walter was a pudgy, affable, mild-mannered man, whose most marked trait, a talent for finding the path of least resistance, was rooted in a low sense of efficacy. In college, Walter majored in English because English was easy for him; later, he went to graduate school because everyone else he knew was going. And he married his first wife, Margaret, because he had known her for all his life and everyone expected them to get married.

For a period of time, like Lucinda Fredericks, Walter led the kind of life that kept his vulnerabilities, which also included a proneness to depression, muted. His wife made decisions for him and took care of his social needs, and his job was tenured. Most of the time, the biggest demand in Walter's life was just showing up.

However, the pretty, flirtatious, and manipulative Sophia Lifton, who appeared in one of Walter's classes one September afternoon, changed that. Sophia pursued him and Walter feebly resisted, until Sophia got herself hired as a live-in baby-sitter by the unsuspecting Margaret Clayton.

"Walter makes it sound as if Sophia kidnapped him," Margaret told me a few months after Walter left her. "The other night, he burst into tears on the phone and said, 'I've lost everything, Meg—you, the kids, my house, my good name.' You'd think he was the victim in all this."

People with an external locus of control often think of themselves as being innocent victims at the mercy of others and rely on others to prop them up. Walter had been fortunate in always having strong, supportive women in his life—his mother, Margaret, and then Sophia—who looked after him and made decisions for him. But four years after leaving Margaret, when Sophia decamped for New York and a SoHo artist, Walter finally ran out of props and his life fell apart. Alone, he became deeply depressed, ignored his appearance, was unprepared for classes, saw less and less of his children, and spent most of his free time staring at the television set, smoking dope, or drinking. At the twenty-year follow-up, Walter was still single, still depressed, and still Defeated.

The Paths Taken

The early postdivorce years are painful and confusing for everyone—adults, children, even the men and women who initiated the divorce. People feel empty and disoriented; they flounder, they pine for former spouses, they feel overwhelmed. "How do you raise a child alone?" they wonder, and if they are men, they also wonder, "Will I lose contact with my children?" The practical problems of living—establishing new household routines, getting good day care, having money to provide for their families—add further to the stress of the newly divorced.

During the difficult first year, some people became Libertines, who drank and danced their nights away; others sank into despondency and despair and became Defeated; while still others, craving the security of a new intimate relationship, became Seekers. But during the second year, as new relationships formed and old angers and resentments faded, many men and women settled into a more constructive path.

The planners, the self-disciplined, the future-oriented began to blossom into Enhanced or Competent Loners, while people who were muddling through and doing a reasonably good job of it became Good Enoughs.

By the end of the second year, a substantial number of women were on a road that, one day, would lead them to independence, self-discovery, fulfillment, and enhancement; it was also a road many women would never have traveled without divorce. Most men were also adjusting reasonably well to their new situation. Loneliness was common in both men and women, but the support and love of a new partner helped to enhance feelings of self-worth, validation, and happiness. A new partner was more essential to the well-being of men, however, who plunged into new relationships and remarriages faster than women. By six years after divorce, many of our men and women were cohabitating or remarried, and their new relationships were playing a major role in reshaping their lives.

Points to Remember

- Look at divorce as an opportunity for personal growth and to build more fulfilling relationships.
- Think carefully about choices. The consequences of early decisions about work, friends, lovers, and children may last a lifetime.
- Don't focus on the past, focus on the future. Set priorities and goals, and then work toward them.
- Goals are personal. For some, they may mean building a stimulating career; for others, building a new intimate relationship or becoming a homemaker again.
- Capitalize on your strengths and the resources available to you. You may discover competencies you didn't know you had.

- Don't expect to win all the time or at everything. The road to a more satisfying life is bumpy and it will have many detours.
- You are never trapped on one pathway. Most of those who were categorized as Defeated immediately after divorce gradually moved on to a better life, but moving onward usually requires some effort.

6

Incompetent Bullies and Undisciplined Disciplinarians: Children and Parents in the First Two Years After Divorce

*A*dam and Bethany Pennybaker were very different children before the divorce, had different experiences following the divorce, and were showing extremely different patterns of coping in the first two years after the breakup.

Bethany had always been closer to her father than to her mother and his departure for her was cataclysmic. In the first year when James tried to leave after a visit, she would cling to him and sob.

James said, "We would have to peel her fingers off me. It was devastating." The previously placid Bethany also would fly into rages, hitting and biting her mother, whom she blamed for the separation. In her distress, she began to wet the bed again, had night terrors, and would wake crying or crawl into bed with Liddy three or four times a night.

Bethany later said, "I had to keep checking to see if Mom was there. If Dad could leave, why couldn't she?"

Adam, who was only four at the time of the divorce, was confused about the changes in his life, but he was overtly upset with his parents' bickering and his mother's increased irritability with him. Adam began to complain about how much time and attention Bethany got and how biased Liddy was as a mother. "Whenever Bethany gets in trouble, it's always someone else's fault," Adam told me one day. "Whenever I get in trouble, it's always *my* fault. That's not fair of Mother. The only one that treats us the same is Grandma."

James's close relationship with Bethany further sharpened Adam's sense of isolation—his sense of being, as he later put it, "the unfavored child in the family." In James's defense, I have to say that once the early postdivorce skirmishes with Liddy had simmered down, James did make an attempt to move close to Adam. But their sensibilities did not mesh the way his and Bethany's did. However, it was more than that. James said, "You know my marriage with Liddy was fine until Adam was born. I know it's not the kid's fault, but I resented him. I used to wonder how much of what I felt for Adam was real love and how much of it was guilt for not loving him enough."

At one year after the divorce, Adam's exuberance and playfulness with other children and adults had an aggressive edge not present earlier. Although both Bethany and Adam were adjusting reasonably well two years afterward, Adam, who was a remarkably attractive and popular child, carried with him a sense of insecurity and low self-esteem that was compounded by the presence of a reading disability when he entered school.

Children at Two Years Past Divorce

For adults, divorce brings *a* world to an end; for young children, whose lives are focused in the family, it seems to bring *the* world to an end. Yet the adjustment patterns of adults and children are remarkably similar: a decline in function in the first year and a notable improvement in the second. Still, at two years, many youngsters remained anxious and whiny, and clingy and oppositional, while others had school and social problems. And children, like their parents, showed wide variation in how they coped with divorce. Some sailed through a turbulent divorce and emerged relatively unscathed; others showed permanent emotional or behavioral problems; and still others appeared to be adjusting well initially, but delayed problems emerged in adolescence or young adulthood.

As with adults, how well children coped with divorce depended on the stresses they encountered and the personal and social resources they had to deal with in their changing life. For some children, who had moved from conflictual, hostile, or abusive homes into a more harmonious family situation with a capable, involved parent, divorce was in the long run advantageous. By two years after divorce, these children were happier and better behaved than they had been before the breakup. For others, who had come from homes in which they felt secure and where marital conflict was concealed or muted, the breakup was unexpected, incomprehensible, frightening, and these children had greater losses to deal with. For all young children, divorce led to changes in their life that were difficult to cope with, and how well they coped to a large extent depended on the behavior of the custodial parent. An involved, competent custodial parent was the most effective buffer a young child could have against postdivorce stress; an irritable, punitive, uncaring, or disengaged parent put the child at great risk for developing problems.

Challenges and Changes

For a young child, psychologically, divorce is the equivalent of lifting a hundred-pound weight over the head. Processing all the radical and unprecedented changes—loss of a parent, loss of a home, of friends—stretches immature cognitive and emotional abilities to the absolute limit and sometimes beyond that limit.

Twenty years later, many of my young adults from divorced families still recalled the pain of the early years.

One young man remembered how horrified he was to see his mother kiss another man for the first time, and how sad he felt when his father told him he was getting married again. "That ended my little dream of reuniting my parents," he said.

Another remembered crying as the movers carried out their furniture from the family home and they moved away from the neighborhood and friends they had known to their first cramped apartment.

"Are you eight or nine now?" one child recalled her father asking the first time he introduced her to his new girlfriend. The girl was ten. Another remembered being afraid to go to school in case his mother had gone by the time he returned.

For many children, postdivorce stress included an abrupt transition from a predictable, orderly, and financially secure life to its opposite: poverty, disorder, and unpredictability—dealing with an altered and often less competent parent, attending a chaotic school, being given age-inappropriate chores, moving from apartment to apartment, or coping with the serial live-in lovers or spouses of a parent.

For most, it included seeing parents they loved fight or become hostile and distant, and seeing one parent intermittently or not at all. For all, it involved a loss of trust. Children are dependent on and attached to parents, even not very competent parents. When their parents seem unreliable and untrustworthy, the very bedrock of children's well-being is shattered. How can you rely on parents who quarrel, leave, become preoccupied, or don't seem to care about the pain they are inflicting on you?

It is not surprising, then, that unmoored from the security of their predictable world, young children become anxious and angry. They may become non-compliant or unruly or dependent, regress and wet the bed or suck their thumb, or fight with their friends or cry at things that never used to bother them. Many are afraid of being separated from their parent—of going to school or being left with a baby-sitter or in day care. Some blame themselves and wonder what they did to drive their parent away.

The problems are not confined to relationships with parents and in the home. They flood into behavior with friends and siblings, teachers and other adults. Some children become loners and fringers. They play alone or hang around watching at the edge of a group of other children playing; young boys in particular may become incompetent bullies, making ineffective aggressive forays against other children. The incompetent bully may grab for another child's truck: if he is unsuccessful or the other child resists, the incompetent bully may start to cry or complain to the teacher. Competent bullies are sometimes popular in adolescence, but incompetent bullies are never popular. Even in the preschool setting, the incompetent bully is rejected and often finds himself exiled to the nursery school equivalent of Siberia. Rejected by his same-aged male peers, he ends up playing with younger peers or playing house with the girls.

It has often been reported that young boys in divorced families temporarily show more feminine patterns of play. In part, this is because preschool boys in divorced families are rejected by the male peer group and so spend more time playing with girls. In part, it is because boys in mother-headed families may not experience the boisterous rough-and-tumble play found between fathers and sons. And in part it is also because mothers, more safety-conscious than fathers, are quicker to shout "Stop" when a boy climbs a tree, crosses a street alone, or engages in other forms of risk-taking behavior.

The incompetent bully pattern usually is a temporary affliction and begins to diminish in the second year following divorce. But even in nursery school, reputations die hard. So, often the child's social problems don't end when his behavior improves. Even recovering incompetent bullies continue to be shunned by their male schoolmates.

Normally, change should be avoided after a divorce. At a time when their world is in flux, children need the stability and continuity conferred by familiar relationships and settings. However, since rejection also is harmful, as the Incompetent Bully syndrome recedes, it is sometimes a good idea to transfer the boy to a new nursery school where he can start afresh.

Distressed Parents

A child's most potent buffer against postdivorce stress is a competent, involved custodial parent; but old hurts and new worries often sideline mothers and fathers whose parenting skills decline during the first year, though they begin to recover in the second and third years.

Custodial Mothers and Their Children

Preoccupied by guilt, some custodial mothers put few limits on their children and allow them to run rampant; others, because of depression or self-involvement, may neglect their children's needs and withdraw from them. But in the most common pattern, parental affection, positive involvement, and time spent with the child diminish, while parental irritability, punitiveness, and unpredictable, erratic discipline increase.

When a youngster misbehaves, instead of explaining why the misbehavior is wrong or trying to distract the child, the tired, preoccupied woman barks out a command: "Don't do that!" or, "Stop it!" If the command is ignored, the woman nags or explodes or both, and if the child still ignores her, she usually gives up or blows up.

Young sons, especially, pose a problem for divorce-depleted mothers. Divorce to some extent makes most young children dependent, whiny, aggressive, and defiant—just generally hard to manage. We found this combination of noxious behavior most common in our preschool boys in the first year. We actually clocked one boy performing demanding, aversive behaviors such as a cry, a hit, a whine, a nag, at the rate of one every thirty seconds. It is no wonder that some of our mothers described their early relationships with their children after a divorce and what they saw as constant harassment by the child as "a fight for survival," "like the old Chinese water torture," or "like getting bitten to death by ducks."

Inconsistent cranky maternal commands and threats are a common feature of the divorced mother–son relationship and only serve to escalate hostile exchanges. Often, when a woman issues a command, boys respond by escalating their misbehavior. This leads to a counterescalation: the woman ratchets up her ineffective, irritable threats or yells or spanks the child, who becomes even more angry and unmanageable, which leads the already depressed, helpless mother to conclude: "I really am incompetent. I can't even control a four-year-old." The endpoint of the cycle is further erosion in the woman's parenting competence and a deepening of her depression and sense of helplessness.

We observed an example of this coercive cycle with Lucinda Fredericks and five-year-old Dickie during one of our home visits. Lucinda was trying to talk on the phone. Dickie was making loud "brroohm, brroohm" noises while he played with his truck.

"Dickie, stop doing that. I'm trying to talk on the phone."

Dickie continues more loudly.

"Dickie, knock it off. I can't hear a thing."

Dickie draws closer now, banging and crashing two trucks together. Lucinda kicks at Dickie. "All right, no TV tonight."

Dickie runs the truck over Lucinda's foot with an especially loud "brroohm!"

At that point an already depressed Lucinda "lost it." She yanked Dickie by the arm and slapped him.

Aggrieved, Dickie threw himself on the floor, screaming. Lucinda dissolved in tears and cried: "I can't take it. I can't take it! I just can't take it anymore."

A few minutes later, in order to get a little peace, Lucinda had seated Dickie, still sobbing, in front of the television with a plate of cookies.

Lucinda in this interchange had not only gotten into a coercive cycle with Dickie, but had fallen into a trap we frequently found with our stressed, overburdened mothers. In order to get a little relief from a child's aggression, nagging, or tantrums, they gave in or actually rewarded the child for his bad behavior. This exchanges short-term gain for long-term pain, since the child learns that misbehavior pays off, and it increases the chances that he will disobey and act out again.

The importance of containing these destructive, hostile exchanges was underscored by a related VLS finding. The VLS was not originally designed to examine the effectiveness of therapy, but when we found that in over a third of our families at least one of the parents or the child had been in counseling or psychotherapy, we decided to see if it was helping them. We found, as others have, that therapy was less effective in single-parent than in two-parent families. We also found that traditional talk therapies didn't offer much solace in the early years after a divorce. The reason? A slow and lengthy intrapsychic examination of feelings and the past seems a little beside the point when you've got three weeks to find a place to live or a job or child care and "are getting bitten to death by ducks."

What did enhance the mental health of newly divorced women was behavior modification programs for parents. These programs were designed to teach parents how to control a child via techniques like consistent rewards and punishments, explanation-oriented discipline, and time-outs. We noticed that women who were involved in behavior modification programs became less vulnerable to coercive cycles. We also noticed that as a woman gained more effective control over her child, she felt more confident and validated. These programs worked for children, too; their behavior improved at home, in school, and on the playground.

Girls show many of the same problems as boys in the first year after a divorce, but parents are more supportive with girls, and mothers and daughters learn to get along quickly. By the end of the second year, the mother-daughter relationship was similar to that in non-divorced families, although it was to become more fractious in adolescence.

Custodial Fathers and Their Children

Custodial fathers face many of the same challenges that custodial mothers do in trying to deal with and support a distressed child; but fathers have fewer problems in control. Children are more likely to obey fathers than mothers, and fathers and children are less likely to get involved in coercive cycles. Where fathers fall short is in communication—in encouraging children to talk about their feelings and problems—and in adolescence, fathers often don't monitor their children's behavior well. They don't keep track of what their teenagers are doing, where they are, and who they are with; and this is associated with antisocial behavior.

Both custodial mothers and fathers can be affectionate, involved, competent parents, but there is more continuity from before the divorce to after the divorce in the parenting of mothers. Fathers' parenting is less predictable, probably because their situation alters more dramatically. If they get custody of the child, they become the primary caregiver, which they were unlikely to have been before. Some previously uninvolved fathers who gain custody of their children rise to the occasion and show a sort of *Kramer vs. Kramer* effect, in which they learn to be caring, adept parents. A critical factor here is whether the father sought custody of the child himself or had custody foisted upon him because of a neglecting, incompetent, or abusive mother. Fathers who reluctantly accept custody are often resentful and unaffectionate, and don't expend the effort and time essential to being a good parent.

Robert Reeves was shamed by his family into assuming custody of his two children, Jane and Ricky, after their mother, a long-term cocaine abuser, was charged with neglect. He complained, "It isn't that I don't care about the children, but I'm just not a touchy-feely kind of guy. I just don't know what to do with them. They make my life too complicated."

For a year, Robert warehoused the children, with long hours spent in shifting child care arrangements—with relatives and neighbors, in day care, school, and after-school programs.

Finally, he just gave up. At our last interview, the two sad-faced children stood silently, four-year-old Ricky clinging to his ten-year-old sister Jane and sucking his thumb, as Robert discussed his plans to send the children to live in another state with his older sister.

Non-Custodial Parents and Their Children

We saw many accomplished men in our studies of divorce: professors and deans, doctors and lawyers, entrepreneurs and "techies" from Internet companies, businessmen and officers in the armed forces. Some days, every man I spoke to seemed to have a Ph.D. or an M.D. at the end of his name. But there was one thing that few of these very intelligent, skilled, and accomplished men knew how to do: how to be a good non-custodial father.

When non-custodial fathers talked about parenting, they often ended up talking about how frustrated, confused, and uncertain they felt, and how painful and difficult visitation days and intermittent parenting were.

In the first year, many men adopt an "Every day is Christmas" attitude. They never visit the child without a gift, plan entertainments, and bite their tongue whenever the child does something wrong. What little time they have with their children they want to be pleasant. Although this holiday attitude declines a bit later, non-custodial fathers remain the most lenient of all parents, including non-residential mothers. Part-time dads rarely set rules or act as disciplinarians or, as non-divorced fathers do, help with homework. Their role is companionate rather than parental.

For most men, not being a daily presence in a child's life is a difficult hurdle to overcome. Planned visits often seem contrived and awkward. As one man said, "Most fathers don't spend eight hours eyeball-to-eyeball trying to entertain their children." Most of the time, parents are available to children but not necessarily interacting with them. Many of the tender times in the relationship are informal. Children are playing by themselves or with friends and wander in to show or give the parent something—a new drawing or a flower or rock found in the garden—to get comfort for a scraped knee, or to complain about the injustices of older siblings. Other times are part of the daily routine of talking over the dinner table about what happened at school that day, of a few moments of wild, rambunctious play when Dad gets home, of helping with homework or reading together before bed.

Being a sometime tour guide father and rainy Sunday mornings spent at Wendy's are unlikely to lead to such tender moments. This is why overnight stays become so important. Overnight stays help youngsters think of their father's place as a second home and foster more relaxed relationships and routines that can draw fathers and children closer together. When regular overnights happen, fathers are more likely to remain involved with their children and less likely to drift away as so many non-custodial fathers do.

Because the father's nurturing role is so fragile and because the role of non-residential parent is filled with obstacles and uncertainty, the behavior of the non-custodial father is harder to predict. Initially, at least, most men stay around. At two months after divorce, non-custodial VLS fathers were having as much face-to-face contact with their children as they had before the divorce, and for a quarter of the men, there was more contact. But since some men were using the visits as an excuse to see a wife they still felt attached to or to annoy a wife they were still angry at, this contact did not last.

Eventually, three types of response patterns emerged. The first group was of men, like Simon Russell, who were consistent in their pre- and postdivorce parenting. Simon had been an active, involved parent before the divorce. After the divorce, when Connie had custody of the children, he phoned them each evening to talk about their day and say good night, and the children stayed with him from Friday to Sunday. Other men were consistent in their neglect. They didn't spend time with their children before the breakup, and they made no room for a child in their new lives.

The second group was composed of what I call divorce-activated fathers. These men had to lose their families to realize how much they loved them. They began attending soccer games and school plays and PTA meetings; they began doing all the things they were too busy to do before the divorce or had relegated to their wives.

The third group, divorce-deactivated fathers, was composed of formerly attentive men who gradually drifted away from the parenting role. During the two-month interview, I remember one member of the group boasting about his hands-on parenting. "I'm the one who put Sybil to bed and read to her," he said, "and I'm the one she ran to when she hurt herself." However, at the two-year interview, when I asked about Sybil, the man said, "I haven't seen her in awhile."

I asked how long "awhile" was.

"Three months," the man replied. "It's hard for me; having her, but not really having her. It's to the point now where I've begun dreading visiting days. I know I'll only be with Sybil for the day and then have to give her back."

Although lethargy, lack of attachment, or preoccupation with their new lives accounted for a lot of paternal dropouts, a surprising number of men stay away because, like this father, they find being all the way out of a child's life less painful than being only halfway in it. But others disappeared because of conflict with their wives or obstacles their wives presented to visits, and the lack of control they had over decisions about their children. They felt shut out of their children's lives.

By the end of the second year, most divorced fathers had settled into a regular visitation pattern. In my study, the norm was biweekly or monthly visits; at the two-year point, only a quarter of non-custodial study dads were still seeing their children once a week or more. Our six-year assessment produced an even bleaker outlook: we found that a quarter of our children saw their fathers once a year or less. However, there is a silver lining.

In our studies, those fathers who divorced in the last decade maintained more regular contact with their children. Almost a third were seeing their children at least once a week. This may be because men are beginning to participate more actively in their children's lives and are reluctant to give them up after divorce, or it may be due to the increase in joint custody and mediation. We found that both joint custody and mediation were more likely to make a man feel satisfied with the settlement. And a man who was happy with his divorce settlement was more likely to remain an engaged parent and to pay child support. But alas, a happy dad often meant an unhappy mom: women were less happy with mediation than men, often because they felt mediation weakened maternal control.

Non-custodial mothers are more likely than non-custodial fathers to remain active, engaged parents. They visit their children twice as much and are less likely to act as a "tour guide" parent. They advise, set rules, encourage mature, self-controlled behavior, and discipline their children more than non-custodial fathers do. Non-custodial mothers also are more likely to rearrange their lives to accommodate a child. Overnight stays are more common with non-custodial mothers, and they often provide a special room for the child, stocking it with clothes, toys, and books.

Children report feeling closer to non-custodial mothers than to non-custodial fathers; they say that they can talk about their problems more easily with their mother and think the mother cares more about them. Still, these relationships are not as close as those in non-divorced families. Shelley Noble at first had physical custody of her children, Christopher and Glenda; but her double shift as a waitress in two different restaurants didn't allow her to provide the supervision or the kind of home and neighborhood setting she thought essential to their well-being. Drug use was high and achievement low in the local schools, and delinquency was rampant in the neighborhood. When ten-year-old Christopher got in trouble with the law, Shelley reluctantly gave the children over to the care of their more affluent father.

"I know it's for the best, but there's never a moment I don't think about them and miss them. I keep in touch by phone and see them on Sundays, but with two jobs it's hard to squeeze more time in. I just feel them slipping away."

What about the children themselves? How do custody arrangements affect them?

On average, youngsters do equally well in mother, father, and joint custody families, provided the parent responsible for the child's care is loving, supportive, and firm about discipline. Not surprisingly, a custodial parent has far more influence on a child's well-being than a noncustodial parent.

Points to Remember

- Divorce, stressful for adults, is usually even more stressful for children. In the early postdivorce years, many youngsters display emotional, social, and behavioral problems.
- However, children are resilient; two years after divorce, most boys and girls are beginning to function reasonably well again. Happily, the tendency to "self-righting" is strong in the young.
- Some developmental problems associated with divorce actually originate earlier. For example, we found that youngsters who lived in high-conflict families often displayed such classic divorce symptoms as aggressiveness, non-compliance, anxiety, and a lack of social responsibility *before* their parents separated.
- Parenting skills decline in the first year after a divorce but begin to revive in the second and third years.
- Divorce is particularly challenging for women with young sons. In the early years, often they get caught up in a series of escalating hos-

tile exchanges, which feeds the child's anger and the woman's sense of being an incompetent parent.

- Custodial fathers are often better at control; custodial mothers are better at communication and nurturance.
- If children move from a conflicted, non-supportive, or abusive situation before the divorce to a more harmonious one with a competent custodial parent after the divorce, their adjustment improves.
- Divorce puts children at risk for encountering many stresses, and for young children the most potent protection comes from a caring, competent custodial parent.
- If parenting is loving, firm, and consistent, and conflict between divorced parents is low, children can thrive in a mother, father, or joint custody situation.
- If you're having trouble, try programs geared toward improving parenting skills. Being a better parent is good for you as well as your child.
- Children usually want to maintain contact with both parents, but many non-custodial parents drop out. Try to facilitate visits if you can control your fighting and animosity. In the long run, it will help you and your children.

7

What Helps and What Hurts:
Children's Adjustment Six Years After Divorce

Six years after the divorce, Bethany Pennybaker's anger, anxiety, and resentment were gone. She had emerged as an unusually mature and responsible child, who was accomplished both academically and socially. And much to her parents' delight, she was showing an interest and talent in the arts—in writing poetry and drawing—that drew them together. "With Bethany, there are never any problems," James said to me one day.

With Adam, in contrast, there often were problems. At six, Adam had been diagnosed as hyperactive and having an attention deficit disorder. Although his hyperactivity had abated by age ten, his problems lingered in the form of a severe reading disability. "It breaks my heart to see him struggle so," Liddy said. "Adam's so bright and he's hurting so much and nothing we do seems to help with his reading. He's being absolutely turned off school by his dyslexia."

Sadly, Adam's problems were just starting. His grandmother, Ginny, had met a Mr. Atwood on an Elderhostel tour. They became friends and then more than friends, and married when Adam was nine. In many ways, Adam had been closer to his grandmother than his parents; with her he had never felt like "the non-preferred child." Although Ginny saw Adam twice a week and phoned almost every day, Adam said that when Ginny moved out, "It was like going through another divorce."

Under the best of conditions, the separation from Ginny would have upset Adam. But it occurred just as his problems in school were intensifying. With no gratification in academic attainment, he turned to his areas of success—sports and the peer group. Adam, a funny, extroverted, uninhibited, and good-looking boy, had always been popular. In addition, he was an exceptional young athlete and eventually in high school won letters in baseball and track. "Not in my game, soccer. He never played soccer," James complained. Adam also became increasingly involved with a group of disruptive junior jocks who were more interested in sports and mischief than school or academics. They spent most of their free time kicking or throwing a ball around, tracking athletic records, or glued to the television watching baseball, football, and basketball. And their high-spirited acting out was becoming serious.

The Pennybaker children illustrate some of our important findings about how children cope with their parents' marital breakup that were emerging six years after divorce. As with adults, how well children were doing depended on risk and protective factors, and as we found with Adam Pennybaker, these factors could shift over time. It was the current stresses and resources, rather than the ones that had surrounded the divorce, that were now most important. These factors were so individual that as in the Pennybaker case, we often saw siblings from the same family take very different paths out of divorce. In addition, by the six-year follow-up, a dramatic change had occurred. The cloud of anxiety and depression that hung over children in the first year usually had diminished or evaporated. Some boys and girls remained deeply troubled, but three quarters of the children from divorced families were now functioning well within the normal range. Like their parents, children were showing diverse patterns of adjustment and had taken varied routes to get there.

By six years after divorce, we were gaining a clearer understanding of how social relationships within and outside the family, as well as individual characteristics of the child, could undermine or promote the child's well-being. When the children were ten, the behavior of the custodial parent was still the most significant influence on their adjustment. But other relationships with siblings, peers, teachers, and mentors were becoming increasingly important. And to a large extent this was influenced by the attributes and behavior of the child. Was the child easygoing or hard to get along with, pretty or plain, shy or outgoing, and did the child have particular skills in academics, social relations, or athletics that might make him feel better about himself and be well regarded by others?

Risk and Protective Factors in the Family

The Invaluable Role of Good Parenting

Parenting is not only the most important but often the sole protective social factor in a very young child's life. But even six years after divorce, when our ten-year-olds were beginning to have access to other potential buffering factors outside the family, we found that a custodial parent—which in most cases meant a mother—remained the first line of defense against the stresses of postnuclear family life.

The parenting and behavior of divorced custodial parents is especially important because if it deteriorates, no other parent is present in the home to buffer the child from the day-to-day hassles of living with an inept parent. Rejection, irritability, or neglect floods directly onto the child, with no second parent able to deflect or lessen the impact.

The good news about parenting six years after divorce is that most divorced women had recovered from the initial dramatic collapse in their parenting skills and had developed reasonably close, constructive relationships with their children. The bad news is that even this long after divorce, because of the many stresses in their lives, divorced women were on average less competent parents than women in non-divorced families. This is in part because authoritative parenting, which requires a great deal of energy and focus, is harder to do when there is no assistance and cooperation available from another partner.

Parenting Styles That Help or Hurt

How do we define "competent" or "incompetent" parents? Four common parenting styles were found in both divorced and non-divorced families: *authoritative, permissive, authoritarian,* and *disengaged/neglecting*. Authoritative parenting, combining warmth and control, has a significant protective effect against the stresses children encounter in all types of families, whereas permissive child rearing and to a much greater extent authoritarian or disengaged/neglecting child rearing make children more vulnerable to risks and postdivorce stresses. Unfortunately, authoritative parenting is found less often in divorced homes, especially in the first year.

Balancing Warmth and Control: The Authoritative Parent

Warm, consistent, and supportive, authoritative parents are also skilled communicators, and firm but responsive disciplinarians. The discipline techniques they use, such as verbal controls, time-outs, deprivation of privileges, and explanation and reasoning, often work on two levels. They snuff out the immediate misbehavior and also teach a child how to control himself when a parent isn't there to do it for him. Authoritative parents also respect their children, which may not sound like much of a compliment; after all, isn't every parent respectful?

Most mothers and fathers think of themselves that way; but during the study, I was surprised at how often a preoccupied, emotionally upset, distracted parent would ignore or bark at the child or interrupt her conversation, criticize the youngster in front of a friend, embarrass her in front of strangers, or unwittingly inflict some other petty humiliation. These same parents would never behave that way with another adult, nor would they tolerate that behavior in their children.

The protective effects of authoritative parenting are threefold. First, parental consistency keeps the child's home environment reassuringly predictable, at a time when everything else in his life is changing in confusing and distressing ways. At the twenty-year interview, David Coleman still remembered every one of the moves his family made after the divorce, although the third move, when David overheard the landlord propositioning his mother, and the fourth, when the Coleman family got its first introduction to food stamps and public housing, stood out with particular clarity in his mind.

"I don't know how Mom did it, but amazingly, through it all, Mom was there when Leah and I needed her," David said. "Even when she was first working for Gordon and afterwards when she was putting in long hours building her own business, we'd have dinner at the shop together and she'd supervise us working on homework while she did flower arrangements. No matter what, Leah and I ate with Mom at the same time every night and went to bed at the same time and were read a story before we went to sleep."

Authoritative parenting also protects by fostering the mutual trust and respect that makes controlling a child easier. Parental guidance represents a child's best protection against the temptations of postdivorce life, especially in an impoverished or unruly new neighborhood. But will a child listen to parental warnings and admonitions?

Parents think that children should obey and respect them because they are older, wiser, more powerful; in other words, because they are parents. But parents have to earn the respect of their children by being trustworthy and admirable. An authoritative parent earns the kind of respect that makes her "no's" stick. But inconsistent authority undermines trust and is ultimately destructive. Children of parents who are alcoholic, lose control, or behave in unpredictable or inappropriate ways often are unruly and contemptuous with their parents.

Celia Russell had initially tried to cope with her mother's alcoholism by helping her when she was drunk—getting her undressed for bed, cleaning up after her when she was sick—a heavy burden for a child. But eventually, as she grew older, her concern deteriorated into a seething anger and scorn.

At her six-year interview, when she was ten, Celia said: "You can't believe what it's like to have a mother who drinks too much. You never know what's going to happen and you're afraid to bring new friends home. I remember my seventh birthday party. It was just before we went to live with Dad. I didn't want a party. I was worried about how Mom might behave and what my friends would think. I couldn't sleep the night before. But Mom insisted. She really worked hard on the games and the food for the party. Everyone was having a great time but me and Michael. I could tell Mom had been drinking. Her voice gets louder and she talks funny and laughs too much and her eyes look kind of wild.

"When Mom came through the door with the cake, singing 'Happy Birthday,' she staggered, tripped on the rug, and fell. There she was sprawled out on the floor, covered with cake, looking like she was going to cry. There was dead silence for a few minutes, then a couple of my friends began to cry; some phoned their mothers to pick them up; some just sat there stunned. A lot started to laugh. I guess it was sort of funny, but not to me. I wanted to drop through the floor. Michael just disappeared. We found him after dark still hiding in the barn. That night, I could hear Mom crying in her room and I was crying in mine. I wanted a mom like everybody else's, a mom that you could trust, not a crazy one like mine."

When twenty-four-year-old Celia was asked about her most traumatic experience, she responded, "my seventh birthday party." By that point, Connie, who had been on the wagon for many years, had done a lot of repairwork on her relationships with Celia and Michael, but an element of wariness and unease remained. The adult Russell children had been through too much to entirely trust their mother.

A final and important element of authoritative parenting is that authoritative parents display a fine-tuned sensitivity and responsiveness to the feelings, needs, and abilities of their children. They know when to soothe and support and when to push and demand more. Often in authoritative homes, age-appropriate chores such as setting the table, mowing the lawn, and baby-sitting a younger sibling were regularly used to foster a sense of maturity, responsibility, and competency. But authoritative parents did not consult or seek help from their children in dealing with economic, personal, or romantic problems the child was too immature to understand or helpless to solve.

Overall, children of authoritative parents emerged from divorce as the most socially responsible, least troubled, and highest-achieving children in our own studies. Some were like Bethany Pennybaker, who was eventually strengthened by dealing with the losses, stresses, and changes in her life, with the support of an authoritative mother and grandmother. Bethany, who had been a timid, socially reticent child before the divorce, had become a self-confident, poised, goal-oriented child by age ten.

When Love Is Not Enough: The Permissive Parent

The popular image of the permissive parent is that of a counterculture idealist who believes discipline will lead to neurotic hang-ups or ruin her child's creativity. We had a sizable number of permissive divorced parents in our studies, but not many like that. Mostly, our permissive parents were recent converts to the style, and their conversion was prompted by physical and emotional exhaustion, or by guilt—how could they discipline a child they had just put through a divorce? After a day of work, often it was just easier to ignore or give in to a disobedient child. Women in the permissive group were affectionate and caring, but they imposed few rules, guidelines, or restrictions; and while a lack of control and limit-setting did not produce the anger and hostility we saw in some of our troubled children, it did produce impulsivity and sometimes aggressiveness. Children from permissive homes needed more time to learn emotional self-regulation than other youngsters.

Some children, such as Michael Russell, who was temperamentally self-controlled and inhibited, needed love and support more than regulation; others, like his sister, Celia, who already was showing her mother's intense emotionality and impulsivity, needed a firmer hand, and she was not to get that from her indulgent father, Simon. Because of Connie's alcoholism and her increasingly erratic neglectful parenting, Simon gained custody of the children when Celia was eight and Michael was six. Simon passionately threw himself into the role of a caring parent. He established routines in their previously chaotic life. He listened to their problems and soothed them when they woke crying in the night. He helped them with homework and consulted with teachers and counselors. He took the children to concerts and puppet shows and on trips. Michael and his father were very alike and rapidly grew closer. By the time they had lived together for a year, Michael was a thriving child, with few vestiges of his traumatic past.

For explosive, impulsive Celia, love was not enough, but for the gentle Simon firm limit-setting and discipline did not seem to be an option. "I'm just loving her and trying to make her feel safe and hoping she'll get over it," Simon said.

Celia didn't get over it, and her lack of control was exacerbated by early physical maturing. At the age of thirteen, Celia was a pretty, provocative, mature-looking teenager, very aware of her burgeoning sexuality and its effect on the males around her.

When Too Much Authority Is Bad: The Authoritarian Parent

Authoritarian parents are the opposite of permissive parents. They try to control the chaos of postdivorce family life with harsh, punitive, rigid discipline. But often the angry, anxious, and bullying behavior we saw in their children also had another source: a lack of genuine parental warmth, affection, and sensitivity. The offspring of authoritarians were also quite often duplicitous. They would be conforming and fearful around a parent or other authority figure, but mean and bullying with peers.

The great irony of the authoritarian style is that, often, it ended up producing what it was meant to prevent, a rebellious child who became increasingly confrontational and defiant as he grew older. Authoritarian homes often had high rates of conflict, and significantly, the effects of authoritarianism lingered into adolescence and young adulthood, particularly in boys. Young adults from authoritarian homes often did poorly at school and work; and they frequently had angry, disruptive relationships with friends, children, lovers, and spouses.

One of the tragedies in our divorced women was that even when they attempted to be authoritarian, they often were erratic and ineffec-

tive. Although like other authoritarians they were unloving and punitive, constantly barking out orders and criticism, they often lacked the
firmness and follow-through found in most authoritarians. Their children didn't even get the benefits of predictable, albeit predictably punitive discipline.

Abandoning Your Children: The Disengaged/Neglecting Parent

Disengaged parenting is a form of emotional, psychological, and
sometimes physical desertion. Essentially, the parent abandons children
to cope with the stresses of divorce on their own. Disengaged parents
are focused on their own needs or survival. When a child interferes or
makes demands, the parent responds with irritation or withdrawal. Some
disengaged parents are just self-involved, narcissistic people like
Lucinda Fredericks. Others neglect their children because of alcoholism
or substance abuse or depression. Disengaged parenting is particularly
common among Defeated adults who, overwhelmed by stress, have no
time or energy left over for their children. But sometimes, as in the case
of Katherine Merrill, success can also make a parent neglectful.

Attractive in a shiny, stylishly dressed, professional way, Katherine
was a good example of that much celebrated creature, the "multi-
tasker," except Katherine multi-tasked at an Olympic level. A real estate
lawyer who was also deeply involved in politics and cultural affairs,
Katherine never went anywhere without her two Filofax datebooks and
cell phone, which rang so often at the six-year interview, I finally had to
ask her to shut it off.

It would be easy to turn Katherine into a caricature of a certain kind
of contemporary woman, so her story should be put into context. She
was an intelligent, lively person, who had given up a promising legal
career to marry another lawyer—an angry, controlling man, who
seemed to have spent most of the marriage complaining about Katherine's mother, her credit card bills, and her lack of domesticity.

"I don't know why I waited so long to leave," Katherine commented
at the two-month interview. "I feel like I've wasted the best years of my
life." By the six-year interview, those last years had already been made

up, and then some. But our data showed that busy, self-absorbed Katherine had begun neglecting her daughter, Annalee, though like many disengaged parents, Katherine didn't realize it.

Indeed, at the six-year interview, Katherine went out of her way to call attention to her parenting. She told me that on nights when she had a date or party, she would invite Annalee into the bedroom and the two of them would chat while Katherine dressed and put on her makeup. Katherine was very proud of these "special moments," as she called them. "I treasure them and so does Annalee."

However, as a young adult, Annalee remembered the "special moments" differently. She described them as "twofers" and said that they were her mother's way of "killing two birds with one stone." "Katherine figured she could get her mother thing out of the way while she was getting ready to go out," Annalee said. "Everyone always talks about what a big success Mom's been. But she paid a price and I'm it." This was a not-so-veiled reference to Annalee's adolescent drug problems. "Nothing should ever be allowed to come before your child," Annalee declared. "Nothing."

Children with disengaged/neglecting parents were growing up without anyone to nurture or guide them and it was reflected in their development. The most troubled in the study, these children of disengaged parents were wild, defiant, and unhappy; they had few skills, and as they grew older, they often had problems with work, marriage, the law, drugs, and alcohol.

The Non-Residential Parent

Where there is a low level of conflict between parents, a non-residential father—particularly a supportive one with an authoritative style—can help boost a boy's achievement and reduce his likelihood of participating in delinquent activities or experimenting with drugs and alcohol. Authoritative non-custodial mothers also can have a positive impact, especially on daughters. But the developmental effects of most non-residential parents are limited. Even if they visit regularly and are skilled, such parents occupy too little emotional shelf space in the life of a child to provide a reliable buffer against a custodial parent who goes into free fall. They are not there to protect against the day-to-day hassles of postdivorce life.

It is the quality of the relationship between the non-residential parent and child rather than sheer frequency of visitation that is most important. And in many cases, that relationship is less than ideal. Many women become non-custodial parents either because they have left their children, do not want to care for them, or have been deemed incompetent by the courts because of emotional or substance abuse problems. Many men become non-custodial parents because they do not want the responsibility of caring for a child, even—and sometimes especially—when they remarry.

Moreover, visits from an alcoholic, abusive, depressed, or conflict-prone parent do nothing for a troubled child, except possibly make the child more troubled. We also found that distance, like a child's sex, affects paternal visitation patterns. Seventy-five miles seems to be the point at which paternal inconvenience overcomes paternal guilt. Men who live within a seventy-five-mile radius of their children are more likely to visit regularly than men who don't. The reason? Seventy-five miles is about the maximum radius of a comfortable day trip. Unfortunately, by the time our children were fifteen, the average distance fathers lived from their children was four hundred miles.

Two Special Hazards in Divorced Adults' Parenting

Although diminished authoritative parenting can have dire consequences for children, two other hazards await children in the postnuclear family. The first is "parentification," when the caretaking roles of parent and child seem to be reversed, with children becoming the caretakers. Lonely, overburdened, or needy, the parent pushes the child to perform household tasks or leans on the child for solace, advice, and emotional support beyond that child's capacity. The second is continued conflict between the divorced parents. When divorced parents fight, it increases the child's distress by making the child feel caught in the middle of divided loyalties for each parent. In contrast, a cooperative relationship between parents can be a support to both parents and children.

Children Caring for Their Parents

The fact that an increased number of divorced parents are turning to their children for counsel and support is related to the observation that children in divorced families grow up faster; but this growing up faster may come at a cost. While often mutually beneficial, the close mother-daughter relationship in divorced homes makes girls more likely to be turned to for solace and advice. Many divorced women described their ten-year-old daughters as being like a close friend or sister; they felt they could discuss anything with their girls, including problems of personal relationships, fears, depression, finances, dating, and loneliness. But ten-year-olds need a competent, caring parent more than a friend.

Not surprisingly, children who are confronted with adult problems often become apprehensive or resentful. But the support-seeking of emotionally needy parents has another, deeper danger. Children who feel responsible for problems that they cannot solve begin to develop a sense of helplessness. "What's wrong with me? Why can't I help Mom feel less lonely?" a nine-year-old thinks. By the time our children were fifteen, we found that this kind of helplessness often bloomed into depression and low self-esteem. These problems occurred more commonly in teenage girls who had been emotionally leaned on as children.

Fathers occasionally disclose their apprehensions and feelings to their children, too. But it is harder for a man to get away with displays of what children may regard as emotional weakness, particularly if he is talking to a son. Children have strong notions about how men should behave and are not always charitable when a father violates those norms.

I remember one ten-year-old telling me about a recent conversation he had had with his father. The boy said that his father had broken down and cried when he began talking about how much he missed the boy and his sister and mother. I was touched by this display of paternal vulnerability. I thought it very affecting. But the boy clearly did not. "Dad's gotta get a grip," he said to me. He was uncomfortable when his father revealed his emotional vulnerability. It was not an acceptable "guy thing."

This is not to say that all parental self-disclosure is harmful. As long as it is restrained and age-appropriate, confiding in a child is not only suitable, it actually may enhance development. Children feel proud when a parent trusts and relies on them, and this may help build a healthy sense of mutual caring.

Janet Coleman told me of a conversation she overheard between her son, David, and a man she was going out with for the first time. As nine-year-old David and her date waited for her to appear, David turned to her date and said, "Where are you taking my mother?"

"To dinner and a concert," the man replied.

"When will the concert be over?" David asked.

"Oh, probably about ten," the man said.

David nodded thoughtfully. Then, in a stern parental tone, he said, "I'll still be up."

What is true about the need for emotional support is also true about the need for practical support. Judiciousness and restraint are critical. Chores like table setting, mowing the lawn, doing the dishes, baby-sitting for a younger sibling all have a potentially positive effect. They can make a child more socially responsible and independent. However, when these interfere too much with play, sports, homework, and other normal childhood activities, they often make girls depressed, and boys rebellious and resistant and, ironically, less responsible.

Co-parenting: Battles, Truces, and Alliances

Some co-parenting agreements are formal; others develop over time. But nearly all relationships conform to one of three general types: what we call *conflicted*, *cooperative*, and *parallel* co-parenting. Like parenting styles, each type varies in its ability to buffer a child or to put the child at a greater risk for developing problems after divorce.

THE DANGERS OF CONFLICTED CO-PARENTING. A scene I observed during a pickup at Sheila McCain's home illustrates why the only childhood stress greater than having two married parents who fight all the time is having two divorced parents who fight all the time.

Perry McCain's pickup of David was scheduled for 2:00 p.m., and Perry and I were both on time. I was in the McCain kitchen when Perry rang the doorbell. However, David was not even home yet. He was next door playing with a friend.

"You know she's doing this on purpose," Perry said, while Sheila was getting David. "She hates Bobbi and she knows David and I are going to Bobbi's for a barbecue this afternoon. This is a little advance payback. Watch. When Sheila gets back, she'll tell me David can't go until he's had his bath. It's her favorite delaying tactic."

When David walked in the front door, Perry clapped his hands together. "Hey, buddy, ready for some ribs?"

Sheila took David's arm. "Perry, he has to have a bath first."

When I looked over at Perry, he was staring at the ceiling. "Do you believe this shit?" he said more to himself than to me. "Sheila," he said, "David doesn't need a bath. We're going to a barbecue—in a backyard. C'mon, Bobbi's waiting for us."

Sheila made a mock pouting face. "Oh poor Bobbi . . . ," then she looked down at David. "Better hurry, hon, your daddy's going to be mad at you if you keep his girlfriend waiting."

"Sheila," Perry hissed, "for once, why don't you stop being an ass. You're unpleasant enough when you're trying to be nice."

In fairness to Sheila, it should be pointed out that her provocative behavior had plenty of foundation. Eighteen months earlier, Perry had walked out on her for his secretary, twenty-four-year-old Bobbi. Still, this incident—and his parents' searing anger—left a deep impression on David. Fifteen years later, he still remembered how awful and helpless he felt as he watched the two people he loved most in the world clawing at one another.

Although after divorcing most couples would like nothing better than to have as little contact as possible with each other, if they both want to be involved in their children's lives, this is not feasible. By six years after divorce, in most families conflict and anger has declined, and if the non-custodial parent has not dropped out of the child's life altogether, some tenable co-parenting arrangement has been worked out.

As obviously destructive as conflict is to all involved in this dilemma, it was surprising to discover that six years after divorce, 20 to 25 percent of our couples were engaged in just such conflictual behavior; former spouses would make nasty comments about each other, seek to undermine each other's relationship with the child, and fight openly in front of the child. Aside from being damaging, constant put-downs of the other parent may backfire, producing resentment and a spirited defense of the criticized parent by the child.

One ten-year-old said, "When she goes into her usual routine about what a loser my dad is, I just hate her. I can't stand it. Last night I yelled at her to stop and threw my dinner plate on the floor and locked myself in my room. She tried to make up but started with, 'But you know your dad's really irresponsible.' I cried all night."

Conflictual co-parenting distresses children and undermines their well-being, and it makes parents unhappy, too. They feel guilty about fighting in front of the children, but their preoccupation with their anger and lingering resentment makes it difficult for them to begin focusing on a new, more fulfilling life and on the pain they are causing their children.

THE BENEFITS OF COOPERATIVE CO-PARENTING. Because of the adversarial nature of divorce, a cooperative co-parenting arrangement where parents put the well-being of their children first is often difficult to attain. Sometimes, it comes only through a crisis—the child has a severe illness or an accident, problems at school, or is picked up by the police, or even makes a suicide attempt. Only about a quarter of our divorced parents achieved a cooperative relationship in which they talked over the children's problems, coordinated household rules and child-rearing practices, and adapted their schedules to fit their children's needs. But two decades later, the couples who cooperated were glad they did.

"James deserves credit, too," Liddy said, when I mentioned how well Bethany and Adam were doing at the twenty-year interview. "It was hard for him, working with me after the divorce; it was hard for both of us. But we managed it and it paid off. Thank God."

What brought the Pennybakers together was Adam, who at eight was still reading at a first-grade level, despite an above-average intelligence and constant tutoring.

As Adam's academic problems worsened, James and Liddy began to consult regularly; they organized a kind of joint tutorial. Each would be sure to go over vocabulary lists and reading assignments when Adam was at their home. They also attended teacher conferences together. What pleased Adam, though, was his parents' willingness to share his athletic triumphs. In elementary school, one of them and sometimes both were there when he hit a home run or won a race, and both were beaming at the high school banquet when he received his Outstanding Athlete of the Year award.

One day James said, "You know I think I started to really love Adam and felt needed when I saw how vulnerable he was and how he was hurting behind that laid-back, smart-assed exterior."

THE MIXED BLESSINGS OF PARALLEL CO-PARENTING. Parallel co-parenting is the most common form of co-parenting and the easiest to implement. Basically, the 50 percent of divorced parents who adopted this arrangement simply ignored each other. The former husband didn't interfere with the former wife's parenting, and vice versa, and no effort was made to coordinate their parenting strategies. In fact, in most arrangements, the former spouses didn't communicate at all or sent messages through their children.

Each parent did his or her "own thing," and while sometimes the things they did were very different, parallel parenting arrangements often contained minimum overt or persistent conflict.

Although young children do better with cooperative parenting, we also were surprised at how easily most youngsters adjust to the differences inherent in parallel parenting. As one ten-year-old said, "I don't act the same with Samantha [a friend] as I do with Miss Moore [a teacher]. Why should I have a hard time acting different at Mom and Dad's place?"

However, the lack of parental communication opens the door to problems. One child received an overdose of medication because his divorced parents, who were not talking to each other, both were giving the child a full daily dose of medicine. As a youngster gets older, lack of communication can make monitoring difficult. One parent may think the child is with the other when she is at the mall with her friends, and homework assignments that one parent knows about may be skipped at the other parent's house.

Siblings

After a divorce, a sibling has much less influence on a child than a parent, but that is not to say the sibling relationship is unimportant. The effects of parental contentiousness in non-divorced, divorced, and remarried families frequently flood over into parent-child and sibling relationships. Moreover, stress, preoccupation, and inept parenting in the early stages of a marital transition may make a parent less even-handed in the treatment of siblings, and less sensitive to issues of fairness and equity that are of great concern to children. In some cases, one child may even be targeted as a scapegoat and blamed for the problems the family is encountering, which increases the animosity, competition, and resentment between siblings. In our divorced and remarried homes, only about 10 percent of siblings—and most were sisters—formed relationships supportive enough to buffer each sibling against the stresses in their new family life.

Although in the early stage of transitions like divorce and remarriage, brothers and sisters were less warm and involved and more aggressive and rivalrous with each other, these effects were more sustained for brothers. Even six years after the divorce, male siblings in single-parent or remarried families were more likely than those in non-divorced families to get involved in long bouts of arguing, teasing, insults, name-calling, and fighting, such as we saw in the Jehrico brothers, who were half brothers.

The two brothers' mutual antipathy was rooted in the kind of temperamental differences that divorce and remarriage and living in a congested mobile home exacerbate. The slow-moving, heavy, wide-hipped

Roy was phlegmatic and passive, like his mother, Betty Ann. The skinny, spiky-haired Paul was volatile and impetuous like his father, William, a sometime construction worker, sometime writer of bad checks who was last heard from on Paul's seventh birthday when he sent a birthday card with a Tijuana postmark.

"The two of them are driving me crazy," Betty Ann Jehrico complained at the six-year interview. "Paul calls Roy fat or Roy calls Paul stupid. They fight about nothing. We don't have a moment's peace when they're together."

During the videotaped sibling interaction when Roy was ten and Paul eight, after ten minutes of shouting, name-calling, and pushing, tiny Paul hurled himself at substantial Roy and got a hammerlock around his neck. Roy tossed Paul on the floor and sat on him like a bemused elephant dealing with a rampaging mouse.

Betty Ann was unwittingly fostering the constant fighting between her sons. In homes with a distracted, emotionally unavailable parent like Betty Ann, a kind of Hobbesian competition develops for the few available scraps of maternal attention. And the winner is usually the child who makes the least demands on maternal energy. In the Jehrico home, that was quiet, low-maintenance Roy, who spent most of his time in his room reading comic books or watching television.

The obvious favoritism for Roy by both his mother and his new stepfather, Roger, fed the Jehrico brothers' mutual antipathy. The parents' disdain for Paul was difficult to watch.

Roger began his interaction with Paul.

"So you want to be a fighter pilot?"

"Yeah."

"You're too dumb, you little sucker. You're too dumb to be a fighter pilot."

"Well, I'm smart enough not to be a truck driver like you."

"Whoa, you have to be smart to drive a truck. You'd never make it, you little weasel."

There was much playing to the camera and rolling of the eyes as Roger continued his hostile attack.

Betty Ann put down Paul even more contemptuously.

"So, what did you learn in school today, Paul?"

"We learned to tell the time."

"What, you're in seventh grade, and you're just learning to tell time!" Betty Ann sneered. "The big hand goes here and the little hand goes there. Big deal. You're so stupid you're just learning to tell time." She laughed disdainfully.

Parent-child relationships like those in the Jehrico family would contribute to sibling antagonism in any family, but sibling relationships in divorced and remarried families seem especially vulnerable to such treatment. Why should these boys have more problems? A mutually supportive, protective sibling relationship can help children cope with stresses when a parent is unavailable. However, boys get little support or affection from either brothers or sisters. Their relationships are less congenial; they spend less time in shared activities; and their overtures and requests are more likely to be refused or ignored by siblings. Girls, on the other hand, even those in divorced or remarried families, more frequently develop close, confiding, friendly relationships.

Under stress, especially when a parent is disengaged, unsupportive, or inept, two options seem available to siblings. The first is to think that adults are untrustworthy, that parents can't be relied on, and to draw together and form a sibling alliance to deal with a difficult world. This banding together can enhance both siblings' ability to weather the vicissitudes of their parents' marital transitions. It is a protective strategy, used more often with female siblings, and frequently occurs when an older sister had been given responsibility for caring for a younger one.

The second option is for siblings to compete for scarce resources in a situation where much stress and little parental support and affection is available. The antagonistic, rivalrous relationship that develops can become a breeding ground for antisocial behavior. During adolescence, Paul Jehrico was expelled from school once and arrested twice for petty larceny and later for drunk driving.

It isn't just the quality of sibling interactions that can be a risk or protective factor; the sibling also can serve as a constructive or destructive role model. A promiscuous or drug-using sibling or a self-controlled, altruistic, achievement-oriented older sibling can be a negative or a positive influence on a younger sibling. The behavior of a younger sibling rarely influences an older brother or sister.

Eventually, in all types of families, the majority of siblings have friendly relationships or congenial relationships with a touch of rivalry. Even some of the siblings who persistently squabble in the home will fiercely defend their sibling against outside criticism or attacks. Hostile relationships are unlikely to be sustained in a home with supportive, loving, even-handed parents. As we shall see, in the long run, it is biological relatedness, not whether a child is in a non-divorced, divorced, or remarried family, that influences the sibling relationship in some unanticipated ways.

Grandparents

Adam Pennybaker could easily have taken a more negative life path following his parents' divorce without Ginny Witter, who made Liddy stop using Adam as a dumping ground for her frustrations about James. But to be a major buffering force, a grandparent has to do what Ginny did, live with the child. Even a grandparent who visits frequently has little effect on a grandchild's emotional, social, and cognitive development.

For the most part, grandparents seem to function like volunteer firefighters after a divorce. They are usually called in emergencies when a divorced parent, most often a single mother, is in an economic crisis or unable to handle the child on her own. The grandparents' support of the mother has an indirect effect on the child's well-being by reducing the mother's stress and improving her parenting.

However, there are two situations where a grandparent has a direct effect, one positive and one negative. First, involved grandfathers seem to promote social success and academic achievement in grandsons; second, ongoing conflict between a residential grandparent and parent can produce anxiety, and oppositional and antisocial behavior in a child.

Relationships Outside the Family

As children grow older, relationships outside the family with peers and mentors and in school become increasingly important. These influences were already emerging when the children in our studies were ten and were to become more powerful as they moved into adolescence. Their role as risk and protective factors will be presented in greater detail in the chapter on adolescence.

Adult Mentors

High-conflict, non-supportive families often send children fleeing for the exits. When they do, children become more susceptible to the outside influences of adults, mentors, and the peer group. At age ten, some of our children in divorced and remarried families were already beginning to disengage from the family. By age fifteen, about one third of adolescent boys and one quarter of adolescent girls in divorced and remarried families had become disengaged, a much higher rate than that found in non-divorced families.

Divorce accelerates disengagement from the family. Disengaged adolescents spend little time in family activities and as little time in the home as possible. And if this disengagement is associated with involvement with an antisocial peer group, it can lead to delinquency, drug and alcohol use, early sexuality, and problems in school. A danger in the best of circumstances, as we shall see later, early detachment is a particular danger for a child like Paul Jehrico.

However, a developmental danger can be turned into a plus when an adult mentor is in the picture. Sometimes, when a close sustained supportive relationship with a competent adult such as a teacher, coach, neighbor, grandparent, or a friend's parent was available, disengagement could be the solution to an adverse family situation. The family of a friend often serves as a surrogate family for disengaged adolescents. Mentors also served as role models, as companions, and as advisers who could be consulted in moments of confusion and doubt. But being an effective mentor was no short-term thing. Contact with an involved teacher or caring adult had little effect if the relationship did not endure for at least two years.

Peers

Unpopular youngsters who had troubles at home and were shunned by their peers often found postdivorce stresses difficult to bear. Eventually, the youngster would begin thinking of himself the way he thought his peers did, as unattractive and undesirable, and this would make him behave in an anxious and withdrawn or angry and attention-seeking manner.

Children like Adam Pennybaker, on the other hand, were often buffered by friends. We found that even having one close friend helped to protect against stress and rejection by other peers. The child and his friend could form an alliance against a hostile world.

Limited in the preschool years, the influence of peers to help or hurt increases steadily as a child grows older.

Schools

The VLS, which was the first study to examine the effect of school on the adjustment of children in divorced and remarried families, found that in the context of divorce, a good school means more than just an academically strong school. To buffer, the school also has to make a youngster feel cared for; the teachers have to be open and willing to listen; and the discipline policy has to be loving but firm. Schools with these qualities are the institutional equivalent of an authoritative parent. As we shall see later, they protect because they provide what a divorced family lacking an authoritative parent cannot provide: structure, support, and emotional regulation.

Personal Characteristics That Protect Children or Make Them Vulnerable to Adversity

Some risk and protective factors in children were similar to those in adults. Children who were intelligent, self-regulated, independent, mature, and had high self-esteem, and those who had islands of attainment in academics, sports, or positive peer relations, showed fewer long-lasting problems after divorce. Those who felt helpless or were impulsive, antisocial, or extremely anxious and insecure before the divorce had these characteristics magnified by the divorce. Furthermore, these risk factors fed into other problems in social relations with peers and adults and in academic attainment. They led to a snowballing of risks.

Some characteristics, such as looks, personality, and gender, also either protected or created risk because they influenced a child's ability to attract support. In a perfect world, every child of divorce would receive the help he or she needed. But in the imperfect world in which we live, the pretty and personable elicit the most support from teachers, peers, the parents of friends, and from their own parents.

Here's why.

Physical Attractiveness

Good looks are more important to a girl than a boy, especially in adolescence, but physical attractiveness buffers both sexes. At every point in the study, attractive children received more support from adults and peers than unattractive children did.

What does "attractive" mean?

To a girl, it means having regular features, pretty hair, and a slender body, although boys are more drawn to adolescent girls with a curvaceous build. For a boy, being attractive means being tall, athletically built, and to a lesser extent having a handsome face. Peers and adults, and later the opposite sex and potential employers—everyone seems to respond more positively to tall males. We found at age twenty-four such men were in more responsible jobs and had higher incomes than small men did, and pretty women were more likely than unattractive women to be upwardly mobile in their marriages—to have married better-educated, wealthier men.

Obesity, acne, unattractive features, physical awkwardness were the opposite of tall in a boy and pretty in a girl. They were risks that reduced available support after a divorce. Even preschoolers were sensitive to these flaws, preferring to socialize with more attractive peers.

Physical appearance is not so important in the behavior of parents. Most parents find something attractive about their own children. As the writer and comic Garrison Keillor puts it, in Lake Woebegone, "all the children are above average," at least in the view of their parents. However, we found that under high stress, such as unemployment or an unhappy marriage, fathers were most likely to reject or be irritable with physically unattractive daughters. Prettiness also influenced visitation patterns, with attractive daughters seeing more of their father than unattractive ones.

Temperament

From the earliest days of life, parents identify temperamental differences in their children. One will be easy, one squalling and difficult; one a cuddler, another resistant to being held closely; one smiley and responsive, another slow to warm up; one active, kicking, and batting the mobile on her crib, another sedentary, lying quietly scanning the room.

The poets who claim parental love is blind are right—up to a point. Parental love is blind, but only under conditions of low stress. When things were going well, our cranky, demanding, temperamentally difficult children received just as much parental affection and attentiveness as our easygoing, adaptable children. In fact, they sometimes got more as parents did their best to support a more needy, vulnerable child.

But when things were not going well, parents with difficult children often responded like Lucinda Fredericks, the woman whose life fell apart when she lost her mother and her upper-middle-class lifestyle. Before the divorce, Lucinda had been managing her son, Dickie, but just barely. Very bright, Dickie was also very difficult, and had been for as long as Lucinda could remember. Colicky and irritable as a baby, Dickie grew into an aloof, cranky preschooler, wary around strangers and anxious in unfamiliar situations. Preoccupied and depressed after the divorce, Lucinda was vulnerable, withdrawn, and neglectful with Dickie because neglecting him required less energy than dealing with him.

However, Dickie's problems extended beyond Lucinda. Some children are able to compensate by attracting support from peers or other adults. But although very intelligent, Dickie had a stickman physique—large head, small body—thick glasses, jittery movements, and an almost heartbreaking awkwardness, not the sort of characteristics that elicit support from peers.

In the playground, he usually stood alone scowling and watching others play. He was the last child to be chosen on teams and the one who managed to drop the ball or fall or injure himself and go crying to the teacher.

According to his first-grade teacher, Dickie spent more time alone than any other child in her class. "My heart goes out to Dickie," the teacher wrote in an observational evaluation. "He has the highest IQ in the class but he doesn't know the first thing about getting along with others."

The stresses of divorce magnify the effects of a difficult temperament on destructive parent-child relationships but may increase the positive effects of an easy temperament. Agreeable and adaptable, an easy child is a pleasant companion and rarely makes the mother's life more stressful or makes her feel incompetent or bad about herself. Parent-child relations are a two-way street. It is much easier to be a responsive authoritative parent with an easy child who has few behavior problems than with a difficult child, especially when the parent is stressed. Our findings illustrate that the old adage, "The rich get richer and the poor get poorer," applies to more than just economics. Easy children, inherently adaptable, grow in resiliency as other people respond positively to them; while difficult youngsters, vulnerable to begin with, under the stresses of divorce often grow more vulnerable as the beleaguered parents withdraw and peers shun them.

However, biology is not destiny. Many of the developmental risks associated with a difficult temperament can be lowered or eliminated by an authoritative parent.

Social Skills

Dickie Fredericks's opposite is a child like Adam Pennybaker, who seems born knowing how to get along with people. "Everyone here has fallen in love with Adam," wrote his teacher on his fifth-grade report card. "Adam's warm, funny, empathic, and despite his reading difficulties, intelligent." From preschool through high school, outstanding social skills buffered Adam from stress by attracting a legion of supporters, including teachers, coaches, classmates, and the parents of friends. Glowing recommendations, plus Adam's charm and persuasiveness in an admission interview, gained him acceptance at a prestigious northeastern university in spite of his mediocre academic record.

At twenty-four, Adam had a larger network of both old and new friends than almost any other young man in the study.

Gender

Our work suggests that one reason why young boys have more difficulty in adjusting to divorce is that they get less emotional support from their overstressed mothers, who find that the combination of demandingness, opposition, noisiness, and physicality makes a young son more exhausting and difficult to parent than a daughter. The loss of another male presence may further complicate adjustment; the lack of a father or other intimate male adult seems to affect young boys more. Preadolescent boys often benefit from the continued involvement of a caring, authoritative, non-custodial father, stepfather, or grandfather.

Young girls adjust more easily to divorce for all the reasons boys don't. Until adolescence, girls are less demanding and resistant, easier to parent, and thus apt to receive more maternal support. Additionally, the vast majority of children are likely to find themselves living with their mother after divorce, and the close, companionate mother-daughter relationship common in many of these homes helps to protect girls, who are also less vulnerable to the disappearance of a father than boys are.

The Most Common Postdivorce Adjustment Patterns

Our six-year data on children after divorce, which found three quarters developing within the normal range, stand as a tribute to the resilience of boys and girls, and to the support, love, and good sense of parents. With modest resources and support, a strong "self-righting" process seems to occur in the young. As new experiences and relationships wash away the harmful effects of old stresses, a push toward recovery and positive adaptation emerges.

However, the six-year data also contained sobering news about divorce and the young. Whereas 20 to 25 percent of the divorced group were struggling with emotional, social, academic, or behavioral problems, the comparable figure for children in the comparison group of married families was only 10 percent. Children are remarkably resilient, but this twofold discrepancy is not to be taken lightly, particularly since most troubled youngsters had problems in many different areas, including family, school, and peer relations.

We found four basic adjustment patterns in children at the six-year point and six in early adolescence. At age ten, youngsters who had a great many protective factors in the developmental bank—such as an easy temperament, an authoritative parent, an adult mentor, or a network of friends—usually fell into one of two exceptionally well-adjusted competency clusters: a *competent-opportunist* group or a *competent-caring* group. By age fifteen, another group of unusually well functioning children emerged that we called *competent-at-a-cost*, because although these children excelled in most areas, the stresses they had encountered left them with diminished self-esteem. The boys and girls in these three competent clusters, almost all of whom had the support of at least one caring adult, scored well on academic achievement, were popular, socially responsible, and had relatively few behavior problems.

A third group of children were classified as *Good Enough*, while a fourth *aggressive-insecure* group with multiple problems found at the six-year mark were clearly headed for difficulties. By adolescence, this multi-problem group had broken into two halves, one characterized by antisocial behavior and the other by depression and anxiety.

Competent-Opportunist

Tall and good-looking, Will Livingston likes to be liked, and he has a gift for it. Charming Will is a master of the velvet art of integration, but he only practices his art among the school elite. To be a friend of Will's, you have to be in a position to help him. Will is a good example of a competent-opportunistic child, one of the adjustment patterns to emerge at the six-year postdivorce mark.

The youngsters in the competent-opportunistic group—which was over half male—were adapting exceptionally well to postnuclear family life. Like other "competent" youngsters, they got along well with others in school and were mature, self-regulated children with few behavior problems. But a flaw marred this otherwise perfect picture—a flaw noticed not only by our research staff but by teachers and peers.

These outside "raters" had many good things to say about competent-opportunistic children, such as Will; raters described them as "curious, socially skilled and charming, with a wide range of interests." However, like our observers, the raters also found them to be manipulative. They were oriented to people who were in a position to help them—whether a parent, the parent of a friend, a coach, a teacher, or a high-status peer.

Competent-opportunistic children were also fair-weather friends. Their friendships rarely lasted beyond another person's usefulness to them. At each point in our study, most children in the competent-opportunistic group had a new set of friends.

How do eight-, nine-, and ten-year-olds learn to be competent-opportunists?

Raised in high-conflict homes, competent-opportunistic youngsters got an early chance to learn how to manipulate people. According to their mothers and fathers, as early as six, these children were already playing their parents against each other. Competent-opportunist children often had one close supportive and one rejecting or neglectful parent, and they would often ally with the supportive parent to checkmate the wishes or demands of the other and gain advantage for themselves.

The contentiousness and loyalty conflicts created by divorce, and the alliances that form in stepfamilies, can serve as fertile ground for the growth of manipulative skills. Children in divorced families would bait one parent about being able to stay up late, about having a more lenient curfew or more TV time in the other parent's home. Adolescents sometimes pushed to move in with the more lenient parent. Still, competent-opportunistic children were a relatively small part of our sample; they accounted for about 8 percent and were found equally often in high-conflict non-divorced families, divorced, and remarried families and rarely in low-conflict non-divorced families.

On the whole, they were remarkably well-adjusted, high-achieving, popular, and well-regarded children. Their manipulativeness was an unfortunate but minor flaw, and it was associated with a keen understanding of what others wanted and how to please them. As young adults, their social skills and ability successfully to wheel and deal contributed to their attainment and rapid rise on the professional ladder.

Competent-Caring

"I don't know how Jeannie did it," Julia Sorenson said. "When she was only eight, I came down with chronic fatigue syndrome—I guess from the stress of the divorce. I had a sore throat, swollen glands, and awful muscle and joint pain. I tried to keep working; without my salary, we'd starve. But just getting out of bed was an ordeal. When I got home sometimes, I was so weak I couldn't get up the stairs to go to bed. I'd sit on the bottom step crying, with Jeannie beside me holding my hand, and then she'd help me up the stairs and put me to bed. I couldn't do anything in the house. Jeannie did the laundry and cooked the meals. Thank God for TV dinners! But the most remarkable thing was how she cared for her little brother, Neil. She'd make sure he ate his meals and had a bath each night, and I'd hear her reading to him before bed. I recovered in six months, but couldn't have gotten by without her. No wonder everybody loves her. You don't expect an eight-year-old kid to be so caring. It's almost worth all the waifs and strays Jeannie brings home. At the moment, we have two dogs she found in the park, one very pregnant cat who wandered into the yard, and a pigeon with a broken wing."

Jeannie, like so many competent-caring children, came from a divorced family, had a loving, supportive mother, and through necessity had to assume responsibility for caring for others at an early age. There were more children from divorced than non-divorced families in the competent-caring group, and like Jeannie, many appeared to have been enhanced by coping with the challenges in a divorced family.

Competent-caring children had all the admirable qualities of competent-opportunistic children—they were socially skilled, curious, energetic, assertive, self-sufficient, flexible, and had many positive coping skills—but competent-caring youngsters were not manipulative. Like Jeannie, they were distinguished by a Mother Earth quality—a notable sensitivity and responsiveness to the feelings and needs of others, and a propensity to help vulnerable people. Often in childhood they would befriend a child who was shy or unpopular or scapegoated by other peers. They did not seek out high-status friends or manipulate others as competent-opportunistic children did. The similarities and differences between competent-opportunistic and competent-caring children can be explained in terms of some of the things we learned about stress and coping in our studies.

There are three conditions under which stress enhances a child's development. The first is when the child shows no history of a difficult temperament, severe anxiety, depression, or antisocial behavior. The second condition is when the child is exposed to stress that challenges but does not overwhelm her. Enough to promote growth and learning. The third condition is the availability of protective factors; it was not coincidental that all the children in the competency groups were supported by at least one caring adult.

Many competent-opportunistic and competent-caring children grew up in the kind of divorced family which our data shows comes closest to approximating these conditions: a single-parent household headed by a supportive, loving, working mother, who was not always available and who encouraged mature, independent behavior in her children.

But what distinguished competent-caring children from the competent-opportunistic children is that their homes had a low level of pre- and especially postdivorce conflict, so they had few opportunities—or temptations—to engage in parental manipulation. Also, members of the caring group were assigned responsibility for the care of others early in life. Most often, that "other" was a younger sibling. But in several instances, a competent-caring youngster succeeded at what would seem to be a high-stress, developmentally inappropriate task, such as caring for a lonely, depressed, or alcoholic parent, thanks to the protective presence of a relative, a mentor, or some other supportive adult.

Perhaps because caregiving tasks and emotional support are traditional female functions, the competent-caring group was largely made up of girls. And, interestingly, members of the group often pursued helping others into adult life. At the twenty-year mark, nursing, social work, psychology, psychiatry, medicine, and other "helping" professions were overrepresented in the competent-caring group.

Competent-at-a-Cost

At the twenty-year interview, Sarah Cohen tells me about a recurring dream. As friends and family cheer, an ecstatic Sarah bounds up to the stage to receive her Ph.D. Up to this point, Sarah's dream and reality coincide; a few months earlier, she was awarded a doctorate in anthropology. But in the dream, a professor steps in Sarah's way, raises his hand, and says: "Sorry, Sarah, no doctorate for you. You didn't pass your qualifying exam. You should have tried harder."

Others view competent-at-a-cost children as remarkably able, successful, and likable; but as with Sarah, a lurking sense of anxiety, inadequacy, and of not trying hard enough underlies their overtly unusually competent behavior.

Competent-at-a-cost was a pattern of adapting that didn't emerge until adolescence, and that like our other two competence clusters shared a background of the presence of a loving, supportive adult. Although girls from divorced families were overrepresented on both competent-caring and competent-at-a-cost patterns of coping, they differed in two ways. First, levels of "parentification" and demands by a needy parent for support and solace were much higher and began at an earlier age with the competent-at-a-cost children. Second, the competent-at-a-cost children were more likely to have been more anxious before the divorce and "parentification" began.

Although both groups were exquisitely sensitive, caring, and concerned about the well-being of others, early failure to solve a parent's problems leaves the competent-at-a-cost adolescent or young woman feeling permanently apprehensive in meeting challenging undertakings. The high standards competent-at-a-cost women set for themselves often further exacerbate their sense of inadequacy. No matter how much such a woman achieves, it doesn't feel like enough; so she tries harder, which brings her more triumph, but still the lingering feeling of failure and inadequacy goes on.

As adults, competent-at-a-cost women were among our most successful—having warm friendships, good family relations, and the highest rates of graduate education and recognition for exceptional academic and professional attainments in the VLS. Still, beneath the glittering exterior, a sense of "letting people down," of not being able to do quite well enough, fed a spring of chronic low-grade depression, insecurity, and lack of self-esteem.

Good Enough

Good Enough children, like Good Enough adults, were the average children coping in a difficult situation. This was the group into which about half our children from divorced families and 60 percent from non-divorced families fell. In the middle on almost everything, including risk and protective factors, academic performance, peer relations, psychological functioning, Good Enoughs had roughly the same problem rate as other kids their age—and happily, their problems rarely endured or were immobilizing.

Aggressive-Insecure

Dickie Fredericks, like Sarah Cohen, had a repetitive dream, but his focused on abandonment, not failure. He dreamed he was walking down a long, dark corridor with a row of multiple closed doors on one side, and tall windows with gauzy curtains blowing in the night wind, obscuring his vision, on the other. He knows something terrible is going to emerge from those doors and runs down the hall screaming for help, but nobody comes.

At age ten, Dickie Fredericks was a sad, sullen, angry, lonely child, with nails bitten to the quick. Not adept at sports and shy with peers, he gradually withdrew into a solitary world of fantasy, science fiction, movies, television, and computers. Looking back on his childhood, Dickie said, "You can't believe what it was like wandering around in that big house in the country alone day after day. My mom and Charles [Lucinda's second husband] were all wrapped up in their own lives. They entertained and traveled and went out with friends. We almost never had dinner together or did anything else together. I don't think they really disliked me, they just didn't care about me. I wasn't important in their lives."

Like many neglected children, Dickie's problems increased as he grew older.

Dickie's fifth-grade teacher could find no redeeming qualities in him. "Richard's a hard child to like," she said. "He is by far the brightest child in the class, but it's no pleasure having him as a student. He's disdainful and sarcastic with the other kids. They think he's strange. He doesn't have any friends."

Dickie was also engaging in minor acts of vandalism; he had been picked up twice by the police, once for snapping antennas off cars and once for spraying graffiti across a store window, though he was not charged for either crime, thanks to Charles's social prominence and influence. Dickie also was beginning to sample his parents' liquor supply, a problem that would increase in adolescence.

At ten, Dickie, like other neglected children, had many risk factors in his life, and all pointed toward a bleak future. Unless some powerful protective factor emerged soon, Dickie was on his way to an unhappy life.

Troubled children like Dickie have no islands of succor in their lives. They usually come from homes where authoritative parenting is rare, and conflict, rejection, and neglect common. Quick to anger and prone to depression, their parents frequently had problems with alcohol and drugs, and at work and in marriage. Troubled children were further disadvantaged by their own personal qualities, which rarely attracted the support of an adult who might provide what they were not getting at home.

These aggressive-insecure children (about 10 percent from non-divorced families and 20 percent from divorced and remarried families at age ten) suffered from many problems. They were sullen, oppositional, angry, and tense. In adolescence, drug, alcohol, and delinquency problems became common in the group. Its members also had the highest pregnancy rate and highest attempted suicide rate in the study. Antisocial behavior, unhappiness, and self-destructive behavior often go hand in hand.

In adolescence, the group divided into two subgroups. And while members of both had many problems, in the one subgroup the problems centered on depression and low self-esteem; in the other, on antisocial behaviors. When we finished examining the six-year data, the questions that pushed us on to continued study of our VLS families were, "How will these children adapt to the unique challenges of early adolescence and young adulthood? Are developmental trajectories set and unlikely to change? And if change does occur, what will the agents of change be?"

Children Coping in the First Six Years

Almost all children are distressed by their parents' divorce; initially, they become confused, anxious, apprehensive, and angry. In the home, they often are both clingy and whiny, and demanding, disobedient, and irritable; at school and with peers, they often become distractable, withdrawn, and aggressive. The cycle of coercive exchanges found in homes with divorced mothers and young sons can lead to prolonged problems in a boy's adjustment. Although fantasies of parental reconciliation may continue, both boys and girls show considerable behavioral improvement at two years after a divorce.

By six years later, children show diverse patterns of coping with their parents' divorce and their new life in a single-parent household. Although twice as many children in divorced and remarried families as those in non-divorced families are anxious, antisocial, and lack self-control, the vast majority are functioning within the normal range of adjustment; they have some problems, but none that are overwhelming. Some of our children—especially girls—developed into remarkably competent, responsible, resilient youngsters.

Coping with the challenges of divorce and life in a single-parent family seems actually to enhance the ability of some children to deal with future stresses. But children can't cope alone; there needs to be a supportive adult in their lives to help buffer them from adversity, and that adult is most often a loving, responsive, firm, authoritative, custodial parent.

Children who move from a conflictual to a more harmonious situation with an authoritative parent usually show better adjustment by two years than they had exhibited before divorce. But children who move into a more stressful, contentious situation, with an inept parent, show an increase in distress, resentment, and problem behaviors.

Points to Remember

- Divorce does not inevitably produce permanent scars. Parents can buffer a child against many of the stresses associated with both divorce and life in a single-parent home.
- You don't have to be a perfect parent to be a good buffer. Naturally self-correcting, children can adjust to divorce with a moderate amount of support.
- Parental love is not enough; firm but responsive discipline is also important to a child of divorce. It teaches the child self-control and how to control his or her emotions.
- Just as it is important to prepare children for the divorce before it happens, it is important to talk to them about the changes that are happening after. Get your children to discuss their concerns and fears so you can help them deal with their anxieties. Make your children understand that you will always be there for them.
- Be consistent. It's hard to overstate the importance of a predictable environment after divorce. With so many things changing in children's lives, they need to know there are some things that can be relied on.

- Remember, your child is a child. Don't confide in her or lean on her for support she is incapable of giving. Solve your own problems; the child has enough problems of her own.
- It is difficult for a non-residential parent to protect a child from the consequences of a hostile, rejecting, or neglecting residential parent. Non-residential parents just aren't around enough to buffer the child in the day-to-day hassles of family living.
- Girls are more likely to benefit from contact with a non-custodial mother, boys with a non-custodial father.
- Preadolescent boys have more difficulty adjusting to life in a family where the mother is the single parent; preadolescent girls have more difficulty adjusting to life in the stepfamily.
- Think about cooperative co-parenting; it is a major protective factor for children, and by working together, parents lighten the burden for each other.
- Rivalry and lack of support are common among siblings in divorced and remarried families. When a protective sibling relationship does develop, it is more likely to occur among sisters.
- A completely stress-free environment is not necessarily the best one. Solving moderately stressful problems in a supportive environment prepares a child for dealing with future challenges. However, the support of a caring adult is critical.
- Girls are more likely than boys to be strengthened by coping with the stresses of divorce.
- Although children from divorced and remarried families are more likely than those in non-divorced families to have problems, the vast majority are adjusting reasonably well six years after divorce.

Part Two

Remarriage and Stepfamily Life: Adults and Children at Eleven Years After Divorce

8

Repartnering: High Hopes
and Crossed Fingers

Janet Coleman and Nick Lang met at the dinner party of a mutual friend.

On the phone, the friend, Janet's old saviour, Marcia Link, described Nick as "a plump Antonio Banderas." But if the Nick Janet met at Marcia's a few weeks later looked like anyone famous, it was Andy Sipowicz, the detective on *NYPD Blue*, except Nick had a bigger overbite and less hair.

Anyway, as advertised, Nick was sweet and funny. So when he asked Janet for her phone number at the end of the night, she gave it to him.

About a year and a half later, we made a videotape of the newly married couple describing their first impressions of each other. Janet, who mentions Nick's sweetness and sly humor, says she left the dinner party thinking: finally, a man who would be good for her. Nick, who is sitting next to her, looks a little deflated by the description. "She makes me sound like a sensible pair of shoes!" When I ask Nick for a first impression of Janet, he says he thought she looked just a little like Sally Field, which makes Janet look a little deflated.

"Why doesn't anyone ever say Michelle Pfeiffer?" she complains.

"I was also intimidated by her," Nick continues. "I knew Janet was doing pretty well. Marcia told me she owned a successful flower business. I'm just a bookkeeper. I thought I might be a little out of my league."

Janet laughs. The thought of being a "catch" seems to amuse her.

The banter between them remains relaxed and affectionate until Nick brings up Janet's daughter, Leah, who is giving him problems. "David and I get along fine. He's like my own son," he says. "But I can't get the time of day from Leah. I try talking to her; I ask her what's going on in her life; I buy her presents; I go to all her school events. Nothing works. All I get is the slow freeze."

"Leah just needs more time, Nick." Janet's voice is soothing, but she looks apprehensive. She puts a hand on Nick's arm. "The two of you'll be able to work things out." As I watch the tape, I wonder who Janet is reassuring—herself or Nick?

"I know we will," Nick says, and places his hand on top of Janet's. "Leah's a good kid; she's just a little high-strung, that's all." Then he looks into the camera. "The important thing is that we love each other. As long as we have that, we can solve any problem."

But as Nick and Janet discovered, sometimes even for couples in love, building and sustaining a strong couple relationship in a stepfamily can be difficult. Remarriage, already occurring at the two-year point in the Virginia Longitudinal Study, was increasingly common at year six. Almost 60 percent of divorced participants were already remarried, and many others were cohabiting or contemplating another marriage. These unions turned out to be an interesting blend of hope and experience. People were constantly telling me that this time they were not expecting miracles. One third of our women remarried at least in part for economic security. "I don't need Prince Charming. I'll settle for a guy who just brings home a paycheck and helps me with the dishes," said one woman. But even the most pragmatic of our divorced participants remarried looking not just for security and companionship but also for an opportunity to right old wrongs, to make up for past mistakes, to heal old wounds, to finally find a better kind of love and family life.

How realistic were these hopes? The answer proved to be complex. Some men and women did learn how to trust and love, how to believe in themselves again. But for others, remarriage only seemed to reinforce the hard lessons learned in a first marriage and in divorce: You can't trust anyone; you're not worthy of another's love; human relationships are a source of pain and betrayal.

These findings not only confirmed what I had seen since the beginning of the VLS—that people take many different pathways out of divorce—but also my second major hypothesis: The experiences at one transition point resonate at later transition points. Sometimes they heal, sometimes they exacerbate old wounds; but either way the past is always present in a second marriage. It's there in the old habits of heart and mind, in old loyalties and legacies, in fears and vulnerabilities, in the "ghosts" of past lives and past marriages. And these ghosts can erode the stability of a new marriage unless laid to rest.

Why Second Marriages Succeed or Fail

Stresses in Remarriage

It is not surprising with all the changes associated with remarriage that in the early years negative stresses are high. In fact, they are as high as those found in the early years of divorce, and three times higher than those in non-divorced families. However, the stepfamily, although exposed to many stresses, also in contrast to divorced families experiences more positive changes.

Remarriage is the fastest route out of poverty for a divorced woman, and the addition of a stepparent can offer emotional and social support for divorced parents and their children. Many people said remarriage improved their standard of living. They moved to a better home in a better neighborhood, their children went to better schools, and now there was money for new clothes, toys, and vacations. Remarriage also produced emotional improvement; loneliness and depression declined and people's social lives improved. Perhaps most surprising of all, despite the challenges they encountered, in the early years of remarriage we found that couples in stepfamilies were happier with their marriages than couples in longer-established first marriages, though the satisfaction often deteriorated rapidly.

Why, then, in spite of these positive changes are divorce rates and problems in children's adjustment higher in remarriages than in first marriages? What are the risks that make building an enduring second marriage and a well-functioning stepfamily so difficult? Some lie in the personalities, expectations, attitudes, and behavior of divorced adults. Some lie in the history of past relationships in the family of origin, in the first marriage, and in life as a divorced single parent. Some are inherent in stepfamily relationships.

New Marriage, Old Problems

Connie Russell, with the support of her new husband, Bob Keatly, was able eventually to control her alcoholism, but some of her problems from the first marriage persisted. Bob's complaints about Connie's disorderliness echoed those earlier heard from Simon Russell. "Connie's the world's worst housekeeper," Simon complained to me one day. "The sink is always full of unwashed dishes and food sits in the refrigerator for weeks. I've thrown away bananas that were older than I am." Fastidious Simon was particularly annoyed by Connie's abandoned clothes, which he claimed were threatening to engulf the house. "The idea of putting anything in a laundry basket or hanging anything up is totally alien to Connie. There's underwear and pantyhose and dirty clothes scattered around in the bedroom, and sweaters and coats and purses and shoes everywhere. Connie never puts anything away."

Connie's untidiness also began to upset Bob, whose previous marriage had been to an orderly, almost compulsive wife. Three years into the marriage, Bob said, "It isn't like I want Connie to be Marion—that would be awful. Marion was a crazy neatnik. Nothing could be out of place. But I'd like to have a clean shirt in the morning and I'd like not to spend half our lives looking through the mess in the house for things Connie misplaced." Bob paused, then laughed. "Part of why I love her is for her being a free spirit, but sometimes it gets a little out of control. There are trade-offs in every marriage. I guess I can live with this one."

People who seize the window of change often learn from the past, but people who ignore the window usually don't. They continue to engage in self-defeating, immature, or antisocial behavior, and to exhibit poor problem-solving skills. And unless something else in the new marriage differs markedly, the immaturity, the helplessness, the substance abuse and chronic depression that undermined the first marriage will eventually destroy the second.

Sometimes, a new spouse is more supportive or tolerant of annoying behavior than a former spouse like Simon, whose domestic fastidiousness made Connie's sloppiness unbearable. Another difference we sometimes saw cushion a chronic behavior problem was a change in circumstances. The emergence of a new buffer—say, enough money to afford a housekeeper or a new partner who doesn't mind doing the dishes or helping out with the laundry—can help to reduce the annoyance potential of a trait like sloppiness. But the most important factor in the success of a second marriage was the choice of a mature, stable, supportive spouse, with good problem-solving skills. A stable partner can help a spouse learn to be more self-controlled, sensitive, and constructive in dealing with problems that inevitably arise in a stepfamily.

How Family History and Poor Relationship Skills Affect Remarriage

Even though couples in first and second marriages are equally as likely to describe themselves as happy, our observations show that when discussing problems, remarried couples display more negativity and are less positively affirming of each other. More than couples in first marriages they criticize, ridicule, and goad each another in destructive ways.

Are the remarried lying about their happiness?

No. For awhile at least, second marriages trump both first marriages and divorced life in terms of satisfaction; but many remarried people don't show the kinds of behaviors that would help them solve problems and sustain a happy relationship. Some of these difficulties are due to the unique stresses in a stepfamily that may make it difficult to build up a positive emotional bank account. Some, as in Diana Taine's case, were due to clashes of values and habits that have their origins in a couple's upbringing and may have contributed to one divorce already. Others, as in the case of Abby Richter, may be because of bad habits that one or both spouses picked up in a failing first marriage.

People used words like "stunning," "imposing," "charismatic," and "powerful" to describe Diana Taine. Diana's ex-husbands were more likely to describe her as "domineering," "explosive," "exhibitionistic," and "pigheaded." Diana described herself as "fierce."

On our first interview, Diana, a woman almost six feet tall with a wild mane of curly black hair, dressed in a red cape and high-heeled black patent boots, swept into the room, plopped herself in a chair, and before I could speak said, "So this study is about divorce. Well, you've come to the right person. I come from a long line of fierce women. It's in our genes. I guess that's why we're not good marriage material."

It took no prodding to have Diana go on.

"For the last three generations, half of the women in our family have divorced. I guess it was unusual in Grandma's day, but she was a strong woman. She supported her children by teaching in a one-room schoolhouse in northern Minnesota and my mother was raised there.

"Mom and Dad didn't divorce, but it was like Armageddon—the shouting and fighting and turmoil was constant. And Mom gave as good as she got. We have four sisters in our family—Joan and I are divorced and Peg is separated. But Ginny, our youngest sister, seems to be happily married. She must be a foundling." Diana laughed.

Every family has myths, stories and beliefs about themselves that are repeated and often passed down through generations. Sometimes it is what is *left out* of family myths that is most interesting. Stories about the fierceness and strength of the Taine women sustained their values for combativeness, not giving in, and not appearing vulnerable. The fact that the Taine women were often lonely and embittered was never mentioned.

It was easy to see why men were attracted to Diana—she was a gorgeous, flamboyant, energetic woman, who fairly sizzled when she entered a room. It was also easy to see why her husbands abandoned ship early in the marriage for kinder, gentler women. Diana didn't know how to compromise.

Unlike Diana, whose combative relations came from her family of origin, Abby Richter's difficulty in remarriage stemmed from what she had learned in a first marriage that had been Operatic. For Abby and her first husband, Matthew, aggressive provocation and sexual arousal were intertwined. Fighting usually was capped off by passionate lovemaking. But when Abby married Paul Oppenheimer, a large, physically imposing, but gentle man, her provocation only produced confusion and annoyance.

Abby prodded, Paul was baffled. Abby baited, Paul withdrew. Abby became increasingly frustrated in her attempts to anger and arouse Paul. Paul became increasingly repelled by Abby's frenetic, hostile provocation. Eventually, he left.

On the surface, Paul's decision to divorce may seem like an endorsement of the traditional view of fighting, that conflict is bad for a marriage. But Paul's decision actually underscores a new view of marital conflict, which holds that what makes fighting destructive in a marriage is not the frequency of conflict but rather the compatibility of a couple's arguing styles and the outcome of their fights.

Abby's old habits might have been tolerable to a man with her first husband's affinity for the Operatic fighting-sex cycle and belief that the best outcome for an argument is falling into bed afterward. But Paul Oppenheimer was not that man.

With Paul, Abby's raising of pseudo-problems and playful, teasing conflict led to resentment on his part and eventually to more serious hostility on the part of Abby. Neither understood the motives and feelings of the other, and their misunderstandings and differences were never resolved.

How Secrets and Censorship Threaten a New Relationship

As with Abby Richter, experiences in a first marriage often have a powerful influence on behavior in a second marriage. But because the new mate is given an air-brushed version of the first marriage, in many remarriages, behavior which in context might look understandable, even sympathetic, seems strange and upsetting.

Nick Lang, for example, was puzzled by Janet's unwillingness to discuss disagreements. "I can't even get her to talk about little differences," he complained one day. "Whenever I bring up a disagreement, she accuses me of being 'negative' and says I have to learn to think 'positively.' I thought you were supposed to talk through little problems so they don't become big problems.

"Most of the time Janet is so wonderful and so open to talking about her feelings that I don't understand what's going on—why she can't tolerate disagreements. The whole damn family is afraid to argue, even David. They don't like to confront things. They just clam up. I come from a family where if something bothers us, we let off steam, and then it's all over."

Janet later said, "You know, I never told Nick the whole story about my first marriage. I was humiliated that I had tolerated such violence. I was afraid that if I told Nick about the beatings, he'd want to know why I'd stayed on for five years, and I don't know how to answer that. Or maybe I thought that if I didn't talk about it, the memories would just go away, but they didn't. I never raised my voice to the children or let them quarrel with each other. We're frightened of conflict because of what it led to before. I know that would never happen with Nick but . . ." Janet's voice trailed off and her eyes filled with tears.

The next time I saw Nick, he knew all about Richard. "I don't understand why Janet was so embarrassed," he said. "Knowing what she's gone through makes me want to look after her and love her even more."

In a second common form of censorship, the censor is the other spouse, who, afraid of what he might hear, discourages talk about the past—especially a previous marriage. Though self-inflicted, this form of censorship also can cause marital problems.

I remember the baffled—and annoyed—reaction of one man in the Nonshared Environment Study when his wife refused to co-sign a mortgage. "It's crazy," the man said. "She acts like the bank is going to ask us for the money back next week."

There was an explanation for the woman's refusal. Her first husband, a real estate agent with a gambling problem, lost so much money, the bank foreclosed on the family home. But the new husband didn't know about the foreclosure because every time his wife mentioned her first husband's name, he immediately shut down the conversation by accusing her of marrying "trailer park trash."

Qualified Commitment and Intolerance for Dissatisfaction

Lucinda Fredericks eventually bailed out of her second marriage to Charles. In fact, over the course of the VLS, Lucinda left three marriages. She was in a fairly rocky fourth one to a much younger man at the time of her twenty-year follow-up.

"How does Lucinda manage to find all these guys?" asked one of the young VLS staffers. But it wasn't hard to understand why men liked her. Lucinda was pretty, stylish, sassy, and of course, quite rich.

In describing her decision to leave Charles, Lucinda said, "After all I'd been through, I loved the money and the fast life Charles gave me. But after awhile it wasn't enough; it got so that everything about him irritated me. I hated his loud laugh. I hated the way he kept hitching his trousers up over his little potbelly. I hated him letting his damn smelly dogs into our bedroom. Eventually, I couldn't bear to have him touch me and thought, Why go on with this? I've survived divorce before, I can do it again, and better this time. I knew I could get a big financial settlement and I wouldn't be so foolish with money this time around."

Lucinda's attitude and the high failure rate of VLS second marriages, which eventually approached the 60 percent national average for remarriages, reflected a lesson learned in the first marriage: Divorce can be an acceptable solution to marital unhappiness.

Fear of the unknown keeps a great many husbands and wives together in first marriages; they figure the devil they know—an unsatisfying marriage—is better then the devil they don't know, divorce. But the devil principle becomes inoperative in a second marriage, since one, and sometimes both partners are already on a first-name basis with the devil. The couple know the world doesn't end when a marriage goes, and that knowledge lowers their tolerance for behaviors they might have put up with in a first marriage. This accounts for divorces in remarriages being more frequent and also occurring more rapidly than in first marriages.

Many of our divorced men and women thought they could use living together as a trial run for remarriage or sidestep a second marriage altogether through cohabitation. Said one man who had just moved in with his girlfriend, "If it works, we stay together; if it doesn't, we break up. Either way, we avoid the expense and hassle of another court battle."

He was half-right. Exhausting legal fights rarely accompany the collapse of a live-in relationship. But cohabiting arrangements are also very vulnerable to failure and can cause a great deal of distress when they end. Couples who had lived together for several years often exhibited the hallmarks of a marriage, including shared history, inside jokes, and family rituals, and sometimes a child born to the union added a measure of cohesion, commitment, and solidarity. However, the breakup of long-term cohabiting relationships often caused the same pain as was found in divorce, and as in divorce the children suffer most. Multiple breakups fuel insecurity and behavior problems in children.

Unrealistic Expectations

People bring two competing sets of expectations to a second marriage. The first set tends to inflate expectations. An idealized image of family life and the search for the perfect marriage can be based on romanticized memories of childhood or a wish to rectify errors in a first marriage.

Childhood memories are distorted and inflate marital expectations because what people remember twenty or thirty years later is often a Disneyfied version of childhood: how good and happy their parents' marriage was; how close they felt to their siblings and their siblings to them; how wonderful life was in a loving, tight-knit nuclear family. Even being raised in an unhappy family is no protection against inflated expectations. It may make a person vow not to have a marriage like their parents' or a family like the one he or she grew up in.

Sometimes, the divorced person feels that after an abysmal first marriage, they will only accept a perfect relationship. One divorced woman said, "I've learned from the past. I'll only go into a marriage where we will always love and understand each other and be honest and want to be together forever."

The second set of expectations tends to promote realism. From experience in the first marriage, one or both partners already know that marriage is an imperfect institution, inhabited by imperfect human beings. They know that asking too much—asking your spouse to always look lovely and be agreeable and your children and stepchildren to always be well behaved and respectful—is usually a prescription for disappointment, if not disaster.

In the end, reality generally trumps fantasy. Marital veterans tend to enter marriage with a more pragmatic set of expectations. But the desire to atone for earlier failures—to get the marriage right this time—makes even the most pragmatic of realists vulnerable to a few unrealistic expectations. And in a sizable minority of men and women, the combination of redemptive hopes and aggrandized fantasies produces a dangerously romantic set of expectations.

After a few months of reality, some romantics realize that they need to reconfigure their expectations to include a stepchild whose favorite expression is "You suck," a non-residential parent with an attitude problem, and a spouse with a 300 percent stress level. In the language of risk and protective factors, these born-again realists are exhibiting social maturity. They are delaying gratification by recognizing that while they may get everything they want from marriage and family someday, they are not going to get it now; and they are not going to get it without a lot of work and careful planning.

But some romantics continue to cling to their expectations, despite overwhelming evidence to the contrary. Expecting stepfamily life to be *Ozzie and Harriet Redux* often makes the normal ups and downs of that life—a rude stepchild, a difficult former spouse, a high stress level—feel worse than they really are; and the more tenaciously a person clings to unrealistic expectations, the deeper his or her disillusionment with the marriage and stepfamily life becomes.

Here are four common fantasies that can promote dangerous stepfamily expectations.

The Nuclear Family Myth

The nuclear family myth creates the expectation that a stepfamily will operate like a nuclear family. Adherents expect family members to love and feel close to one another, children to show deference to parents, and discomforting appendages such as a non-residential parent to disappear. The nuclear family myth fosters destructive expectations about cohesiveness. To people expecting closeness, the college-roommate feel of a new stepfamily comes as a shock, and unless they become born-again realists in a hurry, the shock is likely to deepen. Even in long-lasting stepfamilies, tight-knit relationships are not the norm.

The Compensation Myth

The compensation myth, another common stepfamily fantasy, often occurs among people who have had an unsatisfactory first spouse and without quite realizing it, come to see the second spouse as a form of compensation. The new mate is expected to be everything the problematic old mate was not—kind, sensitive, responsible, and true.

Besides setting a person up for disillusionment, since the new mate may have different but as many foibles as the old, the expectation also can produce marital conflict via shoehorning. People prefer to be who they are; when pushed to be someone else, they often become angry and resistant.

Six months into her new marriage, Nora Litton complained, "Tommy's first wife, Sylvia, was a high-powered businesswoman. She wasn't around much and never cooked a meal. I made the mistake of showing off my very limited cooking skills when we were going together, and he got the idea I was a budding Julia Child. I had one meal I could make—broiled steak, baked potato, and salad. I eventually found a recipe for baked cantaloupe that I added and viewed as a culinary triumph."

Nora laughed. "Almost the first thing Tommy said after we moved into our new apartment was 'No more God-damned baked cantaloupe!' I'm trying to learn to be a decent cook to please him, but I don't enjoy it much. If he wants cunning, innovative little dishes whipped up in the kitchen, he'd better learn to be Emeril Lagasse himself. I can't make up for Sylvia's never setting foot in the kitchen."

The Instant Love Expectation

The instant love expectation is almost as common as the nuclear family myth and just as dangerous. Believing marriage to be a form of parental entitlement, new stepparents presume an intimacy and authority they have yet to earn.

Common among previously single men like Nick Lang, the instant love myth often produces disillusionment even faster than the nuclear myth. Nick was hurt when Leah pushed him away after he tried to hug her the first time they met. And he never forgot his new stepdaughter's words as she fled the wedding reception. "You'll never be a real member of this family," she had sobbed.

The Rescue Fantasy

The rescue fantasy sometimes takes the form of a stepparent thinking they will "shape those kids up" and rescue the children from the adverse, lenient, or ineffectual discipline of a custodial parent. Sometimes, it takes the reverse form of trying to rescue a harassed, inept custodial parent from disobedient, obstreperous children.

In a very common case with custodial fathers and stepmothers, the myth involves the expectation that the stepmother will take over primary responsibility for the care and nurturing of a stepchild. Gordon Salisbury, a very busy executive with custody of two children from a previous marriage, found juggling child care and a demanding career impossible. Both his work and his children were suffering. Gordon thought his problems were going to be solved when he married Martha, a warm, nurturant woman, and he reverted to a pattern of working late and going on long business trips.

Martha often found herself alone, dealing with resentful children whose battle cry was: "We don't have to do that, you're not our real mother!" Gordon was critical of his unruly children, and of Martha, who was unable to control them. Martha was bitter about Gordon's lack of support and participation. Martha described her last evening in the Salisbury household.

"I knew Gordon would be home for dinner and spent all afternoon preparing his favorite things. The dinner was a nightmare. The two little princesses complained about the food and wouldn't eat anything. I said, 'If you don't eat this, don't come whining to me saying you're hungry later. This is it until breakfast.' Gordon just sat there. Later, when I came up from doing the laundry, I found him making peanut butter sandwiches for the kids. It was just too much. The kids smirked at me and laughed. I felt betrayed and humiliated. It's hard enough dealing with those two little hellions alone, without him undermining me. I'd had enough!"

Why Stepchildren Can Become a Risk to a Second Marriage

In stepfamilies, value differences typically cause marital divisiveness in two ways. The first way, and the one most directly related to first marriage experiences, centers on different parenting values and previous experience in parenting.

Any marriage may put together men and women with different parenting traditions, but in a remarriage this can become exaggerated. One may be an experienced parent, one a novice with no children from a previous relationship. One may have come from a first marriage in which children were treated permissively and one from a marriage where the parents were martinets. The biological parent may feel a greater right because of biological ties and past history to impose their standards in dealing with the child. The stepparent, because of an ambiguous role or less emotional commitment, may be more reluctant to intervene or get into a conflict with a spouse about discipline. But even a reluctant stepparent can be driven to intervene when a child is making his or his wife's life intolerable.

"I'd love to straighten that kid out once and for all," Daniel Evans told me a few weeks after his stepson, Brian, was suspended from school. "Kathy's miserable. She blames herself. She says Brian is just confused because we married so soon after the divorce."

But Daniel said he had no plans to speak to Brian. "Kathy's better off handling the situation by herself," he replied when I asked him. "You know how messy things can get when a stepfather steps in." In spite of his resolution not to intervene, when Brian was suspended again a few month later, Daniel, who had been an authoritarian parent to his own children, felt he had no recourse but to act.

"No more car privileges. You don't get to take the car out on weekends anymore," he told Brian that night at dinner. "You've upset your mother enough."

"I can speak for myself, thank you," Kathy interjected.

"Someone has to teach this kid right from wrong," Daniel grumbled.

Kathy curtly thanked Daniel for his concern but said that she would decide how her child should be punished.

Religious or cultural differences can also be divisive, but usually only when the husband and wife have a baby in the new marriage. Although a new child generally has a positive effect on a second marriage, drawing a couple closer together, the go-along-to-get-along attitude most men adopt toward a stepchild's upbringing does not extend to a biological child.

What Divides a Couple in a Stepfamily

It is no accident that the rate of divorce is 50 percent higher in remarriages with stepchildren than in those without. Children can be the make or break issue for many second marriages. The task of forming a close marital relationship in the presence of children; the task of building a stepparent role acceptable to the biological parent, children, and stepparent; and the task of blending children from two different families with different biological relationships into one household, are all formidable. If these issues cannot be resolved, they lead to unhappiness and often divorce.

A small group of stepparents, about 5 percent in our study, view stepchildren as an asset to their marriage. One stepfather said, "I'd always wanted to have children and for me it was wonderful to have a ready-made family." The birth of a new child to a stepfamily couple also often cemented the marital bond, making the stepparent feel less marginal in the family and less resentful of a stepchild. Still, in most stepfamilies, negotiating the relationship between stepparent and stepchild is a major challenge that can undermine marital stability.

The only subject newly remarried couples fight about almost as much as children is finances. But in most cases, arguments about money are also arguments about children, since the most divisive financial question in stepfamily marriages is usually: Who bears financial responsibility for the child—the biological non-custodial parent or the custodial parent and stepparent? Children are also often the subtext in arguments about where the new family should live and who works in the family— one or both adults—and what their money is to be spent on.

Another common source of stress in stepfamilies is the tremendous workload associated with children. Stepparents, especially those who have no children of their own and are inexperienced in raising children, are often shocked at the amount of time and effort that caring for children calls for. Tasks like doing the laundry, driving to and from Little League, and mediating sibling disputes can swiftly produce disillusionment in a spouse who imagined he was marrying for companionship.

"This feels more like a second job than a second marriage," complained Wally Hall, one of the 7 percent of men in stepfamilies to leave a new marriage within a year. Wally was unhappy about an aspect of marriage that most women like—a more egalitarian division of labor. Though women in stepfamilies, like women in other types of families, still do more, chores are shared more equitably in second marriages.

Most of the other reasons why early leavers left—feelings of being shut out or alienation from a wife or constant conflict with stepchildren or the ambiguous nature of stepfamily life—highlight how difficult it is to create a happy second marriage without also creating a workable stepfamily. And that is the subject of the next chapter.

In spite of the many challenges encountered in new marriages and in dealing with stepchildren, 40 percent of couples in stepfamilies were able to build stable, reasonably satisfying marriages. Janet and Nick Lang at times felt overwhelmed by the problems of Nick's relationship with Leah. At one point they separated for several months, but were drawn back together by their great love and respect for each other.

"I realized there was no way I could be happy without Janet. She's my life," Nick said. "I'm just going to have to hang in there and work things out with Leah."

As we will see, some stepfamily histories have happy endings. Nick later said he was never as thrilled as when Leah came home one weekend from college and called him "Dad."

Points to Remember

- Try to learn from a first marriage; face your own shortcomings squarely and don't make the same mistakes the second time around.
- Nurture the marital relationship. Nights out and time alone, although difficult to arrange, may be more essential in building a strong couple relationship when confronting the complex challenges in stepfamilies.
- Dream, but carefully. Unrealistic expectations are common in second marriages, but clinging to them can make the ups and downs of family life feel worse than they are.

- Be honest and open about your concerns and what you want in a new relationship, but be wary of being too negative and critical. Negativity undermines any marriage.
- Be sensitive to the past. Certain behaviors, attitudes, and feelings that seem strange or threatening can become understandable, even sympathetic, when their origin and history are explained.
- Don't expect instant love from children. Relationships in stepfamilies have to be built.
- Expect problems. Second marriages, particularly those involving children, are often turbulent at the beginning. Work on it. Don't bail out too soon.
- Don't be intimidated by the high failure rate in second marriages. Remarriage can open the door to a wonderful new life. I've seen it happen hundreds of times.

9

Building a Stepfamily

"*I* have no idea how I'm supposed to behave, or what the rules are," said one distressed stepfather. "Can I kiss my wife in front of my stepchildren? Do I tell my stepson to do his homework, or is that exceeding my authority? Can I have my own kids over for the weekend, or is that going to be an imposition? It's hard living in a family where there are no clear rules or lines of authority."

This man's concerns were similar to those voiced by many parents in stepfamilies when focusing on relationships with the children.

First and second marriages, similar in many ways, differ in one fundamental way. In first marriages, a satisfying marital relationship is the cornerstone of happy family life, leading to more positive parent-child relationships and more congenial sibling relationships. In many stepfamilies, the sequence is reversed. Establishing some kind of workable relationship between stepparents and stepchildren and resolving their conflicts may be the key to a happy second marriage and to successful functioning in stepfamilies. Children can play a critical role in a second marriage; remarried couples cite children as the number one source of marital stress and tension.

One of the great difficulties lies in how to build family roles and relationships that are acceptable to all the members of a new family. About 70 percent of couples agree that a stepparent's role should be similar to that of a biological parent; but there is much less agreement on this point by children, who often do not view a stepparent as having parental rights or even as being a member of the family. Everybody wins when a remarried couple manages to solve these problems. Marital satisfaction goes up. This correlates not only with being a better spouse but also a better parent and stepparent, and eventually with better adjustment for the child. So, resolving these conflicts is paramount if a second marriage is to succeed.

The good news about stepfamilies is that we know some things about what works in terms of stepparenting. The kind of disruptive behavior that can make a child a wedge issue in a marriage is minimized when the biological parent continues to serve as the principal parent—while the new stepparent initially focuses on providing support for discipline and establishing a friendship with the child. In some stepfamilies, this is the best a stepparent can do because of the children's resentment of any kind of control by a stepparent. Stepparents need to move slowly into the role of limit-setter and disciplinarian. Children will not accept the authority of an adult until that adult has won their trust and respect. Only about one third of stepfathers and one quarter of stepmothers, in comparison to 60 percent of parents in non-divorced families, ever become authoritative. And yet, authoritative parenting is as important to the well-being of the child in a stepfamily as it is to the child of a non-divorced family.

The bad news about second marriages is that so many things can make defining the parenting role in a mutually acceptable manner and building a constructive relationship between the stepparent and stepchild especially difficult. This chapter deals with some of the most important obstacles and how they might be overcome.

The Risk of Maternal Resistance

There are several ways a new stepfather's support can enhance a woman's parenting. One is by acting as a sounding board when his wife wants to talk about child-rearing issues and problems. A second is by giving her emotional support when she is having problems dealing with a fractious child or doubts about her competence as a parent. Others are by backing up the mother's discipline, participating in activities with the child, monitoring the child's activities, and helping with child care tasks such as homework which give the mother some time out.

Complaints of being overburdened are so common among single mothers that in theory, they should embrace the opportunity to share those burdens. And sometimes they do. But after years of exercising sole parental authority, women often develop a "Mother knows best" attitude, which can make help hard to accept. Not uncommonly, the upshot is that the man who offers the help is left feeling isolated and unappreciated.

Tamara Evans, like a lot of the single mothers in our studies, tended to be fairly restrictive about her seven-year-old son Timmy's rambunctious rough-and-tumble play and risk-taking activities. When her new husband, Ray, told Tamara that she was babying Timmy, she told him that he didn't know what he was talking about. "Basically, Tamara told me to butt out," Ray said later. "She told me that Timmy was her responsibility and I had no business interfering. I spent a lot of time feeling like a fifth wheel around that house."

This kind of maternal resistance can undermine a marriage in at least two ways. One is by isolating the stepfather and making him feel less emotionally invested in the family. After awhile, the stepfather begins to feel like a visitor from another country; he can see that the inhabitants are fond of one another and are having a terrific time, but since he doesn't understand the local language or customs, he feels excluded. Aside from frustrating him, exclusion limits his emotional stake in the country's success. Which means he is more apt to leave at the first sign of trouble.

A second, more insidious threat posed by maternal resistance involves the child's behavior and the authority of the stepfather. The stresses of early stepfamily life, like the stresses of the early postdivorce period, produce a decline in maternal skill and an increase in behavior problems in children. And these changes can have an important effect on the dynamic within the new stepfamily. Distracted and preoccupied, often focused on her new marriage, the woman's ability to manage the child diminishes. The trap results because many remarried women recognize neither their own ineptitude nor the hostile, resistant behavior of their children. Thus, when the man offers advice or help, the woman who thinks she doesn't need assistance refuses him. Worse still, if the stepfather intervenes, even in a reasonable way, he frequently finds himself undercut. This adds to his problems with the child, who concludes that if the mother doesn't respect the stepparent's authority, why should she? The most common outcome of this process is yet more misbehavior and defiance toward the stepparent.

"It's been a little crazy lately," Amy Pembroke assured me after her remarriage, "but I have things pretty well under control."

However, Stuart, Amy's new husband, told me he was astonished at how little control Amy had over his stepdaughter, Maggie. "And I'm the one who suffers," Stuart complained. "I never know when that kid is going to pop off at me or how long her little explosions are going to last." Even twelve-year-old Maggie agreed with her stepfather about Amy.

"Mom's definitely slipping," declared Maggie, who told me she had violated her curfew a half dozen times in the last few months without being punished.

Stuart later said, "About six months into the marriage, it occurred to me that I didn't have to stay around and take Maggie's abuse. So I left. It just wasn't worth it. I was miserable."

When Stepfathers Withdraw

Paternal resistance is more common than maternal resistance because men usually remarry for love and companionship and are reluctant to become deeply involved with a stepchild. "I married her, not her kids," was a favorite mantra among stepfathers. However, aware that marital happiness necessitates some parental involvement, most men initially try to develop a friendly, constructive relationship with their new stepchild.

Immediate emotional attachment to a new stepchild is rare. Such attachment has to build gradually in both stepparents and stepchildren, and is most likely to occur when the stepfather has helped raise the child from early childhood. The average new stepfather behaves like a polite but wary stranger, trying to ingratiate himself, seeking areas of common interest like sports, movies, and music, rarely criticizing the child but feeling little emotional closeness or rapport. Emotional distancing is common. A disengaged parenting style remains the most common style for stepfathers even in long-established stepfamilies.

Another numerically much smaller group of stepfathers were hard-liners, who actually avoided building a close relationship with their stepchildren. Their attitude is exemplified by Lucinda Fredericks's second husband, Charles, a locally prominent lawyer, who said, "I've already done the parenting thing with my own kids," when I asked him why he spent so little time with Dickie. However, Charles's attitude wasn't as simple as he made it sound. A gregarious, social man in the mold of James Pennybaker, he found the asocial Dickie as inexplicable as a black hole, and Dickie's problems with the law further complicated their relationship.

"I'm a lawyer," Charles told me. "And here I am getting calls from the police about my stepson's behavior. I've told Lucinda, it puts me in a very awkward position."

Hard-liners often made hostile, reproachful stepfathers, and their relationships with their stepchildren were usually turbulent and conflicted. Not surprisingly, their negativity left a mark; they had stepchildren who were at high risk of developing behavior, academic, and emotional problems.

However, hard-liners are the exception. More common are men who, while often reluctant to become active parents, do want to establish at least a congenial buddy relationship in which they can share pleasant experiences with their new stepchildren. In about a third of stepfamilies, these first, tentative efforts to establish common ground eventually led to a close, authoritative relationship, especially with stepsons. In other stepfamilies, the man settled permanently into the role of a buddy, helping to nurture his stepchild by supporting his wife's parenting through activities such as monitoring, and by maintaining a friendly relationship with the child.

Sadly, in a great many other stepfamilies, a steady stream of invective and rejection on the part of a stepchild eventually wore down the man's resolve. This was true even when, as with Nick Lang and Leah, the stepfather made great efforts to promote a positive relationship with his stepdaughter and knew that difficult behavior was to be expected.

"Look, I know I'm supposed to be an adult about these things," Nick said two years into his new marriage. "And I try to be; but I'm also human. There's only so many times I can be sneered at and ignored and told, 'You're not my real father,' by Leah. I never thought I could dislike a child, but I dislike Leah and what she is doing to our marriage."

Two years of rejection seems to be about the average man's limit for abuse. After that, even eager men like Nick lose interest in their stepfather role and withdraw into a kind of cranky disengagement or sullen anger—or both. They avoid the stepchild when possible, criticize more freely, and when attacked, no longer turn the other cheek.

Paternal resistance also can make a stepfamily, particularly a new one, vulnerable to the boomerang effect. Without support, the overstressed woman begins to lose whatever control she has over the child, who becomes even more unruly, which deepens the stepfather's alienation.

Steve Black blamed his departure on his stepdaughter, Renatta, whom he called "simply impossible," and on his wife, Katherine, whom he declared "incompetent," particularly in comparison to his first wife, described as having been "a wonderful mother."

The only person Steve did not blame for the failure of his marriage was himself, even though he had given up on trying to establish a relationship with his stepdaughter at the first sign of resistance.

"I did all I could to help," Steve assured me. "When I couldn't bear it any longer, I left."

Stepparent resistance to the parental role creates a threat to the marital relationship as well. The biological parent gets caught between her desires to promote the marriage and to protect her child. These split loyalties can create impossible choices for the biological parent. It happened to Helen Lolland. After a year of overaggressive and unsuccessful stepparenting, Helen Lolland's husband, Lamar, made an abrupt U-turn and disengaged from even an advising and monitoring role. When Helen's daughter, Leslie, predictably grew even more unruly, Helen was confronted with a stark choice. Either Leslie moved in with her father or Lamar moved out.

The next morning, Helen told Lamar, "You can do what you want. Leslie is staying."

The worst thing about such choices is that whichever one a woman makes, she usually loses.

Denise Beauchamp was a woman who had also confronted a "her or me" choice but made a different decision.

"You know what I got for Mother's Day?" Denise said to me at the twenty-year interview. "Just a message on my answering machine. No card. No gift, just a 'Sorry I missed you, Mom, talk to you later.' I didn't even get a call back. Jane was too busy, I guess."

When I spoke to Jane a few weeks later, she told me she felt "absolutely no guilt" about the Mother's Day call or about all the other times she failed to call Denise.

"I'm sorry Mom's lonely," Jane said. "But she should have thought of that ten years ago, when she shipped me off to boarding school to keep my stepfather happy. You can't imagine what it feels like to be turfed out of your own family. Now that they're divorced, he's gone and she's the one who will have to cope with being alone."

Moving Too Fast

Parental overeagerness can make a child a divisive marital issue for the same reason that maternal and paternal resistance do. It often ratchets up the child's level of resistance, invective, and rebelliousness. But in this case overparenting, not underparenting, is responsible. Overeagerness prompts a couple to violate the rule of having the stepparent establish a positive relationship with the child before exerting control.

Overeagerness on the part of the woman is often caused by exhaustion. After years of parenting alone—as well as serving as her family's sole breadwinner—a mother is eager for a helpmate. So she encourages her often reluctant new husband to begin playing a hands-on role with her child immediately.

Overeagerness on the part of the man often results from an attempt to move in too rapidly to try to build a traditional paternal role. Men like Nick Lang, who have no personal experience with children and come from traditional homes, are particularly prone to a kind of misdiagnosis of their stepchildren's feelings and behaviors, and misdiagnosis may lead to malpractice.

Sometimes, overeager males like Nick may try to use physical affection in building a close relationship with their stepchildren. This can be especially disruptive with adolescent girls. Nick, an ebullient, open, loving man, made this mistake with Leah Coleman, when he tried to hug her on their first meeting and Leah was repelled. The initial wariness of stepchildren often is interpreted by stepparents as active rejection rather than the cautious "let's go slow, stranger" attitude found in many stepchildren.

Male overeagerness also often arises from another kind of misdiagnosis. The stepchild's resistance and unruliness are attributed not to the normal anxieties and stresses of adjusting to stepfamily life but rather to years of living under a pliant female hand. Before having built a close relationship, when the child misbehaves, instead of allowing the biological parent to handle the discipline, the eager stepfather does what Nick did after a school play, when Leah introduced Janet to a classmate as "my mother," then pointed to him and said, "That little fat guy over there is her husband."

"You're grounded for two weeks," Nick said as soon as he, Leah, and Janet were in the car. "Hear me? No anything for two weeks. No going out. No TV. Just in your room and homework."

Nick checked the rearview mirror; Leah was curled up in the backseat scowling. "You hear me, young lady? Two weeks." A raised middle finger appeared in the mirror. "All right, Goddamn it, three weeks."

Leah sulked, storming to her room in the evenings, and one night Nick even had a slipper thrown at him. But then suddenly her behavior improved. "See, I told you firmness works," a triumphant Nick declared.

But a few days later, Nick arrived home to find Janet and Leah sitting in the living room eating popcorn and watching a soap opera. "What's the story?" Nick said, pointing to Leah. "Isn't she supposed to be in her room?"

As Leah smirked, Janet replied sheepishly, "I'm sorry, Nick. I thought you were just too hard on her."

Stepmother families are, if anything, even more prone to overeagerness. As a rule, women, like men, prefer to slip into the stepparenting role slowly; but often they are pressured into immediate active parenting by what might be called the "Mommy gene expectation." Almost all men seem to believe that women are born with a gene that gives them instant access to a ready-made and vast store of parental skill and knowledge.

Crystal Hassard was one of the many stepmothers in our studies mugged by this expectation.

Crystal's new husband, Bill, reassured her when Crystal said she was concerned about her relationship with Trish and Sheila, Bill's daughters, and her inexperience as a parent. "Don't worry," he said. "You'll have the girls eating out of your hand in no time."

"Bill would have been more accurate if he'd said, 'biting your hand in no time,' " Crystal told me a year later. "You should hear the way those girls talk to me."

"How much support do you get from Bill?" I asked. Crystal shook her head ruefully. "Not much, and it's passed the stage of support now. What I need is a vacation from Billy *and* the girls."

Stepmothers like Crystal face the additional problem of parental competition. Unlike most non-residential fathers, who are happy to play a companionate role or no role at all, most non-residential mothers continue to be actively involved in their children's lives. They visit more frequently; even more important, biological mothers set rules, discipline and monitor, advise and act as confidantes and do a lot of other things that can—and often do—undercut a stepmother's authority and interfere with her building a constructive relationship with her stepchildren.

Stepchildren are most likely to be hostile and resistant if they think the stepparent is trying to replace the biological parent, or if the stepparent and biological parent are in competition.

Crystal learned this the hard way. Sheila, her elder stepdaughter, was complaining that her mother, Angela, had promised but not yet helped her pick out a dress for her eighth-grade prom. As the prom drew nearer, Sheila's anxiety and complaints increased. Two days before the prom, Crystal took Sheila shopping and bought her a lovely dress. Even Sheila was ecstatic and appreciative; but Angela was outraged. She phoned Crystal, screaming that she was an interfering bitch butting in where she wasn't wanted. Angela threatened Sheila that she would never see her again if she wore the dress. The dress was returned and Angela purchased a dress that Sheila liked less well for her guilt-ridden daughter.

"I don't blame you for being upset," Bill said when Crystal complained to him. But Bill refused to go beyond moral support. When Crystal asked him to speak to his former wife, he said, "I think it's best if you ladies work out this problem among yourselves."

Why Stepchildren Resist

It would be nice if parents were in complete control of what happens in building happy relationships in a new stepfamily; but they are not. Parenting is a two-way street, and the behavior of stepchildren has an important influence on the responses of stepparents and the quality and duration of a new marriage. Disobedient, contentious, hostile stepchildren can make a misery of family relations. However, although many children initially are somewhat wary about the unknowns in their new family life, only about one quarter in stepfather families are aggressively resistant. These are most likely to be girls, and over time their resistance often abates. The vast majority of children, especially those who have been prepared for the new marriage and have had prior contact with the prospective stepfather, eventually view the move positively if the marital relationship is good and the stepparent is warm and supportive. Although they are aware of some negative changes in their life, they describe their reactions as generally happy, satisfied, or pleased. They are pleased with the practical gains in their life, and adolescent girls are especially appreciative of their improved financial situation.

Said one teenage girl, "We live in a big house in a fancy neighborhood now. I'm proud to bring my friends home and I don't have to wear hand-me-downs anymore. Mom takes me out shopping and charges things. After the hell we went through before, counting every penny, it's unbelievable."

Some children, like David Coleman, were just happy to have a father. "I love Mom," he said, "but it's different having a dad in the family. Nick throws a football around with me and he's teaching me to flyfish and we go to basketball games together. We do guy things I couldn't do with Mom. I talk about different things with Nick."

Other children were appreciative of the changes in their mother. One ten-year-old commented, "Mother's not worrying so much and working so hard now. I've never seen her really happy before. She's a different person. I realize now how tough things were for her."

With these advantages, what makes children resistant? Boys, who often have been in coercive cycles with their divorced mothers, are more likely to see stepfathers as potential allies or companions, and are more accepting than girls, who may view the stepfather as a rival. In some cases, as with Leah and Nick, it is jealousy and fear of dilution of the close mother-daughter relationship that makes daughters resistant. We have found the closer that relationship was before the new marriage, the more unyielding and resentful the girl will be.

As a young adult, Leah said, "I was just jealous, I guess. I missed the times Mom and I spent together sitting on her bed eating Chinese food and watching TV. I resented Nick being there at the dinner table when I wanted to get her advice about something—a romantic problem, an unreasonable teacher, or a fight with a friend. I couldn't stand it when they hugged or kissed. I thought it was disgusting. There wasn't much they could do. I just felt shut out."

Other children were resistant and angry because stepparents moved in too fast or were too immediately touchy-feely. Some were resentful because they thought the stepparent was trying to replace the biological parent and the new marriage destroyed the child's fantasies of his parents' reconciliation. They resisted calling their stepparent "Mom" or "Dad" and usually resolved this issue by calling the stepparent by their first name or by not calling them anything at all.

Children recognized stepparents as marginalized in the family and often liked it that way. Only 25 percent of children in stepfamilies reported that the stepfathers were "the boss in the family," compared to two thirds in non-divorced families. However, children could come to appreciate these marginalized stepfathers if they brought in income, were a support and companion to the mother, and proved a friend or a buddy to the child.

Some stepparents who gradually became more firm and authoritative also were appreciated, and stepchildren with an authoritative stepparent often commented that the extra love and control made them feel safer. Despite all the difficulties stepmothers confront, we saw many women use a combination of patience, skill, and sensitivity to build good family relationships. This good relationship with a stepmother was most likely to occur when the father was an actively involved parent who supported the stepmother's discipline, when the first and second wife did not act like rivals, or when the non-custodial mother had disengaged from the child's life while the child was young.

Fathers who were unemployed, authoritarian, physically punishing, and especially those who were abusive to the mother or children were intensely resented. In adolescence, this resentment could take the form of early leaving in stepdaughters and of violence and fighting between stepfathers and stepsons. It is much more difficult to bully a teenager than a young child.

One stepson, describing his stepfather, said, "For eight years we put up with his shouting and tantrums and being hit with a belt. Then one day when I was fifteen and late getting home from football practice and he started to unbuckle his belt, I knocked him across the room. It dawned on me I didn't have to put up with this crap. I was bigger and stronger and tougher than he was. I said, 'If you ever touch me or Debbie or Jane or Mom again, I'm going to rip you apart,' and he never did. Eventually, he just left. I guess the fun was over for him."

The situation with stepmothers is more difficult and stepchild resentment more intense. Stepmothers, even those who would like to be less involved, rarely have that option: they find themselves in the center of the fray. They are often expected to be nurturers to already difficult and suspicious children. In order to satisfy their husband's expectations, they have to impose some kind of order on the household, which is angrily and bitterly resented by many stepchildren. In our most contentious stepfamilies, a real demonizing of the stepmother often occurred. We heard stepmothers described by some stepchildren as "evil," "malevolent," "wicked," or as "monsters," and nicknamed "Dog Face" or "The Dragon." Stepfathers rarely encountered this level of vitriol. Many well-intentioned but angry, discouraged, and defeated stepmothers gradually gave up and pulled out of the marriage.

Alliances and Scapegoating

When conflict is present, when emotions run high, when people have different expectations and values, the family becomes like a battlefield or political campaign. People take sides, alliances are formed, and there is much blaming, finger-pointing, and scapegoating. Some battle lines are drawn based on family history and some to build or sustain new relationships.

In all human societies, outsiders are the targets of scapegoating. Whenever anything bad happens, the insiders, which in a stepfamily are the biological parent and child, often team up to blame the outsider. In the Coleman family, Janet was caught between her love for Nick and for Leah; she took Leah's side and undermined Nick's discipline. But sometimes alliances and scapegoating can be even more extreme and irrational, and the outsider can be blamed even if he happens to be 30,000 feet over Detroit in a plane when bad things take place. Which is where Ned Kauffman happened to be when his stepdaughter's soccer team lost in the quarter finals in a statewide tournament.

Arriving home the next day, Ned was accused of selfishness even before he had his coat off. "You don't care!" his stepdaughter shouted as he was unpacking. "We lost because you don't care!"

"I don't understand your daughter's logic," Ned told his wife that night. "Even if it were true and I didn't care, how would my not caring make her team lose?"

"Tracy's thirteen and she's disappointed in herself," his wife said. "She missed an important shot yesterday. It would have been nice if you could have been there, though. It would have made her feel supported—and who knows?"

"Who knows what?" Ned asked.

"Who knows? If she felt supported, maybe she would have played better."

Children can also become victims of scapegoating, particularly when they get caught between two unhappy, warring adults as Wilbur Brill did. Never a good student, Wilbur became a very poor student in junior high school; his grades fluctuated between D and D- and he was caught smoking twice in the men's room. At her wits' end, Wilbur's mother did what women with hard-to-control young adolescent sons often do: she sent Wilbur to live with his father. Maybe her former husband could succeed where she had failed.

At first Wilbur was excited; he had always wanted to live with his dad. But a month after moving in, Wilbur was already having second thoughts. All his father and stepmother seemed to do was fight. Worse still, they started blaming him for their fights. "We didn't used to fight until you came here," Wilbur's father told him one night after consuming a six-pack of beer.

A few days later, after a particularly vicious fight, Wilbur's stepmother came into his room and accused him of "destroying our marriage."

In this case, scapegoating had no effect on what was already a failing marriage—it just gave two unhappy people someone new to blame their unhappiness on. But it did affect Wilbur, whose insecurity and troubled behavior accelerated after being returned to his reluctant mother. The depressed teenager said, "I guess I'm just a born screw-up. No matter where I go, I can't do anything right and nobody wants me."

Stepfamily Structure

We did thousands of hours of videotaping of families in our studies, but one set of tapes in those thousands of hours still stands out in my mind. They involve the interactions of a family headed by Marjorie and a stepfather named Paul Drew.

In the first interaction, Paul and his biological daughter, fifteen-year-old Daphne, who was born to the new marriage, are sitting in the Drews' living room talking to one another. The father and daughter joke, laugh, tease, and touch. The affection between the two is palpable. Although they have been asked to discuss their problems, Paul says, "Problems—we don't have any problems."

Reading the instructions for the interaction task, Daphne says, "How do we resolve our disagreements? I just do what Dad says and that's it." Both laugh. Daphne playfully pokes her father in the ribs and ruffles his thinning hair. The touching and interaction are flirtatious and somewhat inappropriate.

In the second tape, Paul is still sitting in the living room, but now his sixteen-year-old stepdaughter, Anna Marie, has replaced Daphne in the chair next to him. There is also palpable emotion on this tape, but it's unremittingly negative. Stepfather and stepdaughter carp and bait and criticize; they avoid direct eye contact and end the session silent, each turned away from the other, staring into a different corner of the room.

Paul and Anna Marie talk directly into the camera, like two complainants addressing a judge.

"Paul hates me," Anna Marie says calmly.

"Liar!" Paul exclaims.

Ignoring the accusation, Anna Marie repeats her charge. "Paul hates me. He expects everyone to treat him like God."

"Another lie," Paul interjects.

"But I won't do it. I'm the only one in the family who won't. So he hates me."

When Marjorie joins Paul on the couch and the couple are filmed discussing their problems, Paul describes the Drews as a "happy" family.

But Marjorie refuses to endorse the statement. She says in a flat voice, "Well, at least two of you are happy."

When we filmed the sibling interaction, the behavior of Daphne with her half sister, Anna Marie, seems almost hysterically animated. In contrast, Anna Marie sits hunched, frowning, looking away from Daphne and speaking in a low, contemptuous voice.

Anna Marie begins by complaining about Paul's preferential treatment of Daphne. "Paul just bought you an ice cream cone. He didn't buy me one. He invited you to go to the mall with him. He didn't invite me."

Then the girls' discussion moves to many of the complaints we find common in siblings—taking each other's things, borrowing clothes without asking, and intruding on each other's private space in their rooms. But the arguments between Anna Marie and Daphne are presented with a vitriol and intensity unusual even in hostile sibling pairs.

Finally Daphne said, "There is no solution to our problems except to keep us apart. We've tried everything."

Anna Marie looks at the camera and says, "Kill her, just kill her. That's the only solution."

The Drew family is a complex stepfamily in which the relationships of children to parents differ. In this case, both were the biological children of their mother, Marjorie, but only Daphne is the biological daughter of Paul. This is a common combination since a half sibling is born within four years of a remarriage in one third of stepfamilies. Other less common complex stepfamilies, since fathers rarely gain custody of children, are blended families in which some children come from the father's previous marriage and some from the mother's.

In contrast to simple stepfamilies, where children share the same biological relationship with parents—for example, where both children were born to a mother's previous marriage and are the father's stepchildren—complex stepfamilies have more troubled family relationships, and more problem behavior in children. Stepfamilies, like machines, are subject to the complexity principle: the more working parts, the greater the risk of a breakdown. And in a complex stepfamily, breakdown often occurs in family cohesion. Alliances, scapegoating, and divisive loyalty issues appear more commonly in families like the Drews. The children in the family clash; each parent sides with his or her biological child; and the unit divides into hostile, sometimes warring camps.

This is more or less what happened in the Drew family. But instead of leading to divorce, as factionalism often does, in the Drews' case, it led to stepparent-stepchild and sibling alienation. The bad feelings between Daphne and Anna Marie eventually polarized the family—but with a twist. While Paul always took Daphne's side, Anna Marie's mother, Marjorie, attempted to be an honest broker in disputes between Paul, Anna Marie, and Daphne. "If someone doesn't play referee," a clearly depressed Marjorie told me, "the family will go flying apart."

But Marjorie's attempts to mediate were insufficient for Anna Marie. Feeling increasingly isolated, she left the upper-middle-class Drew family at seventeen, had a child at eighteen, married at nineteen, and was divorced by twenty-two.

In spite of the difficulties encountered by complex stepfamilies, they can succeed. But success takes more time and effort. Restabilization after a new marriage takes longer than restabilization after a divorce, and the process is more prolonged in complex stepfamilies. It may take as much as five to seven years in complex stepfamilies, and with the high rate and rapidity of divorce in stepfamilies, the new marriage may already have dissolved before restabilization ever occurs.

The Importance of Timing

The timing of remarriage also has a major influence on the success of a second marriage because a child's age affects his or her receptivity to stepfamily life in general and a new stepfather in particular. New marriages that occur before or after the early teen years of ten to fifteen are more likely to be successful and to provide the least resistance. In one of our studies of remarriages that occurred when the children were early adolescents, we found that the relations between stepchild and stepfather, bad in the immediate aftermath of the new marriage, had shown no signs of improvement twenty-six months later, when the study ended. No positive adaptation had occurred.

Why should this be?

Young children and stepparents are more likely to become emotionally attached, and the addition of a stepparent relieves older adolescents of concerns about emotional support for their parents as they prepare to leave the family and go on to college or the world of work. However, in early adolescence, children begin to become more autonomous and to establish an independent identity. This may present difficulties for children in divorced and remarried families who already have "grown up faster," enjoying less adult supervision and earlier independence than those in two-parent households. In all adolescents, but especially in these precociously autonomous children, any pressures that threaten the move toward greater independence—including a stepfather with the nuclear family myth on his mind—are likely to generate a good deal of resistance.

A good marriage often promotes acceptance of the stepparent as well as diminishing behavior problems in preadolescent boys, but not in preadolescent girls, who see a close marital bond as a threat to their status as chief maternal companion. However, in adolescence, all this changes. Both adolescent boys and girls have more harmonious relationships with a stepfather if the marriage is close and happy.

Why this change in adolescent girls? Adolescent girls are very aware of their sexual maturing and the changes in their bodies. They have romantic fantasies and are hypersensitive to issues of intimate relationships and sexuality. As they mature, girls begin to view a good marriage in a stepfamily as a kind of sexual insurance policy. The girl thinks that the closer the stepfather is to her mother, the less likely will be his real or imagined advances toward her. Once the sexual threat is tabled, often a girl becomes more accepting and open. But that doesn't mean her stepfather reciprocates.

Sexual abuse may get the headlines—and it does occur more often in stepfamilies than in nuclear families. However, the more common problem, by a very wide margin, is stepfather avoidance. The adolescent girl's burgeoning sexuality, which makes even biological fathers feel inhibited and begin to shy away, often produces a severe form of avoidance in stepfathers. Even loving stepfathers may avoid showing physical affection or contact, out of fear that anything they do may be misinterpreted by the girl or her mother—or by both of them.

Building a Family Identity

Five years into his new marriage, Jacob Lockard said that he never felt part of a real family while he was married to Miranda. "There was the marriage, which was Miranda and me; and parent-child relationships, which was Miranda and her kids. Somehow they never came together. I share the same address with the kids, but we live such disconnected lives we might as well be living on different planets." Jacob didn't cite this as his reason for seeking a divorce; but such lack of cohesion—a lack of "familyness"—often has an eroding effect on a marriage. It makes leaving a remarriage easier, because the person feels he is abandoning an arrangement, not a family.

"Why stay?" Jacob said, when I asked why he was leaving. "I have all the headaches of family life and none of its benefits."

Routines, Celebrations, and Traditions

Part of what makes a family feel like a family is a shared history and shared family routines, celebrations, and traditions. These are things new stepfamilies lack at the outset but can create, and they help to promote a sense of identity and cohesion.

The regular routines of family life—eating together at six, reading before bed, going to church or for Sunday drives in the country or regularly watching a favorite TV program—help to build a sense of rootedness in a stepfamily. They help to make stepfamily life feel more organized, predictable, and reliable.

Celebrations like holidays, weddings, birthdays, bar mitzvahs, first communions, and other rites of passage also help to define the stepfamily. They provide an opportunity to gather the larger stepfamily together—uncles, aunts, grandparents, cousins, and perhaps even non-residential children—all the people who play a role in the life of the family and who support it. They constitute a kind of living history, a reminder that, despite its newness, the stepfamily does have a distinctive past. It serves as a way for the family to say, "Here is who we are and here are the people who belong in our family."

But how and where to celebrate special occasions can also create divisiveness in divorced and remarried families. Resolving issues such as where the children will be spending Christmas or birthdays, eating Thanksgiving dinner, or going on summer vacations may be difficult. And when the weddings of offspring occur, the inclusion of a divorced non-custodial spouse and his new family may be particularly contentious.

As one woman said, "Max [a stepfather] and I raised Susan. We cared for her as an infant, looked after her when she was unhappy or ill, and shepherded her through adolescence. Max now is her real father. Susan loves Max. We're a close family. And now she wants to have that bastard Leon, who never did anything—never paid child support and rarely saw her—at her wedding. I don't get it. I don't want to ruin the day for Susan, but Leon being there will certainly ruin the day for me and Max. Even though Max will walk down the aisle with her, I know Leon will be swanning around as if he's the real father of the bride."

Family traditions are a third form of cohesion-producing rituals. They are a symbolic way for a family to say not just, "Here is who we are," but, "Here is what is unique about us, what makes us different from other families, what makes us special." A tradition can mean having special decorations on a Christmas tree, the kind of cake we choose for a birthday party, putting a tooth under the pillow for the tooth fairy, or who sits where in the car. What makes a tradition a tradition—what gives it emotional resonance, makes it a unifying symbol—is its repetition and its history. So, in stepfamilies, traditions have to be developed.

One of our newly remarried mothers put it well: "You know, I'm sick of arguments with my family and in-laws about where we spend Christmas. I want us to have our own special Christmas, with the kids stringing popcorn and making their own ornaments to decorate the tree. I want them to sneak down in our house in the morning to see if Santa has been there, and for all of us to open our presents together. We're going to stay home. We want to start our *own* Christmas traditions."

Points to Remember

- Insecurity and disagreements are a normal part of early stepfamily life; most people feel stressed but hopeful.
- If a stepfamily is to be successful, family members must reach a mutually satisfactory agreement on family roles and relationships, but there may be little initial consensus between parents, stepparents, and children on this issue.
- Don't expect instant love from stepchildren. Go slowly; it takes time to build a relationship.
- Don't try to replace the non-custodial parent. Children can love and benefit from supportive relationships with both stepparents and biological parents.
- Authoritative parenting benefits all children, including stepchildren, but stepchildren are often unwilling to accept discipline and control from a stepparent. Don't force it. Support the biological parent's discipline, monitor the child's activity, and be patient and supportive with the child.
- Support your spouse. Parenting is often difficult in stepfamilies.
- Sometimes problems in stepfamilies are not the parents' fault. Resistant children can cause rifts in marital relationships as well as in parent-child relationships.
- Learn to be flexible. Change is a constant in stepfamily life. And since much of the change is generated by factors not entirely within your control—children and stepchildren moving in and out of the home, dealing with non-residential parents and in-laws—the best policy is to go with the flow.
- Try to be understanding and not take sides with family members. Hostile alliances and scapegoating can destroy a stepfamily.
- Time the remarriage. The best time to remarry is before a child's tenth birthday and after his or her sixteenth; couples who marry in

between often find themselves on a collision course with the teen's developmental agenda.

- It takes a longer time to build positive relationships and constructive functioning in a stepfamily than in a first marriage or even in a single-parent family following divorce. Be patient and work at it.

10

Welcome to Peer World: Why Teens from Divorced and Remarried Families Leave Home Earlier and Get into Trouble More Often

When Celia Russell turned fourteen, she announced she wanted to live with her mother, which thrilled Connie, who couldn't believe her good luck. "I never thought Celia would give me another chance," she told me later.

Frankly, neither did I. Something just didn't ring true about Celia's decision. In our annual telephone interviews, Celia had continued to speak coldly about her mother, but with great affection although also considerable condescension about her father, Simon.

Simon was reluctant to give Celia up, but her defiant, uncontrollable behavior defeated and saddened him.

"Nothing I do seems to help," he said mournfully. "I'm afraid she's going to get into serious trouble. Maybe a teenaged girl just needs her mother. Without Bob being there, I wouldn't let Celia go. But look what he's done for Connie. Maybe he can turn Celia around, too."

Turning Celia around proved to be difficult.

An angry and disappointed Connie came into the eleven-year interview a year after the move. "Bob and I were had," she said, when I asked about Celia. "She was never interested in living with us; she just wanted to be near her boyfriend, and our house happens to be closer to his than Simon's."

The boyfriend's name was Reese Pierce and Connie described him as "the Einstein of dysfunction." "He's been arrested twice for drunk driving, once for shoplifting, and I know he does drugs. He's a real prince. A few weeks ago, I told Celia, 'No more Reese.' So what do I find in my front hall floor the other day? Reese's naked backside! It was the first thing I saw when I opened the front door; then Celia's head pops out from under one of his shoulders and says, 'Hey, what are you doing home? You're supposed to be working late tonight.' It was like she was accusing me, like I was at fault! Can you imagine?"

Connie sighed. "We try to control her and set curfews, but I know she sneaks out at night after we're asleep and she never comes home when she's supposed to. We ground her for that, then she just goes out and does it again. What can you do? You can't chain her to her bed! I've almost given up on her. I'm afraid I'm going to land up a thirty-eight-year-old grandmother."

Many of the parental worries and conflicts in adolescence center on the early adolescent's increasing independence and involvement with peers. Conflict between parents and children increases in most families during early adolescence; but the increase is especially marked in divorced and remarried families. Parent-child relationships that have been troubled earlier, such as those between stepparents and stepchildren or divorced mothers and sons, are likely to become more contentious in early adolescence. However, even the relatively congenial relationships between divorced mothers and daughters deteriorate and their conflict rises to the same levels as that of divorced mothers and sons.

Although most families may gain some comfort in the knowledge that this too shall pass, since conflict tends to peak at fifteen and begins to decline at sixteen, in divorced and remarried families this may not be the case. Sometimes, parent-child conflict in divorced and remarried families is sustained throughout adolescence and doesn't diminish until the adolescent leaves home.

A second comfort may lie in the fact that annoying as it is, such oppositional behavior does have a legitimate developmental purpose. It is part of the process of individuation, of adolescents beginning to recognize themselves as highly individual human beings with particular needs, competencies, tastes, views, and idiosyncrasies. But teenagers cannot discover who they are or who they want to be without a broad range of people and varied experiences. So at about ten or eleven, adolescents begin to push out of the family and become increasingly involved in the Peer World. Often the teenager wants to move into the Peer World faster than the parents are prepared to let her go, and this creates problems.

We frequently heard comments from mothers such as "I miss my little girl" or "I miss her depending on me and confiding in me. She has secrets now." As early adolescents mature and strive to become more independent, parents and children spend less time together. The closeness and parental control diminishes as the disagreements increase.

One of the reasons that parents may be apprehensive about their child's increasing independence is that parents often see Peer World as a place of potential danger and temptation, while most children see it as an important step toward adulthood and freedom.

Who's right? It depends.

The influence of some Peer Worlds can be beneficial. The right kind of friends can promote achievement, security, a sense of belonging and responsibility in a child. But other Peer Worlds can be a parent's worst nightmare. They expose a child to influences that can lead to teenage pregnancy, academic failure, substance abuse, and juvenile delinquency.

A number of factors determine children's choice of a Peer World and how constructive or dangerous that choice is for them.

The most positive shifts occur when a child still remains emotionally attached to his family while he moves into Peer World. In stable, authoritative families, although parents and early adolescents may argue, the adolescents still love their parents, want to please them, and value their opinion; unlike unattached adolescents, they are unlikely to get involved with a markedly deviant peer group.

The timing of the shift to peer allegiances is also important. Does the shift occur before or after the adolescent has developed the maturity to handle common temptations like alcohol, drugs, and sex? Most studies agree: the earlier disengagement occurs, and the more completely it removes a child from parental guidance, the more likely a youngster is to end up in over his developmental head.

Critics of the postnuclear family argue that children in divorced and remarried families disengage in a way that puts them at special risk. They point out that a stressful, conflicted home setting with inept parents is more likely to push a child out the door early, and since these are more common in divorced and remarried families, their children are particularly likely to disengage prematurely. Many critics also contend that high-stress and non-authoritative parenting fails to promote protective factors that can help buffer against the hazards of adolescence, such as self-control, self-esteem, academic achievement, and social skills.

Our studies of over 2,500 adolescents and their families suggest that on these points the critics are correct. But what explains why only about a quarter of children in divorced and remarried families disengaged prematurely, and why only one quarter showed deviant patterns of emotional and behavioral development?

Again, it is a question of risk and protective factors that every child, within his or her specific family context, does or does not have. Some are carryovers from childhood, but some are new as the child becomes increasingly involved outside the family.

Risk and Protective Factors in Adolescence

The Parent-Child Relationship

Celia Russell arrived for her eleven-year interview late and unrecognizable.

Her black-dyed hair erupted from her head in lacquered spikes. Adorning one nostril was a pearl-colored stone, and on the outer lobe of each ear a row of earrings. Everything else Celia had on was the same shade of Addams Family black as her hair—her eyeshadow, lipstick, halter top, motorcycle jacket, boots, and skirt. The skirt, precariously short to begin with, rode up to reveal black underpants when Celia sat down, her legs splayed and one arm looped over the back of the chair.

"How are you?" I said.

"Huh?"

"Why don't you turn off your Walkman, Celia?"

"Oh yeah, I forgot." Celia's head stopped bobbing.

"Can you hear me now?"

"Uh-huh." Celia removed a Tootsie Pop from the pocket of her motorcycle jacket, unwrapped it, and took a lick. "Sorry I'm late, Dr. Hetherington."

Adolescent girls sometimes are full of rude observations about their parents, but Celia's observations about Connie transcended rude. They were full of disdain and anger. "I suppose Connie told you about Reese," she said, pulling one corner of her halter down to reveal a heart-shaped tattoo on her left breast: REESE.

"Your mother mentioned him," I said. "Why don't you tell me about Reese?"

Celia rolled her eyes and waved her Tootsie Pop like a baton. "God, Mom has some nerve. She keeps telling me what a bad influence Reese is. I mean, here's a woman who's humped half the men in the western hemisphere and now she's all hot and bothered over a little teenage romance between me and Reese. She's going to give hypocrisy a bad name. All the kids have sex now. I mean, it's just like eating and sleeping. What's the big deal?"

After my interview with Celia, Connie's worry about becoming a thirty-eight-year-old grandmother didn't seem unreasonable. Celia appeared to have been swept up in the forces that make pregnancy a serious risk for girls in divorced and remarried families.

Celia's observations about Connie, full of personal pique and hurt, illustrate a key finding in our longitudinal studies. Children continue to need parental guidance and advice in adolescence, but to be in a position to provide both, a parent has to be respected and to have a long history of engaged parenting. A history of firm discipline, caring, and nurturing imbues parental "no's" with the moral force that even an increasingly independent-minded, peer-influenced teen will heed. Conversely, a history of non-authoritative parenting makes parental "no's" ineffectual with a headstrong adolescent.

The influence of parenting is especially important in divorced and remarried families because their teenagers face some special risks. In relation to early sexual activities and the high teenage pregnancy rate among girls like Celia, what occurs might be described as the Catch-22 of postnuclear family life.

The Special Challenge of Early Physical Maturing in Girls from Divorced and Remarried Families

Life in divorced or remarried families promotes early maturation, measured by the onset of menarche, and hence the risk of early pregnancy. While only 18 percent of girls from non-divorced homes went into menarche by eleven or younger, the comparable figures for girls in divorced and remarried homes were, respectively, 25 and 35 percent. On average, girls in stepfather families menstruated nine months earlier, and in divorced homes four months earlier, than girls from non-divorced homes.

Our findings on the age at which adolescents first have intercourse illustrates what happens when early menarche occurs in girls with weak self-regulatory skills. At fifteen, 65 percent of early maturing girls in divorced homes and 54 percent in remarried homes had had sex at least once, compared to only 40 percent of early maturing girls in non-divorced homes. And since early teenage sex often goes hand in hand with teenage pregnancy and sexually transmitted diseases, these girls also more often encountered such hazards.

What makes early menarche and sexuality more common in adolescents from divorced and remarried families?

The new discipline of evolutionary psychology may provide an answer. Evolutionary psychologists argue that since a species's survival depends on the ability of its members to pass on their genes, behaviors that facilitate reproduction and survival persist and evolve because the people who employ them produce many offspring, while ineffective reproductive strategies disappear because the people who employ them produce few offspring.

Many evolutionary psychologists believe early menarche may have evolved as a strategy to solve a particular problem: life in a hostile environment. Over the eons, the theory goes, early maturation in females in dangerous environments such as a stressful family situation gave them a reproductive advantage because they were physically able to reproduce earlier. Moreover, the precociously mature girl developed breasts, curvaceous hips, and other secondary sexual characteristics that made her attractive to potential mates at a younger age. And the earlier she mated, the better her chances of producing children, which is to say, of passing on her genes before succumbing to the dangers of the environment.

But why does an adaptation designed to deal with the threat of a dangerous environment surface in divorced and remarried families? There are two possible explanations. One is that the high rate of stress and conflict in divorced families and stepfamilies may mimic the characteristics of a hostile environment, thereby sending ten- or eleven-year-olds into menarche. The other explanation is the "strange male" phenomenon. In many animal species, the presence of a strange male is one of those environmental cues that induces sexual readiness in a young female. Since menarche occurs earlier in girls from stepfamilies than divorced families, it may well be that a stepfather has some triggering effect on early maturation in a stepdaughter.

About one thing, however, there is no doubt. There is a link between early maturing and sexual activities, but that link is modified by characteristics of the adolescent and the family and by relationships outside the family.

As in other studies, we found a relationship between early maturing, association with older male peers, early sex, and high risk of pregnancy. The early appearance of sexual characteristics like breasts, once designed to facilitate early mating by attracting potential partners, still facilitates early mating by attracting potential partners—except now the partners come in the form of older male peers like Reese Pierce. A thirteen-year-old who looks thirteen often can't buy trouble even if she is in the market for it; but a thirteen-year-old who looks seventeen not only can but often does. And when trouble hits the young teenager, she has neither the cognitive maturity, good judgment, nor emotional self-control to deal with it.

As every parent and teacher knows, in the first decade of life, boys have more trouble mastering self-regulation—a particularly important life skill. Boys have more difficulty learning to sit still, to wait their turn, and to control their anger and impatience. But in adolescence, the burden of emotional self-regulation shifts to girls, who not only must learn how to control their own sexual feelings but those of an often ardent teenage boy.

Girls in divorced, remarried, and high-conflict families often have problems with self-regulation that compound the problems of early physical maturing. Sometimes, they have disengaged from home early, before they have developed the requisite emotional maturity to deal with male peers like Reese Pierce. They also tend to come from homes where distracted or stressed adults fail to teach emotional self-control and the other skills a girl needs to manage her sexuality effectively. These skills include thinking through the consequences of an action (unprotected sex leads to pregnancy, for example), the ability to plan (pregnancy will make it harder for me to go to college), and social adeptness (being comfortable in saying no and saying it effectively).

Clarice Taine's story illustrates what can—and often does—happen when immaturity and skill deficits are packaged in a womanly body.

Clarice Taine, the daughter of Diana Taine from her first marriage, was not one of the "fierce" Taine women. She looked like her mother, but in personality she took after her father. From an early age she had been shy and withdrawn, and she was made more insecure by her demanding, volatile, flamboyant mother.

Pretty and already curvaceous at thirteen, Clarice caused quite a sensation among the upper-class boys during her freshman high school year. Socially inexperienced, Clarice was flattered when she was invited to a party by a popular senior named Talbot Quigly. At the party, a junior girl introduced her to daiquiris, and later in the evening, Talbot introduced her to sex.

Clarice said she rebuffed Talbot's first advance, and was shocked when on the way to the party he had playfully touched her breasts as he reached over to close the car door. But half a pitcher of daiquiris later, she found herself in the backseat of a car with Talbot on top of her. Ten weeks later, she was sitting with her mother filling out forms in the waiting room of an abortion clinic.

"Does the boy know?" I asked, when Diana Taine called to tell me about the abortion. "Yes, Clarice told him," Diana said. "Talbot just shrugged and said, 'Sorry. It was an accident.' "

I could hear Diana choke up on the other end of the phone. "I don't understand how this could have happened. Clarice is such a good girl."

Our work suggests that it is often the inexperienced good girl who is not expecting to have intercourse and who is unprepared with contraceptives who gets pregnant.

Early maturing boys are also more likely to engage in norm-breaking behavior for all the reasons early maturing girls are. But looking fifteen when you're twelve isn't as risky for a boy for a number of reasons, including biology; boys don't get pregnant and aren't stigmatized for being "easy." Moreover, boys normally mature later than girls, and early maturity may put boys in step with their female peers.

Parents may be unaware of the latest wrinkle in evolutionary theory, but they do know trouble when they see it. In divorced and remarried homes, as in non-divorced homes, parents step up their monitoring during adolescence in response to their children's behavior. But as the influence of the peer group grows, a parent's influence on the teen becomes increasingly dependent on the past. What kind of mother or father were they when the teenager was eight, nine, and ten? Sensitive, engaged, dependable parents build up a large emotional bank account that they can draw on in adolescence, while parents with a history of disengagement and undependability usually go into overdraft as soon as the child becomes a teenager. For parents who have not been authoritative earlier, by the time the child is an adolescent, the horse is out of the barn. Even if they change their parenting behavior in response to an adolescent's runaway behavior, it may be too late to exert effective control.

The reason why authoritative parenting remains important in adolescence is that it represents the best counterweight a parent has to the dangers and temptations of Peer World and to the risks of early maturing. In authoritative homes, we found that early maturing girls were no more likely to engage in sexual activity than late maturing girls. So the point is to sow the seeds of authoritative parenting early.

Leah Coleman was an early maturing girl, and her conflicts with Nick could have led to early disengagement and early entry into a dangerous peer group, with all the attendant risks that carries for a young girl.

But thanks to Janet's sensitive, consistent, and loving parenting, although Leah was sometimes difficult at home, she didn't disengage until she had the maturity and life skills to handle the dangers of Peer World. Even then, she continued to take advice and seek support and solace from Janet.

This continued willingness to listen is one of the principal benefits of an authoritative style, which builds respect and goodwill a parent can draw on during adolescence. When an authoritative parent warns about a Reese or a Talbot, the adolescent may roll her eyes and scowl, but she also is likely to listen and heed.

Although previously inept parents like Connie also frequently step up their control attempts in the teen years, they can never entirely escape the shadow of the past.

Celia in many ways was like her mother: impulsive, warm, sensation-seeking, and except in her punk phase, very pretty. But in childhood she never got the firm discipline she needed, either from her loving, indulgent father or her neglectful, alcoholic mother, to help her develop the kind of self-control she needed when she hit puberty at ten. Celia's problems were compounded not only by maturing early and the presence of Reese, but by Connie's own earlier promiscuous behavior. We found the combination of early puberty, non-authoritative parents, associating with older peers, and a flagrantly sexually active mother to be the pattern of greatest risk for early and promiscuous sexual activity in girls.

Parents who behave in undesirable ways—who smoke, drink, use drugs, lie, or have many sexual partners—may hope that the old adage,

"Don't do as I do, do as I say," works. It doesn't. Children are more likely to imitate the behavior than to heed the admonitions of an irresponsible role model.

What saved Celia was a combination of Reese getting into trouble with the law and leaving town, and her relationship with her stepfather, Bob Keatly. Until her rebellious adolescence, Celia and Bob had gotten along well and been close. They had a teasing, affectionate relationship. Celia called Bob "Big Bad Bob," after a character in a children's story, and he called her "Lamb Chop." Since their marriage, Celia had turned to Bob to talk about her troubles, not to Connie or to her sweet father, Simon, who seemed baffled and personally distressed when she even touched on issues of sexuality or her flirtation with drugs.

"Nothing shocked Bob," Celia said. "Maybe policemen are like that, they've seen everything. Bob always listened. He never hesitated to point out what the dangers were and he made suggestions, but he never said I 'had' to do anything."

But Big Bad Bob's patience was wearing thin with Celia's adolescent shenanigans and he finally drew the line.

"If you're going to live in this house," he told Celia, "you're going to play by house rules. No skipping school or not doing homework. No breaking curfews on weekends. The first time you break the rules, you're out."

Celia at first laughed, but then sobered as she realized how serious Bob was. It was easier with Reese gone, but the first time Celia tried to test the limits and stay out late, she found the door locked. A frightened and penitent Celia appeared at the door the next morning. Celia later said, "Somehow it was like turning a corner. Here was this guy I loved and admired saying, 'Shape up or ship out.' It shocked me and started to turn me around. It took me awhile but I made it."

The Value of Adult Mentors

We found that the more marital and divorce transitions a child experiences, the more emotionally and psychologically fragile the child becomes. And Dickie Fredericks had gone through many of them. After

Lucinda had been left by her first husband, Dickie's father, she in turn left her second husband, Charles, the wealthy lawyer whose generous divorce settlement subsidized her next two husbands. One was a handsome rock musician who was eight years Lucinda's junior; the other an even handsomer horse trainer who was six years younger.

Any child who emerges from a marital history like that deserves to be called a survivor. And despite some lingering problems, when we saw Dickie in adolescence and young adulthood, in many areas he was functioning at an exceptionally high level.

Often, Dickie had seemed well on the way down the path of a destructive lifestyle—isolated, angry, defiant, and already at age ten participating in delinquent activities. With a neglectful mother, a rejecting stepfather, and no close friends, he seemed to have no resources to deflect him onto a healthier trajectory.

But Dickie's unexpected turnaround illustrates why it is always unacceptable to give up on a child, even a troubled one. The door to hope remains permanently open, thanks to the emergence of new protective factors, such as a new skill or a new relationship. One of them walked into Dickie's life one hot July afternoon shortly after his thirteenth birthday. His name was Ed Dooley. He was a counselor at Dickie's summer computer camp and a graduate student in computer science.

Ed was quite taken by Dickie the mathematician, though not Dickie the person. Dickie, who was at his blustery, arrogant worst that summer, made a poor impression on Ed, and according to Ed, an even worse impression on his bunkmates.

One morning a few weeks after the camp began, Ed found Dickie strapped to his bunk, naked and sobbing; someone had tied him up and smeared black shoe polish all over his genitals and backside. "We got tired of Dickie's big mouth," one of the perpetrators said when he was caught a few days later.

Ed told me that after this incident, he got frightened for Dickie. "I thought that if this kid doesn't get help soon, either someone's going to kill him or he is going to kill himself. So I took him under my wing. We ate and walked and talked together, and we worked on computers every night until lights out. It's hard to describe a talent like Dickie's—it's amazing, awesome. It took me awhile to see that under Dickie's arrogance and talent was a frightened, unhappy, insecure little kid."

Ed and Dickie became friends, and the friendship continued after the camp disbanded. When they returned to Richmond, Ed tutored Dickie and got permission to have him sit in on some university computer science classes. What was even more important was that Ed and his wife, Jeanie, began to do other things with Dickie—had him over regularly for Sunday dinner, took him on picnics and to concerts and movies. Dickie later said, "It was the first time I knew what a real family felt like."

Dickie never became a paragon of good adjustment, but the boy I saw at age fifteen was much different than the ten-year-old Dickie. At fifteen, he came in the room and announced that his name was Richard, not Dickie. "Dickie sounds too much like a tweetiebird," he said. He no longer hung his head and scuttled into the room. He looked directly into my eyes when we spoke, and even laughed, something that never occurred in the interview when he was ten. He still was explosive and had some problems with teachers and peers at school, but he had made friends with some other boys who also were computer jocks.

At twenty-four, Richard was living in Silicon Valley—a place he described in his acerbic manner as having five hundred thousand nerdy computer geeks and a thousand ugly women. "I fit right in," he said. He was successful, wealthy, and ran his own computer consulting firm. He worked too hard and drank too much. But his talents were valued and he had obvious pride in his attainments. He had some friends who shared his interests and was in the first tentative stages of a relationship with a woman, Hayden Moore, he had met on the Internet who worked in a high-tech firm in the Valley. He was in regular contact with Ed, who was now a professor in a Colorado college, and he spent what little vacation time he could muster with Ed and his family.

One important characteristic all of our successful children shared was the support of at least one caring and loving adult. In most cases, the adult was a parent, but a biological connection was not required for an adult to make a difference in a child's life. Adult mentors like Ed shepherded dozens of our children safely through childhood and adolescence, and through parental divorce and remarriage.

How do adult mentors buffer?

One way is by providing a child with an alternative to the peer group. Because he had Ed in his life, Richard was never forced to make the Faustian bargain so many lonely, neglected children make with Peer World today: I'll give you my future, if you give me your validation and companionship.

Mentors like Ed give the child a sense of being cared for, valued and of worth. Many also can foster skills the child may not be learning at home. They offer role models and advice about what behaviors are acceptable or unacceptable, and what works and doesn't work in social situations. Children in divorced, and even in remarried, homes may not get to see a man and a woman communicating effectively, negotiating differences, seeking compromises, putting a cap on potentially explosive arguments, working together to build a better life for each other and their families. Adult mentors may also represent a more neutral way for a child to accept an authoritative model of parenting. A well-functioning family or parents of a friend can provide an alternative place to learn these skills; this was a lesson learned by Samantha Doyle. Samantha's mother, explosive twice-divorced Mary Doyle, lacked both the husband and the temperament to model these skills. But Carol Keogh, the mother of Samantha's best friend, Katie, did not.

"I learned a lot from Carol," the recently married Samantha told me at the twenty-year interview. "Steve [Carol's husband] would sometimes come home from work in a black mood and could be a big pain . . . demanding and full of himself or sullen and withdrawn. But Carol could always sense what was wrong and was wonderful with him. She could get him to talk about his problems and she knew how to make Steve laugh at himself, how to get him to do stuff he didn't want to do, when to push him and when not to. I used to think these were little things, but now that I've got my own big pain, I'm finding that a lot of the things I learned from watching her come in handy."

An adult mentor can also be a valuable ally for a parent.

One divorced mother spent most of the twenty-year interview describing all the "wonderful" changes in her daughter. The girl's surliness and negativity, rampant in early adolescence, had disappeared, and—what particularly pleased the woman—the two of them were becoming close again. "Chris has finally grown up," the woman told me. But at her twenty-year interview, the daughter credited her high school guidance counselor for these changes. "Whenever I complained about Mom," the young woman said, "Mr. Frazier would remind me of all the things you don't think about when you are sixteen—like how hard Mom worked to support us and the sacrifices she made so that I could go to college. He'd tell me I was lucky; not many kids had a mother like mine."

Along with parents of friends, neighbors, coaches, Scoutmasters, and stepparents also can play a mentoring role; and as Timothy Wiggins found, a caring stepfather can make a critical difference in a boy's life.

Timothy Wiggins's mother, Rebecca, dark, willowy, and elegant, had the arrogant, careless air you sometimes see in very pampered women—the wives of wealthy husbands or the daughters of wealthy fathers. She grew up the indulged only child of a wealthy Maryland surgeon, and her divorced husband had been a well-to-do stockbroker.

She was also a recovering drug addict.

Rebecca blamed her addiction on the prescription painkillers she took for a college skiing accident. But I think the story was more complicated than that. Rebecca, impeccably dressed and perfectly spoken, had a willful "bad girl" quality about her. One of Timothy's earliest memories was of catching her and a friend of his father's kissing on the back porch. Another was of the arrest warrant a burly detective shoved in his face one afternoon. The detective told seven-year-old Timmy that his mother was wanted for writing illegal drug prescriptions for herself.

Rebecca's present to Timothy on his ninth birthday was her sobriety. But a maternal promise, no matter how heartfelt and well kept—and Rebecca's was well kept—cannot wash away years of rehabilitation clinics, police at the door, nasty fights, or doltish lovers. At the six-year follow-up, ten-year-old Timmy had acquired all the hallmarks of a troubled child: consistent bad grades, frequent truancies, and fistfights.

The teacher reports that preceded Timmy to the interview were full of dire warnings. "I fear for this child's future," wrote one worried teacher. "Timothy is a bright child," wrote another, "but very disruptive and scattered. Adolescence will be a very difficult time for him."

But a year later, Timothy got his own Ed Dooley. As stepfathers go, Paul Costos was unusual. A concert violinist with a long, Ichabod Crane face and a taste for flamboyant bow ties, Paul knew next to nothing about sports—the tool many men use to bond with a new stepson. Nor did Paul score high in other areas of that indefinable quality, "guyness."

An agitated Paul could get as fluttery as Big Bird. But he did know something many men don't know and something the brittle, high-strung Rebecca often forgot. He knew that the best way to teach a child how to get along with peers, how to control his temper, how to organize his day, how to focus on a task—how to do all the things that ten-year-old Timothy did not know, but needed to learn—was to provide him with a warm, involved, adult role model.

Sometimes mentors become more than just mentors. At the twenty-year interview, when I asked Rebecca about Paul and Timothy's relationship, she corrected me.

"It isn't just a relationship," Rebecca said. "It's a mutual admiration society. They're real buddies, best friends. I don't know how they ever got along without each other."

Picking the Right School

In urban settings, selecting the "right school" for your child has become ludicrous, with prenatal enrollments and frenzied applications, testing, and petitioning. Still, in spite of Americans' disenchantment with their education system, schools do matter, and they matter a great deal for children from stressful family environments.

At the start of the VLS, I hypothesized that, like mentoring, a school would be an important buffer for a child of divorce and remarriage or for other children undergoing stressful situations. But I imagined that the school's protective effects would be limited largely to younger children—to children in elementary schools. The VLS endpoint data proved me only half-right. School was, indeed, an important developmental asset, but its buffering effects were felt as keenly in adolescence as in childhood.

Many of the characteristics that promote academic quality, the measure by which schools are traditionally judged, also promote buffering. So the two qualities often correlate. But they are not synonymous. An academically good school can have no protective effect at all, and in rare cases, can actually exacerbate a stressed child's developmental problems.

Over the course of my research, I examined over 150 schools—some public, some private, some large, some small, some rural, some urban inner-city—ranging from preschool to high school. I found that schools can be divided into different categories similar to those in parenting. Some of these schools help to protect against the adverse effects of inept parenting and stressful experiences; some exacerbate them.

AUTHORITATIVE SCHOOLS. Authoritative schools, like authoritative parenting, are characterized by an organized predictable environment, standards, expectations for appropriately mature behavior from students, and a nurturant, responsive faculty. They make students feel safe and valued, that certain behaviors will not be accepted, and that their positive efforts will be appreciated. However, the benefits of authoritative schooling are not experienced by all children. For children who had two authoritative parents it was like "carrying coals to Newcastle." These children already were stable and adaptable and could adjust in almost any kind of school environment. For children with less fortunate family situations, an authoritative school often provided the structure, predictability, and organization unavailable at home. The biggest gains in academic achievement and social competency, and decreases in behavior problems as a result of an authoritative school environment, were attained by children who had non-authoritative single mothers or who were in stepfamilies or non-divorced families where neither parent was authoritative. In high-stress environments, the quality of schooling had its most marked effects.

Clarice, Diana Taine's shy daughter, was sent off to a private boarding school after her unfortunate pregnancy and abortion.

"Mother was furious at me," said Clarice. "Sending me away was supposed to be purgatory, exile. Some exile! I had always felt overwhelmed in our family. Our house was always full of people shouting and laughing and arguing. It was chaos. The first thing I noticed at St. Elizabeth's was how peaceful it was. The teachers were strict and expected you to work hard and didn't put up with any guff, but they listened to you. At first I was a bit afraid of them, but you felt they cared about you and appreciated the things you did.

"I didn't know I had any artistic talent until I went to St. Elizabeth's. Then I walked into the art room. The silence was wonderful. I thought, this is where I want to be. Everyone was concentrating on drawing a still-life of a bowl of fruit and three brass candles with a paisley shawl draped behind them. Sister Maria Theresa took me by the hand, led me to an easel, and started talking quietly to me about the fundamentals in drawing. It changed my life. For the first time, I learned being fierce isn't the most important thing in life."

AUTHORITARIAN SCHOOLS. *Such, Such Were the Days*, George Orwell's acerbic memoir of his years at a rigid British preparatory school, vividly captures the regimentation, coldness, and often brutality of an authoritarian school. Highly coercive, such schools are punitive, overly controlling, and they enforce rules and standards by way of power assertions and threats. Public humiliations and reprimands are favorite disciplining techniques. In these schools the gulf between teachers, who criticize frequently and praise rarely, and students, who are expected to display a herdlike submissiveness, is wide. Assertiveness, divergent thinking, and creativity are not only discouraged, they are smothered.

Authoritarian schools may make good incubators for colonial administrators and professional military officers, but they have little to offer children going through the stresses of their parents' marital transitions.

Many parents with acting-out children seek out stricter schools for their children. However, there is no evidence that "boot camp" schools improve the long-term adjustment of wayward or stressed adolescents. Firm controls may help, but only in combination with support and responsiveness to the child's needs.

At one point, Lucinda Fredericks had sent Dickie to a military school. It lasted two months before Dickie ran away. Dickie said, "I knew if I didn't get out of there I'd kill someone or kill myself."

PERMISSIVE SCHOOLS. Permissive schools are the opposite of authoritarian—lenient, unstructured, often warm and supportive. Teachers repeatedly say they are focused on the whole child and the needs of the individual child. There is a great deal of responsiveness, questioning, reasoning, and communication between teachers and children. In permissive schools, especially in the preschool and elementary school years, many of the classroom activities are student-initiated and children are encouraged to pursue their own interests. When you enter a classroom in a permissive school, there is often a sense of excitement, with students talking to each other, working on group projects, and involved in active exchange with each other and the teachers. It sometimes seems like a happy pandemonium. These are child-focused schools, with an emphasis more on creativity and process than on the acquisition of traditional skills and knowledge.

Permissive schools can provide a positive setting for secure, mature, goal-directed children. But for the insecure, stressed children in our study, the lack of structure and guidance often proved anxiety-provoking. Our children and adolescents from divorced and remarried families functioned much better in authoritative than permissive schools.

CHAOTIC, NEGLECTFUL SCHOOLS. The large number of children from divorced homes who end up in chaotic, neglectful schools, which can exacerbate the effects of a stressful family life, highlights a major theme of my work: how frequently divorce sets in motion a series of interrelated events that can end up propelling a person onto a particular life trajectory.

Before William Jehrico disappeared, leaving a vapor trail of bad check charges behind him, Paul Jehrico lived in a modest but neat, middle- to lower-middle-class neighborhood, which included a decent if not outstanding elementary school whose student body was made up of the sons and daughters of policemen and firemen, bank clerks and car salesmen, and assistant managers at stores like Home Depot and Wal-Mart.

Betty Ann remarried more to hang on to this life than anything else. With two paychecks, she thought she could keep the house and all the precious intangibles—a safe neighborhood, good parks, and good companions for Paul and his brother, Roy—that went with it. But when Roger Little turned out to be as unreliable as William Jehrico, the family began the downward progression I saw in so many other divorced families. Betty Ann, the only steady breadwinner in the family, eventually lost the house, and the Jehricos had to move into a double mobile home in a trailer park three miles away.

Their new neighborhood contained all the things that go with poverty and near poverty: run-down homes, cracked sidewalks, potholed streets, a high crime rate, no after-school facilities, an irregular police presence, and no adult males to speak of, except itinerant alcoholics and men like Roger.

Paul's potential line of defense might have been an authoritative school. But like many poor neighborhoods, his new neighborhood had a chaotic, neglectful school. Physically decrepit, academically disastrous, it was as unsafe as the neighborhood surrounding it. The halls were a floating drug bazaar; fistfights were common in the schoolyard, and knife and even gunfights not unheard of. In eighth grade, one of Paul's classmates was shot, and pregnant female classmates were ubiquitous.

The teachers we interviewed in such chaotic, disorganized schools regarded the student body with a blend of fear, contempt, and indifference. They had low expectancies for either mature, responsible behavior or academic achievement in their students, and rarely encouraged them to consider going on to college. Their attempts to control students were ineffective and erratic, and often harsh and belittling. Lessons were disorganized, and frequently disrupted by inattentive, bored, or aggressive students. In many of these classrooms, as much as 80 percent of the time was spent attempting to gain disciplinary control and only 20 percent in active teaching.

Teachers in chaotic high schools often report their environment to be dangerous and depressing. They show the least satisfaction in their role as teachers, complain of feeling burnt out, and have the highest rates of bolting from the teaching profession.

The children in these schools were not insensitive to their teachers' discouragement, disregard, or animosity. By a wide margin, children in chaotic, neglectful schools had the highest rate of truancy, pregnancies, substance abuse, fighting and acting out at school, and problems with the law, and the lowest level of academic achievement. These problems were compounded if the children came from single homes or stepfamilies with non-authoritative parents.

Although such chaotic schools were more prevalent in poor inner-city areas, we also encountered chaotic schools with better physical plants but with the same disorganized, uncontrolled, hostile environments in more affluent areas. Usually headed by an incompetent principal, these schools had demoralized, poorly trained teachers and an overrepresentation of uninvolved and single parents. In contrast, we found some authoritative schools, with fine, committed principals, motivated, caring teachers, and competent, well-performing students, in the heart of poverty, and these schools played a major protective role in sheltering students in high-risk families from adversity.

In sum, an authoritative school does not add much when there are two authoritative parents at home. But if a child has a chaotic or neglecting or disorganized home life, as the child of divorce often does, an authoritative school can make an important contribution to healthy development.

Points to Remember

- For all adolescents, peers can be a powerful constructive or destructive force, and adolescents from divorced and remarried families are more vulnerable to peer influence than those in non-divorced families. Try to monitor who your child associates with.
- Adolescents who receive authoritative parenting are less likely to become involved with a delinquent peer group.
- Girls in divorced and remarried homes are often sexually precocious. These girls show an early onset of menstruation and early maturation, often accompanied by association with older peers, which can predispose a girl to early sexual initiation.

- Sexual discretion is advised for all parents, but particularly for single mothers. An adult has a perfect right to an adult sex life, but most parental teaching, including teaching about sex, is done via role modeling. An overtly sexual parent predisposes a child to early sexual initiation. The child heeds what the parent does, not what she says.

- Parental "second chances" are rare with adolescents. Parents who try to compensate for a history of disengaged parenting by stepping up their control when a child becomes a teenager are rarely successful.

- Adult mentors often play a valuable role in a child's life, especially for children with a difficult home situation. They can make a child feel worthy and valued, and can serve as confidants, advisers, role models, and surrogate parents.

- Although it has become fashionable to downplay the effectiveness of schools, a structured, supportive, authoritative school can help to protect against the adverse effects of non-authoritative parenting often found in divorced and remarried families. Choose your child's school with care and stay involved with teachers and school activities.

Part Three

In the Home Stretch:
Adults and Children
Twenty Years Later

11

Mostly Happy:
Children of Divorce as Young Adults

*D*avid Coleman has his father's imposing height and muscularity, but whereas on Richard, size added to his air of menace, making him look explosive even at rest, the son's six-foot-three frame has the opposite effect. It underscores his gentleness, makes you notice it in a way you wouldn't if he were a smaller, more delicate-looking man.

At a time when genetic theories threatened to reduce human development to a branch of biology, the difference between gentle David and violent Richard reminds us of the powerful role nurture plays in development. Genes are important, yes, certainly, but life experiences—especially with those closest to us—can take a given set of genes and make them add up in many different ways.

Much of the credit for the way David and his older sister, Leah, have ended up goes to Janet. Both benefited immensely from her ability to maintain a stable, loving, emotionally safe environment through Richard's stalking, through the family's sojourn on welfare, and through Nick and Leah's fights. When the VLS ended, David had taken over much of the responsibility for running "Janet's Garden," and Leah was a happily married mother, with a young daughter.

In the 1970s, a fierce debate broke out about the future of children like David and Leah. Critics of the divorce revolution believed that as the generation of children from divorced families matured, American society would descend into disorder and chaos. The collapse of the two-parent family, the traditional engine of socialization, critics argued, would lead to a *Clockwork Orange* generation of unstable, reckless, indulgent young adults, who would overrun the nation's prisons, substance abuse centers, and divorce courts.

"Nonsense," declared supporters of the divorce revolution, who saw divorce as a kind of cleansing agent. At last, the dark gloomy oppressive Victorian house that was the nuclear family would get a long-overdue spring cleaning, one that would produce a new and more egalitarian, tolerant, and fulfilled generation of men and women.

While I found evidence to support both views, the big headline in my data is that *80 percent of children from divorced homes eventually are able to adapt to their new life and become reasonably well adjusted.* A subgroup of girls even become exceptionally competent as a result of dealing with the challenges of divorce, enjoy a normal development, and grow into truly outstanding young adults. The 20 percent who continue to bear the scars of divorce fall into a troubled group, who display impulsive, irresponsible, antisocial behavior or are depressed. At the end of the VLS, troubled youths were having difficulty at work, in romantic relationships, and in gaining a toehold in adult life. They had the highest academic dropout rate and the highest divorce rate in the study, and were more likely to be faring poorly economically. In addition, being troubled and a girl made a young woman more likely to have left home early and to have experienced at least one out-of-wedlock pregnancy, birth, or abortion.

However, coming from a non-divorced family did not always protect against growing into a troubled young adult. Ten percent of youths in non-divorced families, compared to 20 percent in divorced and remarried families, were troubled. Most of our troubled young men and women came from families where conflict was frequent and authoritative parenting rare. In adulthood, as was found in childhood and adolescence, those who had moved from a highly contentious intact home situation to a more harmonious divorced family situation, with a caring, competent parent, benefited from the divorce and had fewer problems. But the legacy of the stresses and inept parenting associated with divorce and remarriage, and especially with living in a complex stepfamily, are still seen in the psychological, emotional, and social problems in 20 percent of young people from these families.

A piece of good news about our youths was that their antisocial behavior declined as they matured. Much of the adolescent exploration, experimentation, and sense of invulnerability had abated. Although excessive use of alcohol remained a problem for one quarter, drug abuse and lawbreaking had declined in all of our groups; but the decrease had been most marked in those who married.

What about the other 80 percent of young people from divorced and remarried families?

While most were not exactly the New Man or New Woman that the divorce revolution's supporters had predicted, they were behaving the way young adults were supposed to behave. They were choosing careers, developing permanent relationships, ably going about the central tasks of young adulthood, and establishing a grown-up life.

They ranged from those who were remarkably well adjusted to Good Enoughs and competent-at-a-costs, who were having a few problems but coping reasonably well to very well.

Finally, it should be a reassuring finding for divorced and remarried parents, and their children, that for every young man or woman who emerged from postnuclear family life with problems, four others were functioning reasonably or exceptionally well.

I think our findings ultimately contain two bottom-line messages about the long-term effects of divorce on children. The first is about parents, especially mothers. If someone creates a Nobel Prize for Unsung Hero, my nominee will be the divorced mother. Even when the world was collapsing round them, many divorced mothers found the courage and resiliency to do what had to be done. Such maternal tenacity and courage paid off. Despite all the emotional and financial pressures imposed by marital failure, most of our divorced women managed to provide the support, sensitivity, and engagement their children needed for normal development. And while divorce creates developmental risks, except in cases of extraordinary stress, children can be protected by vigorous, involved, competent parenting.

The second bottom line is about flexibility and diversity. Divorce is not a form of developmental predestination. Children, like adults, take many different routes out of divorce; some lead to unhappiness, others to a rewarding and fulfilling life. And since over the course of life, new experiences are being encountered and new relationships formed, protective and risk factors alter, and the door to positive change always remains open.

We turn now to look at how some of these changing experiences and relationships contributed to the well-being of our younger generation from divorced and remarried families.

Parent-Youth Relationships in Perspective

At age twenty-four, Leah Coleman was a high school history teacher in a happy marriage to Brad Norton, and the mother of two-year-old Cindy. She commented, "I can't believe what a bitch I was to Nick. He tried so hard, but I just wanted to destroy him. When he gave up and avoided me, I thought it was a major victory. But you know, I gradually started to envy David and be jealous of Nick and David's relationship. David would go to Nick with things he didn't want to talk about with Mom, and they had such fun together, and I don't know, their relationship seemed so special."

Leah's reassessment of Nick advanced another step when she brought home Brad, her future husband, for the first time. "It would have been so easy for Nick to be standoffish and nasty," Leah told me later. "Instead, he was a real sweetie with Brad, friendly and warm and welcoming. He and Brad spent the whole afternoon drinking beer and working on an old beat-up wooden sailboat Nick had bought. They just hit it off right away. I felt absolutely terrible. I mean, here's this lovely man, and I've given him nothing but trouble since he stepped in the door."

Motherhood finally produced a complete rapprochement. "Nick's turned out to be the world's best grandfather," Leah declared. "Cindy's crazy about him, she calls him Gee-pa. She'll stop in the middle of playing and say, 'Where's my Gee-pa?' Did you ever think you'd hear me talk this way about Nick?"

Actually, I did.

Family relations do tend to improve in young adulthood. It may not always be the "Whoopie" experience described by some empty nesters, but it is often a mutually gratifying time for both parents and children. This is a time with more autonomy for both generations, less responsibility for parents, diminished conflict and acrimony, and continued affection and interest in each other's well-being. Parents get the satisfaction of launching a young life into the world, one they don't have to pay for or wait up for any more, while children are finally free of Mom and Dad's annoying foibles and demands. That, along with their growing maturity, allows them to begin appreciating Mom and Dad's sacrifices and good points. Distance helps, too. When parents and children live apart, there are fewer opportunities to step on each other's toes, and when a toe is stepped on, everyone has a neutral corner to retreat to.

When our younger generation totaled up the balance sheet on how they felt about their parents, the mothers did well. Eighty percent of youths in non-divorced families and 70 percent in postnuclear families reported feeling close or very close to their biological mothers. Men didn't do as well. Although 70 percent of youths in non-divorced families felt close to their fathers, less than one third of males and one quarter of females reported being close to their stepfather or non-custodial fathers. Remarks like, "He was never around," "He never showed any interest in me," or, "He never played a real part in my life" were common.

Why do children feel so distant from fathers after divorce? Two reasons. First, often divorced fathers are not around because the kids are usually in the custody of their mothers, and children feel closer to custodial than non-custodial parents. Second, the disengaged parenting style common in stepfathers fails to promote close emotional bonds with stepchildren. In youth as in adolescence, when asked to list members of their family, only one third of those in stepfamilies included their stepparents. However, even these relationships in young adulthood were more likely to be characterized by disengagement than by confrontation and conflict.

Cross-gender parent-child relationships were found to be more fragile. Divorce was more likely to have undermined the quality of an adult son's than an adult daughter's relationship with their divorced mother, and of an adult daughter's relationship rather than an adult son's with their father.

Stepmothers, especially those in complex stepfamilies, had been able to build up the least closeness and goodwill with their stepchildren, with less than 20 percent of young adult stepchildren saying they felt close to their stepmothers. The competition between non-custodial mothers and stepmothers was remarkably enduring, and youths with close ties to their non-custodial mothers were less likely to be close to their stepmothers.

A partial exception to the generalization that parent-child relations improve in young adulthood occurred in complex stepfamilies. Although relations did warm in some cases, in most, such as the Drew family, they did not.

The Drews were the complex stepfamily we met earlier. Anna Marie, the daughter who left early to escape her stepfather and half sister, grew into an embittered and alienated young woman, who refused to accept her mother's help even though, as a divorced single mother, she desperately needed it. "Anna Marie won't budge an inch," her mother told me the last time we talked. "I've offered to pay the tuition if Anna Marie goes back to school. But she says she doesn't want my help; she says she doesn't want to have anything to do with anyone related to Paul Drew."

Anna Marie later said, "Maybe I still love my mother, but I don't trust her. She never saved me from the Dastardly Duo." She laughs, rolls her eyes, and twirls an imaginary mustache like a villain in a Victorian melodrama. The laughter cuts off abruptly and is replaced by a scowl. "I'd rather stay away than put up with that cockroach Paul and that smug little pissant Daphne. She got all the advantages and went to medical school. I made some mistakes and I'm trying to put my life together now. But it's tough when you have a kid."

The intensity of the sustained hostility in the Drews' relationship was unusual. What distinguished families where relationships improved or at least mellowed from families where they did not? Usually, one of three protective factors that promoted family harmony was at work.

Distance

At the time this book was written, almost three quarters of our parents in the VLS were still living in Virginia, but only one third of their young adult children had remained in the state. They were dispersed across thirty-eight states, and two had moved to Canada and two to London. Those who were better educated were the most mobile. They had gone away to college, met new friends, sometimes married a spouse from out of state, and taken jobs where the best opportunities were found.

At the time of her twenty-year follow-up, at age twenty-four, Celia Russell was living on an organic farm co-op in Vermont. Except for the liquid Tidewater vowels, the Celia I interviewed there bore little relation to the angry punk teenager I had seen a decade earlier. The new, Vermont Celia was a bit plump, her spiky black hair now its natural light brown color and trimmed in a boyish cut. She was wearing a tailored blue button-down shirt, loose-fitting khakis, and a pair of thick-soled Birkenstock sandals.

I wasn't totally surprised by the transformation. Dramatic emotional change often produces dramatic physical change. Besides, a few weeks earlier, Connie had warned me to expect "a big change" in Celia.

"Celia looks like Pat now," Connie said at her twenty-year interview.

"Pat who?" I asked.

"Pat on *Saturday Night Live*. Pat, you-don't-know-whether-she's-a-girl-or-a-boy Pat."

"I'm sorry," I said. "I don't watch *Saturday Night Live*. What's Pat got to do with Celia?"

Connie frowned. "I think Celia's a lesbian, Mavis. She dresses like one. And that co-op she belongs to; it's all girls." Connie sighed. "Something else to blame myself for."

"Does Celia seem happy?" I asked

"Yes."

"Well . . ."

Connie shrugged. "Well, better a boy's haircut and an all-girl co-op than Reese Pierce, I guess."

The relationship between Connie and Celia never became really loving. There was too much history between them for that. But those six hundred miles and intermittent contacts and phone calls ended up serving mother and daughter well. Living in Virginia, Connie didn't have to confront her daughter's sexuality, which made her uncomfortable, and that allowed the adult Celia's good qualities to shine through—her newfound stability, independence, and determination to make something of her life. Up in Vermont, Celia didn't have to be embarrassed by her mother's impulsiveness and showgirl makeup and fondness for tight Lycra pants, which left her free to appreciate her mother's good points.

As their phone calls became more frequent, Celia came to enjoy her mother's enthusiasm and ability to find humor in some pretty dire situations. Celia also added a new detail to her birthday party story. She said the next morning as she was getting dressed, Connie came into her room. "I thought Mom was going to start cracking jokes about falling into the cake; she always tries to be funny when she does something stupid or embarrassing. But this time she didn't. She sat down on the bed and said, 'I know I humiliated you in front of your friends and I'm really sorry.' Then she promised to stop drinking.

"It took Mom five years and a marriage to Bob to keep the promise," Celia said. "But in the end, she did, didn't she?"

As time passed, Celia and Connie grew comfortable and congenial with each other, and the six hundred miles between Virginia and Vermont was a major factor in this.

Distance can operate in two ways to promote good parent-youth relationships. In those cases where parents and their sons and daughters are already close and loving, being able to see each other frequently sustains this relationship. In contrast, as for Connie and Celia, distance may improve bad parent-child relationships. Poets may believe that absence makes the heart grow fonder, but our findings suggest a more pragmatic reason for its salutary effect: mother and child have fewer opportunities to fight or otherwise annoy one another when one of them lives in Virginia and the other in Vermont. "He's still screwing up his life," said one mother, whose son had finally gotten his own apartment, "but at least I don't have to watch him doing it every day anymore."

An Outstanding Achievement

Graduating with honors, acceptance to medical or law school, a big promotion, a jump shot that gets the whole town talking—any notable triumph by a child can help heal a troubled parent-child relationship. However, one of the greatest antidotes to a troubled relationship, especially between mothers and daughters, is a new baby.

Sophia Eames stopped talking to her daughter when Madeline dropped out of college to marry. Sophia said she wanted to show disapproval of "a thoroughly stupid decision." But I think what she really disapproved of was that Madeline's new husband, a second-year law student at UVA, was African American.

About two years after the wedding, Sophia was out shopping one afternoon when she ran into an old acquaintance. "Congratulations!" said the acquaintance, whom Sophia had not seen in several years. "Isn't it wonderful having a grandchild?"

Sophia held herself together until she got to her car. But, fumbling for her keys, her self-control snapped and she leaned her head against the car and began to weep. "I thought, Enough," Sophia told me later. "My pride isn't worth this. Nothing is worth this."

The next day, Sophia held her new granddaughter for the first time.

A Good Relationship with a Son- or Daughter-in-Law

A new son- or daughter-in-law can also help change a negative parent- or stepparent-child dynamic. In some instances, if the in-law is a person of obvious merit, the new spouse validates the child's worth or even raises the parent's prestige. Diana Taine, who had become distant after her daughter Clarice's pregnancy and abortion, became enthusiastic and involved when Clarice married a prominent judge. In other cases, as with Leah Coleman and Nick, the new spouse may actively heal the rift. In still others, a mutual fondness for the spouse gives the wary parent and child some new common ground to stand on.

However, the opposite can happen, too. Mutual antipathy between parents and in-laws can undermine the parent-child relationship and make congenial visits difficult. Preoccupation with work, a move to a distant location, or a serious depression can also have a negative effect. But parents and offspring who have had good relations in childhood and adolescence seldom have adversarial or disengaged relations in young adulthood, and when temporary perturbations occur, they usually are soon righted.

The Sibling Relationship in Early Adulthood

Tom Oglethorpe's decision to take a job on Wall Street upset his mother, Lisa, who was very close to handsome, ambitious Tom. "I miss him," Lisa would say at least once during every annual telephone check-in call. "I wish he'd come home."

At the twenty-year interview, Lisa announced that she was getting her wish. Tom was moving back home to Alexandria.

"Mom's thrilled about the move," Tom's older sister, Jan, told me a few weeks later.

"And you?" I asked. Jan and Tom had a long-standing love-hate relationship.

Jan sighed. "I love Tommy. But he's compulsively competitive. He's got to have the best car, the best apartment—and he never stops bragging about how much money he makes. He thinks he's Johnny Wall Street, but what he really is is a pathetic little four-year-old. Tom's world view is basically 'mine is bigger than yours.' "

Over the years, Tom had made similar remarks about Jan's academic competitiveness. Always the better student, her 1500 SAT score was the great tragedy of Tom's fifteenth year. "Talk about a big head," he complained at the eleven-year interview. "Jan acts like she's Alberta Einstein."

But a videotape we made of Jan and Tom in early adolescence captures the complexity of their relationship. The first part of the tape is full of negative behavior. Tom and Jan shout and quarrel about trivia, talk simultaneously, and don't listen to each other.

However, the mood on the tape changes abruptly when they begin to discuss their parents' divorce and Tom talks about how he felt after his father moved out. As Tom describes his pain and confusion, the noisy, combative Jan suddenly quiets down and stares intently at her younger brother; for the first time in the interaction, there are no interruptions or complaints or sarcastic remarks. When Tom begins to sob and say repetitively, "I'm sorry. I'm sorry. I'm sorry," Jan leans over and puts her arms around him, kisses him on the cheek, and says gently, "Tommy, you didn't do anything wrong. You have nothing to be sorry about."

Mixed feelings for siblings like those of Jan and Tom are common, but such relationships sometimes take a marked turn in young adulthood. As siblings move out of the home and contact becomes optional, the emotional intensity declines and hostility is often replaced by the disengagement common to all sibling relationships. Positive relationships are more likely to be sustained than are hostile ones. However, contact between most siblings diminished dramatically between adolescence and young adulthood as they went away to college, married, and took jobs in other states. Continued involvement was most likely to be sustained by the women in the family. Mothers attempted to draw the family together for shared activities, holidays, and special occasions, and to defuse disharmony between their children. Sisters also attempted to promote contact, especially with another sister. Eighty percent of phone calls between siblings were initiated by women, and in young adulthood more women than men were involved in close, warm relationships.

Congenial and Congenial-Competitive Relationships

Most young adult siblings had a congenial relationship and managed to remain warm and involved in each other's lives, even though they might be living at a distance. However, about half of these congenial relationships, while characterized by affection and support, also—like that of Tom and Jan Oglethorpe—had a strong element of rivalry.

These more rivalrous relationships tended to appear in families where parents had been warm and supportive but had high expectations and demands for good performance. Although these young adult siblings often compared their educational and professional attainments and the qualities of their partners or children in a laughing or teasing way, there was an underlying seriousness to their comparisons.

Siblings in non-divorced families are more likely to have harmonious relationships than are those in divorced families or stepfamilies in the early years following a marital transition. However, as we found in adolescence, increasingly in young adulthood, biological relatedness influenced the quality of sibling relationships. There is not only more engagement and support between biologically related siblings but also more rivalry, especially in half siblings, than is present in stepsiblings. We found that although stepsiblings were friendly, they were more likely to drift apart in young adulthood. The involvement of biologically related siblings is just more emotionally intense and sustaining. Over half of the biologically related siblings in any of our family types had congenial or congenial-competitive relationships, in contrast to 25 percent of step-siblings, who were overrepresented in disengaged sibling pairs.

Hostile or Disengaged Relationships

With younger siblings in the early stages of their parents' divorce or remarriage, sibling negativity and conflict rather than closeness were characteristic. However, in young adulthood, when siblings have the choice of whether to maintain contact, such conflict and aggressiveness are usually replaced by avoidance and detachment. About one quarter of our disengaged youths had little contact with each other because of lack of interest and attachment rather than any active animosity. However, another quarter had hostile, conflictual relationships, and these usually showed a long history of stress and conflict.

The main change in Paul and Roy Jehrico's relationship was that instead of hitting and taunting one another, they now avoided each other. But when they got together, the sparks still flew. For the most part, the only contact that the brothers had was when Paul needed money, was too drunk to drive home, or had been thrown out by his current girlfriend and needed a bed for the night. On such occasions, Roy usually provided assistance, but not out of brotherly love or concern. "Roy figures if he throws me a few bucks or puts me up for the night, I'll leave him alone for a couple of months," Paul said to me.

"Paul's right," Roy told me later. "I don't want that loser hanging around my family. He's pathetic."

The Jehrico brothers' pattern is typical for hostile-alienated adult siblings. They avoid each other when they can, and when they can't, are cold, critical, and aggressive.

Hostile-alienated relationships, most common among half siblings, often grew out of a rivalry between a favored sibling born to the new marriage, like Daphne Drew, and a rejected or scapegoated sibling, like her half sister, Anna Marie.

One surprising byproduct of the rivalry was its effect on the winner. As you might expect, scapegoated youths like Paul Jehrico and Anna Marie Drew often became hostile toward the favored sibling but, more unexpectedly, victors like Daphne Drew and Roy Jehrico were just as likely to become aggressive and contemptuous with the losing sibling. At her last interview, Daphne used the same word to describe Anna Marie as Roy used to describe Paul. She said her half sister was leading a "loser's life."

Although positive relations among female siblings continue to serve as a protective factor when they confront stresses, the effect of young adult siblings in any type of family proved minor. Just as was true in parent-child relationships, sibling relationships become less important as the influence of academic and occupational attainments, and relations with friends and romantic partners, grows more important with the move into young adulthood.

Social and Romantic Relationships

Are children of divorce marriage-challenged?

In the 1970s, when critics began warning about the effects of divorce, one of the things they feared was a generation of Linda Reids.

Linda spent most of her twenty-year interview complaining about Steve Frankel, the young stockbroker she was living with.

"I had a pretty good relationship with Steve at first, but now I'm struggling to find anything I like about him," Linda said. "It's just too boring. Steve's only interest in life is making money. I could walk into the room stark naked and it wouldn't turn him on as much as a rise in the NASDAQ. Talking about the market every night isn't my idea of stimulating dinner table conversation. And he wears his socks to bed. Yuck! It's repulsive to make love to a man with his socks on. How can he be so out of touch with the way I feel?

"I've made up my mind," she declared, "I'm getting out of the relationship. That was Mom's big mistake. She waited too long; I'm not wasting the best years of my life like she did."

Specifically, what critics worried about a generation ago was that young adults like Linda, conditioned to think of marriage as a disposable commodity, would desert a relationship at the earliest possible moment and for the most trivial reasons. And, interestingly, many of our target children began to share this fear as they grew older. "It left me 'marriage-challenged,' " is how one young man explained the effects of his parents' now distant divorce. Even Linda, in a fleeting moment of introspection, said she believed her intolerance of Steve's foibles had "something to do with Mom and Dad's divorce," though when I asked what, she said, "I'm not sure."

At the twenty-year interview, divorce had metamorphized into an all-purpose villain for some of our young men and women. They not only blamed their romantic problems on it, but also every failure, defeat, and dissatisfaction in their lives. However, this had more to do with what they were reading about in magazines, newspapers, and popular books than with reality. The media, aided and abetted by pop psychology books based on very thin data, encouraged a cult of victimization, producing apprehension and a wave of divorce hypochondria among our young people from divorced and remarried families.

I do not want to downplay the risk that a family history of divorce plays in predisposing to marital failure. The risk, though easy to exaggerate, is real. But the contributing factors are complex.

The logical way to assess how a family history of divorce affects an individual's risk of marital failure is to look at the incidence of divorce among men and women with such family histories. But we had a problem. Although we had followed the marital and cohabiting relations of the youth in the VLS until the time of the writing of this book, when the average age was thirty, of the 900 young people from the sibling pairs studied in our 450 families, 690 had married, but only 189 had gone through divorce. These rates are slightly higher than national norms since two thirds of our sample were from divorced and remarried families, and these young people do marry younger and divorce more rapidly and frequently. Still, the sample size of divorced youth was smaller than we would have liked in order to reach any definitive conclusions about the contribution that a parental divorce does or does not make to marital instability.

So, we used an additional method to assess divorce risk: the Marital Instability Scale, which has been found to be an extremely effective predictor of divorce. It includes questions about thoughts of ending a relationship and about behaviors that usually lead to divorce. It asks people to rate such factors as how often they have thought they would be better off alone, how often they have thought of leaving the relationship, how often they have separated, whether they have ever talked to friends or family about the possibility of separation or divorce, whether they have ever contacted a lawyer about divorce, and so on.

Young people from divorced families may think of themselves as "maritally challenged," but in fact the majority are doing reasonably well in their marriages. Still, married youth from divorced and high-conflict intact families were more likely to divorce and to score high on the Marital Instability Scale than those from low-conflict non-divorced families. Of those who had married, 36 percent of those from divorced families, 29 percent of those from high-conflict intact families, and only

18 percent of those from low-conflict intact families had broken up. A similar pattern was obtained on the Marital Instability Scale.

In addition, the more divorce there was in the background of a marriage, the more likely the marriage was to fail. Risk of breakup was increased if one spouse came from a divorced family, but it was highest if both partners did. Still, the female partner's family history was more important than the male's. As I noted earlier, women act as emotional regulators in the family. And since young women from low-conflict non-divorced homes make better regulators than young women from divorced, remarried, or high-conflict non-divorced homes, marriage to such a young woman is more likely to benefit a man like Richard Fredericks. Richard's online relationship blossomed into a full-blown romance and marriage with Hayden Moore, a remarkably sensitive, stable young woman. Richard said, "The only person I ever trusted other than Ed and Jeanie Dooley is Hayden. I feel really safe with her." Hayden, who came from a non-divorced family, gave Richard the love, support, and privacy and space he needed; she also recognized the importance of his involvement in his work. With Richard, some explosions were inevitable, but Hayden was careful not to reciprocate his irritable outbursts. Eventually, they were able to disagree, talk about, and even laugh over some of their differences. They called Richard's irritable, stressed days "black cloud days." When things were getting tense, Hayden often joshed, "I think I see a black cloud coming," and Richard would give a sheepish smile and calm down a bit or withdraw.

What Makes Children of Divorce More Vulnerable to Marital Failure?

Non-traditional Values

It is often argued that young people who grow up in divorced families have a set of attitudes—including a greater acceptance of divorce and a wariness about commitments—that contributes to their greater marital instability. We did find that these attitudes were more prevalent in those from divorced families. The two most common themes that came up in conversations with these young men and women about relationships involved issues of trust and safety. Children of divorce displayed a reluctance to commit and an uncertainty in relationships. But there was also a countervailing concern—"I don't want my children ever to go through what I did when my parents broke up"—that influenced their behavior. Usually, however, the focus on adult needs rather than childhood needs prevailed, and coming from a divorced family was associated with a commitment wariness and a sense of conditionality in relationships.

"What do I need Steve for?" Linda Reid declared. "I had a great life before I met him and I'll have a great life when he's gone. My job pays wonderfully, and I have everything else I want: tons of friends and a really neat apartment. Married I can always get."

This willingness to bail out of relationships was also found in attitudes toward divorce. Seventy percent of our young people from divorced families versus 40 percent from non-divorced families said that divorce was an acceptable solution to an unhappy marriage, even if children were present.

Their view was that marriage is forever "if" things work out—but only "if." There is something to be said for maintaining a measure of reserve. It makes people less tolerant of physical and emotional abuse, philandering, alcoholism, or financial irresponsibility—of many behaviors that once made marriage a prison for some men and many women—and could instill a heightened sense of autonomy. But an ever present "if" can also promote a dangerously low tolerance for the merely annoying and unpleasant; it can make divorce seem like an acceptable solution to the transitory problems and minor irritations that are part of every marriage, good and bad.

On the surface, one subgroup of our study children seemed to defy the wariness rule. Its members searched frantically for love and admiration; but once found, they grew skittish and doubtful, eventually rejecting commitment.

Sylvia Elzroth was concerned about her relationship with men. "I guess I'd have to admit I'm promiscuous. I was lying in bed the other night trying to remember all the men I've had intercourse with. Sort of like counting sheep. I got to thirty-eight, but I know I forgot some. I know I'm very attractive to men. Attracting them isn't a problem. But when they get too attached to me, I bail out.

"My dad was a wild womanizer. He screwed everything in sight— our housekeeper, his secretary, a seventeen-year-old *au pair*, even Mom's best friend. It eventually broke up their marriage. But I loved my dad and I guess I'm like him. I learned two lessons from him: that you can't trust anyone and that it's better to leave than to be left."

Some of the non-traditional values associated with being in a divorced family would seem to be positive. We found that sons who grew up with divorced working mothers were more likely to accept a wife's economic independence and career, and to be more tolerant of the inconveniences her work caused, than men raised in nuclear families. Although there may be a wariness about relationships that can lead to more ambivalence about marriage, this wariness doesn't seem to delay getting married. Our youths from divorced and remarried families remarried at an earlier age than those in non-divorced families, in part because of their earlier disengagement from the family.

Weak Relationship Skills

"Peter always says that I have to have my way," said one young woman at her twenty-year interview. "That's not fair. I give a little when I get a little in return." The young woman was wrong. In a problem-solving interaction with her husband, she showed no inclination to negotiate or compromise. She dug in her heels and more or less told Peter, "My way or the highway."

The roots of marital instability, what the American psychologist John Gottman calls marriage's Four Horsemen of the Apocalypse— hostile criticism, contempt, denial, and withdrawal—seem to run across generations and to undermine marriages for young people from divorced and non-divorced families alike. But VLS data show that youth from divorced and high-conflict non-divorced homes do have more trouble controlling the Horsemen. The reason: a contentious home life and early disengagement, the source of so many other problems, often prevent young people from developing the relationship skills needed to keep the Horsemen in check. Many of our young men and women from divorced or acrimonious non-divorced families entered marriage not knowing how to negotiate and compromise, how to make their partner feel valued, how to control their emotions, or how to use humor to defuse hostility. Belligerence, contempt, criticism, denial, and withdrawal occurred more often in the marital interactions of young people from these families, contributing to their relationship problems and marital instability. And they sometimes seemed to have acquired their destructive interaction styles from their parents.

On occasion, as when we examined the tapes of the marital interactions of a parent like Hillary Martin with her husband, Bennet, and those of her adult child, Meredith, the similarities were striking.

In Hillary's marital interaction observed in 1974, she and Bennet are discussing a leak in their cellar. When Bennet complains that fixing it will cost "a fortune," Hillary says, "You've always hated me for making you buy the house, haven't you?"

Confused by the non sequitur, Bennet protests, "But I love the house."

"That's not what I said," Hillary snaps. "I said, you've never forgiven me for insisting we buy it. You thought it was too expensive. You don't care about my happiness; you never have. You're too selfish." Bennet, who looks confused again, tries to placate Hillary, but she pushes him aside and storms out of the room crying.

History repeats itself more than twenty years later in a 1995 videotape between daughter Meredith and her husband, Seth, who comes under attack when he brings up the couple's money problems. "Why don't you just come out and say it?" Meredith declares. "You think I spend too much money. You think I'm a little ninny who doesn't know the first thing about money."

When Seth tries to defend himself, Meredith says, "I think you're a very unhappy and angry person; you're not capable of caring about anyone else." Then she leaps out of her chair and runs out of the room crying.

Genetic Predispositions

Environmental influences may be one reason why children of divorce are more prone to divorce themselves, but it is not the only reason. There is growing evidence that behaviors that to some extent are genetically based, such as irritability, impulsivity, antisocial behavior, and depression, are handed down from one generation of a family to the next. These attributes in turn lead to poor relationship skills that can erode a marriage; they let the Four Horsemen out of the gate.

Behavior geneticists would argue that it is the inheritance of such genetic vulnerabilities that contributes both to the intergenerational transmission of divorce and to behavior problems in children from divorced families. People who have these high-risk characteristics are more likely to bring troubles onto themselves and those around them. They provoke difficulties in social relationships, undermine their marriages, make incompetent parents, and have children who also show personality problems that contribute to the instability of their marriages. Thus, the offspring of parents with these personality characteristics are exposed to a double risk—the genetic risk of inheriting these personality traits and the environmental risk of being exposed to poor parenting and inept role models.

Diana Taine's daughter, Amy, from her second marriage was the opposite of her eldest child, the reticent, shy Clarice. She was, as her mother said, "a real Taine woman"—feisty, contentious, stubborn, opinionated, and divorce-prone. Amy's second husband, Everett Taylor, whom Amy had met on a trip to London, said, "Marrying into that family was like diving into a shark frenzy. I've never met such a bloody-minded group of women. They weren't happy unless things were stirred up. When I'd think things were going along well, Amy would go out of her way to pick a fight over trivial things—the kind of cat food I bought or a new black jacket I had that she said made me look like a mortician, or how I put on a new roll of toilet paper. She said I put it on backwards. What the hell is putting toilet paper on backwards and why is it such a big deal? I had to get out before she destroyed me."

A number of general factors also contribute to marital instability, and by "general," I mean factors that affect everyone, regardless of family history. They include gender, sex, in-laws, and what we call the "second shift."

Gender

One of the most surprising findings to emerge from the VLS is that gender has a more important influence on the decision to divorce than coming from either a divorced or non-divorced family.

Young women, but not young men, in all families whose mothers had been employed were 150 percent more likely to divorce. They were more autonomous and self-sufficient, and more likely also to be employed themselves. Many regarded working as a kind of marital insurance that would prevent economic constraints from locking them into an unhappy marriage.

For our youths in the 1990s, as with their parents in the 1970s, we found that male withdrawal and denial, two of Dr. Gottman's Horsemen, are particularly likely to drive a woman out of a marriage; while criticism, contempt, and reciprocated aggression—counterattacking when attacked—act like marital Mace on a man.

The average man, particularly if he's from a divorced family, wants an optimistic, cheerful, non-contentious wife, who will nurture him and make him feel good about himself. What he doesn't want is a depressed, irritable spouse, who looks for fights, carps on his failings, and wants him to do more around the house. Women, on the other hand, dislike husbands who are cold and unaffectionate, belligerent, poor providers, irresponsible, or who drink heavily.

Interestingly, the Pursuer-Distancer pattern in which the woman pursues intimacy and the man flees it contributed heavily to divorce in both the original VLS parents and, two decades later, their adult children. However, the Pursuer-Distancer pattern is more likely to be found in young men and women from divorced and high-conflict non-divorced families. Although many of the complaints of the Pursuers were similar across generations, more contemporary young working women with children were vociferous about their husbands not doing their fair share of child care and tasks around the house.

Sex

Sex also creates issues for couples, regardless of family background. Unsatisfying sex, often tolerated by women, makes men very unhappy. We found that women who had a positive relationship with their father in any type of family were more likely to experience orgasms in sexual relationships. Here women in divorced families and stepfamilies were clearly disadvantaged by their more alienated relationship with their fathers. My original interest in this topic was provoked by a review of a book, *The Female Orgasm*, that I had read when I was still a graduate student in the early fifties. The review was entitled "My Orgasm Belongs to Daddy"—and apparently it still does.

A spouse's infidelity produces unhappiness in both sexes, though when it comes to their own infidelities, men and women respond differently. Men are master compartmentalizers—a fact reflected in the number of males who had both high marital satisfaction and an occasional casual sexual encounter; indeed, for some men, a girlfriend seemed to function as an aphrodisiac, increasing their desire for married sex.

Women, whose infidelities were usually driven by marital dissatisfaction, are less likely to compartmentalize. When women had an affair, it was less likely to be a one-night stand and more likely to be a committed relationship that could lead to divorce. However, one aspect of female sexual behavior has changed. Now that work has put women into daily contact with other males, they stray almost as much as men!

In-Laws

"Our problems started with the wedding," Adam Pennybaker said. "Moira and I wanted a small wedding with family and a few intimate friends, to be held at a friend's farm, but my mother-in-law, Sheila, had a different definition of intimate than we did. We ended up having a big formal church wedding and a reception in the ballroom of the Jefferson Hotel with a lot of people I didn't know. It was awful.

"Then she phoned Moira every day and would talk for an hour and stop by without calling late in the afternoon. She's a drinker, and when I got home from work, half the nights she'd be there smashed out of her mind. And the more she drank, the more critical she got about me, about Moira, about the way we lived. The main reason we moved to San Francisco was to get away from Sheila."

Aside from moving physically to another part of the country, the key to resolving in-law problems is learning how to manage interference. Split loyalties between the family of origin and the new family can be corrosive to a marriage. Firm boundaries around the new family need to be set to protect against inappropriate outside pressures. But this is not always easy. We find that while most people can live with an occasional snide remark or criticism, direct in-law interference in the marriage or in the family produces marital instability in people from all kinds of family backgrounds.

The "Second Shift"

The modest change in two decades in the distribution of household labor between husbands and wives was surprising. In 1972, when the VLS began, only 30 percent of married women with children worked; by the 1990s, over 70 percent of the young mothers and 90 percent of the childless wives in our younger group were employed at least part time. Yet, in that period of over two decades, the average man's contribution to household chores went from ten hours in 1973 to only fifteen hours in 2000; the working woman's contribution, on the other hand, remained constant over the two decades, at thirty-eight hours.

Apparently, a generation of feminist rhetoric and wifely exhortation about the "second shift" has failed to penetrate the male world view: which is that men work and women keep house—everything else women do, including work, represents an "in addition to." Over two thirds of married women complained about sharing a disproportionate burden of child care and housework. One woman said, "If the kids have to go to the doctor or if they're sent home because of a snow day, I'm the one who has to take time off work, and I'm the one who squeezes in time to watch some of Jason's baseball games. It's as if my work doesn't count or as if they're somehow more my children than his. We're both assistant professors working to get tenure. It's damned well intolerable."

A few years ago, the Berkeley psychologist Arlie Hochschild identified another consequence of unfair burden sharing. For many young women with children, work has replaced family as a "haven in a heartless world." Our data support Dr. Hochschild's position. Our young working women reported that their happiest time was at work, whereas for men it was at home.

"That's no big surprise," said one young woman, when I mentioned our findings to her. "I work at home; he plays or rests. I'd be happy at home too if all I did was sit in front of the television and drink beer or play with the kids. Scrubbing out toilets and changing diapers isn't exactly a big esteem builder. At work, I feel appreciated. I feel I'm doing something useful. It's not the same old repetitive drudgery."

One other social change which is beginning to produce marital instability is the financial and occupational success of the working wife. Today, an increasing number of wives out-earn their husbands, and while men from divorced homes are more accepting of disparities, probably because they grew up with a breadwinner mother, men raised in nuclear families are not. They often feel threatened and emasculated, and not infrequently they respond by becoming even more reluctant to help around the house.

However, it is the spouses' attitudes and acceptance of the distribution of work rather than the actual amount of work done by husbands and wives that influence marital stability. We found a substantial number of young working women who carried the predominant burden of child care and housework, but did not view it as unjust. They saw it as a reasonable part of a woman's role, even of a working woman's role. If husbands and wives both find the distribution of labor acceptable even when it is unbalanced, this does not increase the risk of marital breakup.

What Protects Against Marital Instability?

There are a number of ways to look at the higher divorce rate among young people from divorced families. Critics imagine that divorce-prone behaviors are being institutionalized and warn of a snowball effect: with each succeeding generation, a larger and larger proportion of young people will come of age knowing more about how to destroy a marriage than how to make it work.

But you can also look at the divorce rate as a triumph. When the study ended, there was less than a 10 percent difference in the marital failure rate between those from divorced and non-divorced families. Given all the developmental vulnerabilities that divorce creates, I think that is a remarkably small difference.

What promotes such resiliency?

Our research shows that several factors can protect against the inter-generational transmission of divorce.

The lessons children learn from adult mentors, authoritative parents and schools, and pro-social peers about self-respect, respecting others, and the importance of self-control all help them socially, in a marriage, and in dealing with the vicissitudes and setbacks of life.

Supportive friends with stable marriages also contribute to marital stability. Our youth were often helped through marital bad patches by other couples who acted as friends, advisers, sounding boards, and role models. And since immaturity can compound the effects of skill deficits, marrying later also has a protective effect.

However, the most important potential protective factor is the selection of a mate. Marriage is a relationship, not a one-person show. When a young person from a divorced family marries a stable, supportive spouse from a non-divorced family, his or her risk of marital failure falls back to that of a young man or woman from a non-divorced home. The reason? A mature spouse can teach skills like problem solving, sensitivity to others' needs, how to offer support in times of stress, and how to be a better parent.

In describing their marital histories, for young people from divorced families who were married to a caring, stable spouse, as well as those in other well-functioning marriages, the marital relationship seemed to be an entity in itself. These young people more often used the integrative "We" and "Us" and less often used the pronoun "I" in describing their marriage than did people from divorced families who had not married a supportive spouse. Moreover, like others in fulfilling marriages, they more often glorified and celebrated the building of their relationship. They spoke warmly and nostalgically of painting their first apartment, of early shared financial struggles, and of the births of their children. In discussing their marriage, couples in mutually supportive relationships also seemed to have a different timeline. They shared vivid memories of their initial meeting and past history, excitement about the present, and plans for the future. Their less happily married peers seemed focused entirely on the present.

Twenty Years Later

The adverse effects of divorce and remarriage are still echoing in some divorced families and their offspring twenty years after divorce, but they are in the minority. The vast majority of young people from these families are reasonably well adjusted and are coping reasonably well in relationships with their families, friends, and intimate partners. Most are moving toward establishing careers, economic independence, and satisfying social and intimate relationships. Some are caring spouses and parents. Although the divorce may resonate more in the memories of these children, most parents and children see the divorce as having been for the best, and have moved forward with their lives.

Points to Remember

- Parent, child, and sibling relationships that have been close in childhood seldom deteriorate in adulthood.
- Even if absence doesn't make the heart grow fonder, conflict usually diminishes once the protagonists are apart and contact becomes

optional. Disengagement often replaces conflict in stepparent-stepchild and sibling relationships in divorced and remarried families in young adulthood.

- Biologically related siblings, whether in divorced, non-divorced, or remarried families, tend to have both more attached and more rivalrous relationships than those found in stepsiblings.

- Men remain reluctant to do their fair share. In most first- and second-generation VLS homes, the burden of household labor continued to fall predominantly on female shoulders. After a demanding eight- or ten-hour day at the office, many of our women would come home to cope with unmade beds, unwashed laundry, unfed children, and the morning's unwashed breakfast dishes in the sink.

- A family history of divorce does leave children of divorce relationship- and marriage-challenged. Children of divorce are often reluctant to commit wholeheartedly to a marriage, have fewer relationship skills, and in some cases show a genetic predisposition to destabilizing behaviors like antisocial behavior, impulsivity, and depression.

- Gender affects a person's divorce risk more than the kind of family the person was brought up in. In divorced, remarried, and non-divorced families alike, male belligerence, withdrawal, and lack of affection often produce thoughts of divorce in a woman; female contempt, nagging, or reciprocated aggression, thoughts of divorce in a man.

- Although marital instability is higher in offspring from divorced families, marriage to a stable, supportive spouse from a non-divorced family eliminates the intergenerational transmission of divorce. A caring, mature spouse can teach their partner from a divorced family skills they never learned at home.

- Young adults from complex stepfamilies continue to have more adjustment and family problems than young adults in other kinds of stepfamilies.

- For most youths, the legacy of divorce is largely overcome. Twenty years after divorce, most men and women who had grown up in divorced families and stepfamilies are functioning reasonably well. Only a minority still exhibited emotional and social problems, and had difficulties with intimate relationships and achievement.

12

Win, Lose, and Draw:
Adults Twenty Years Later

"*I*t happened a few weeks ago. Jimmy was pretty low-key about it. He said he just wanted me to consider it. To tell the truth, it didn't come as a total surprise. We've gotten close again since Jimmy's been sick. Still . . ." Liddy stops and smiles. "Sometimes, life takes the strangest turns, doesn't it?"

When the two of us met for the first time, the country was still recovering from the wounds of the Vietnam War, women were rallying to the feminist cause, Richard Nixon was still a year away from resigning, and the divorce rate was soaring. Liddy Pennybaker was twenty-eight then, very pretty and blond, and for 1973 dressed demurely. She wore a flowered summer dress to her first interview. I remember the dress because I so seldom saw anything other than a miniskirt or jeans on our female participants at that time.

I also remember thinking how untouched Liddy seemed by the sixties. So many others I met, back then, were bristling with righteous anger and sexual swagger. Soft-spoken and a little prim, Liddy could have stepped out of a John Cheever short story from the 1950s, one about a naive, sheltered young woman, whose perfect life explodes when she discovers her husband has betrayed her.

If there is an inspirational message in what happened to Liddy after that betrayal, it is about the power of the personal. VLS participants like Liddy who won big at divorce, won more because of who they were than what they had. When you look at the trajectory of a life after divorce over two decades, money and education certainly do matter; but personal traits like determination, maturity, resourcefulness, ambition, self-discipline, and the capacity to endure hardship and sacrifice matter far more.

When the study ended, Liddy had been remade by her divorce experience. She was vice president of a national brokerage firm, on the boards of several local companies and foundations, and active in local politics. Materially, too, hers was a success story. She owned a large, comfortable home, had a sizable investment portfolio, took winter vacations in the Caribbean and summer vacations in Europe. And what mattered most to her, at the end of the study, was that Liddy had two well-adjusted, successful children: Bethany was beginning to gain recognition as an author of children's stories; and Adam was a sought-after contractor and builder who specialized in restoring old houses.

During our last talk, I found myself wondering what the young Liddy would make of her older self. I'm sure she'd be very surprised, and maybe even a little intimidated at how competent, independent, and worldly she had become. The Liddy I met twenty years ago was a small-town girl raised to be a wife, and when that role ended, she seemed temporarily disoriented about what steps to take next.

Now, the mature Liddy seemed disoriented by the prospect of becoming a wife again. Three weeks earlier, James had asked her to marry him.

"I wish the proposal hadn't happened," Liddy said at her last interview. "Jimmy and I still love one another, maybe in a better way now. But I'm afraid that marriage would ruin what we have. Besides, I think I've become unmarriageable. I'm too used to doing what I want when I want."

Liddy smiled. "You know what Katharine Hepburn said. Men and women ought to just live next door to one another. They'd get along better. I'm with Kate on that one. I don't like to disappoint Jimmy. But we already have something wonderful. We'll go to our graves best friends. And if that isn't the definition of a successful relationship, what is?"

The 20 percent of our participants who were Enhancers like Liddy clearly won at divorce. Its opportunities and challenges changed them in ways that would have been unimaginable to their predivorce selves. At the other extreme were our clear divorce losers, those who twenty years after the divorce found themselves Defeated. For many people, defeat was merely temporary; they moved up and out, when they got a new job or remarried or solved a substance abuse problem. But the 10 percent of men and women who remained Defeated at the end of the study were leading empty and often troubled lives. Some, like Betty Ann Jehrico, had no sources of solace or satisfaction in their lives; they worked, they ate, they slept. Others were still going to singles bars, mixing with people who were half their age; still others had had a second and third divorce. A number of the Defeated were addicted to alcohol or drugs and many in the group saw little of their adult children.

Most others in the VLS emerged as a Good Enough of one type or another. Two decades later, most members of this group still felt good about the decision to divorce—said one Good Enough woman, "My divorce was the best thirtieth birthday present I could have given myself." But because few people in the group took advantage of the window of change, Good Enoughs didn't get new lives; divorce merely rearranged the furniture of their old lives. By the end of the study, most Good Enoughs had reverted to a version of their predivorce selves. They were doing all right; they were getting by in marriage, at work, and with their adult children.

When we looked at what made people satisfied with their lives twenty years after divorce, the most striking thing was warm intimate relationships with friends and family and children, but especially with spouses. People in long-lasting, gratifying first and second marriages were better off economically, and had the lowest rates of depression, substance abuse, conduct disorders, health complaints, and visits to the doctor. Married people also reported that their sex life was more satisfying and they had intercourse more often than divorced men and women who remained single. They were healthier, happier, wealthier, and sexier. In short, being in a satisfying intimate marital relationship made a large difference in personal well-being.

Our cohabitating participants, who now accounted for only 9 percent of the study sample, and single women, who accounted for 35 percent of our postdivorce female sample, had the next-lowest rates of physical and psychological problems. Single men, as they had throughout the study, continued to have the most problems with alcohol, antisocial behavior, and health.

Most of the parents in the VLS were now in their late forties or fifties, a time when people are often reevaluating their past life and assessing the prospects for their future. For the vast majority, their divorce was a dim memory, and irrelevant to their current concerns. Many of our middle-aged adults no longer expected any notable changes in their life situation. Some looked back on their attainments with pride and expected to move on into a gratifying future. Others had given up the struggle and just expected to go on as they had. Many were beginning to be concerned about retirement, financial security, and old age. Those who had had a serious illness or who had friends or family members die had a heightened sense of vulnerability and mortality. Among people who were still single, concerns about being elderly or ill and alone began to surface frequently in our twenty-year interviews, which were the most thoughtful, forward-looking interviews in our study.

Single Women: Resources and Vulnerabilities

At the end of the study, as at its beginning, single women were leading more satisfying, meaningful lives than single men. While men seem to need a partner to feel complete, women are better able to rely on each other. Most of our now middle-aged single women were living largely in the company of other women, and they played many roles in this female world—friend, traveling companion, dinner date and movie mate, and crisis adviser.

The orientation toward helping that is part of female socialization makes women better able to adapt to the single life. Women are brought up to be interested in and care about others, and that not only leaves less time for the kind of emotional isolation and self-destructive behavior single men are prone to, but also acts as a source of self-esteem. Our single women accompanied one another to important medical appointments, did volunteer work for charity organizations, devoted time to their children and parents. Helping others gave many women a way to feel good about themselves. Religion was another important source of strength for single women. Like Liddy, who was a deacon at her church, at the end of the study many of our single women were involved in a religious network of some type or other.

But this relatively bright picture also contained some dark spots. Even twenty years after divorce, divorced women were not only found more often than unhappily married women in the Enhanced group; they also continued to be substantially overrepresented in the Defeated group. The Defeated had been overwhelmed by stresses and by the failure to exercise personal initiative in shaping their choices in life.

When her sons Paul and Roy were adolescents, Betty Ann Jehrico's second marriage to Roger had ended in a wild, tumultuous divorce and a final nasty bout of physical violence. Roger had blackened both of Betty Ann's eyes and broken two of her ribs; Betty Ann had laid Roger out with a blow to the head with a poker.

Roger now lived with a woman at the end of Betty Ann's block. There were some disparities in Betty Ann and Roger's reports of how the romance had developed. But apparently Roger, no longer a truck driver, had become a mailman. On his delivery route he was smitten when he saw Georgia gardening in a pair of cut-off jeans, and eventually began delivering more than just the mail at her address.

"The hell with Roger," Betty Ann snarled at our last interview. "I've had it up to here with men."

By the end of the study, Betty Ann was managing a convenience store, but otherwise she was leading an almost pitifully stripped-down life. The only people she saw regularly were her coworkers, and she rarely socialized with them outside store hours. There was no new man in her life, and her relationship with her children consisted of holiday dinners at Roy's.

Moreover, unhappiness was beginning to take a toll on Betty Ann's health. Despite a serious case of hypertension, she was smoking two packs of cigarettes a day and consuming a six-pack of beer each evening as she sat watching television alone. Stocky when I first met her, she weighed almost 270 pounds when the study ended.

Betty Ann, like so many Defeated men and women, had settled into a life of victimhood. Rendered inert by chronic depression and a low internal locus of control, she felt powerless. She believed everything bad that happened to her was someone else's fault. And while she was, indeed, often "acted upon," the larger truth was that passive-aggressive Betty Ann both allowed herself to be "victimized" and drove people off with her sullen, sarcastic demeanor.

About a quarter of our single women were single out of choice and leading satisfying lives. These Competent Loners almost always had a gratifying job and sustaining relationships, but relished their freedom as a single person. Most of our other single women, even many of our unmarried Enhanced women, would like to have had a new relationship, if a "Mr. Right" came along. The Defeated often were indiscriminate or made bad mate choices. Most people have a need for a loving, emotionally supportive relationship. Going it alone was often hard for both men and women, but men seemed to have greater difficulty.

Single Men:
Isolation and Vulnerabilities

Some of our single men ended the study in states ranging from melancholy to despair. Age had something to do with this. One divorced single man of fifty-four said, "I don't like the way I live, but I can't see my life changing now. The chances of a new marriage or a new job at my age are pretty slim. I guess I'm going to be stuck in the same old rut—

working at a job I don't like, wondering what to do with my free time, occasionally watching a ball game or going out drinking with the guys. You know, the hardest part of getting old is you have to learn to live without a future."

By the end of the study, some single men had built up enough of a support system to avoid a bar existence. But others were still going out—for the excitement and for the alcohol. Over one third of our single men had serious drinking problems, and accident rates, in part a result of the drinking, were three times higher in single than married men. Single men also had more health problems than other adults their age. At the twenty-year mark, many of the single men had suffered from serious illnesses, and because they had estranged adult children and men don't support each other the way women do, the sick had to endure their illness alone.

I remember one man with prostate cancer who wanted to hire a student to drive him to and from chemotherapy. The man said he could get himself to the hospital all right but not back; the chemo made him too nauseous to drive.

I knew the man had not spoken to his adult son in years. But I wondered about his friends. "Wouldn't you feel more comfortable having someone you know drive you?" I asked.

"I usually vomit on the way home," the man said. "I don't want my friends to see me like that. It'd make me uncomfortable and it'd make them uncomfortable."

Being alone and ill was a big worry for both single men and women as old age started to come into view. Those who were still single were beginning to wonder who would take care of them if they become too sick or infirm to care for themselves. "There's this lovely old woman who lives across the street from me," said one fifty-two-year-old woman. "Except for the visiting nurse, I never see anyone at her house. And she never goes out; she can't get around without a walker. Her whole life is sitting on the front porch and watching soap operas. Every time I see her, I think, Is that going to be me in thirty years?"

I think the fear of being ill and alone may have had something to do with James Pennybaker's proposal. In spite of James's regrets about the breakup of his marriage, he had gone on to build an extremely successful career, a satisfying social life, and close relationships with his two children, Adam and Bethany. He lived alone with a weimaraner named Hindenburg in the penthouse of a condominium building he had designed. His relationship with Liddy had evolved from contentiousness to cooperation and mutual concern about caring for Adam and Bethany to friendship. However, when James developed heart problems, their relationship became more intense. Liddy, Adam, and Bethany stayed with him in shifts around the clock in the hospital after his heart surgery, and Liddy arranged for nursing care and stopped by daily when he was recovering at home.

At our twenty-year interview, six months after his surgery, I was impressed by how James Pennybaker had matured and mellowed. In spite of his recent illness, although gaunt and a bit pale, James still moved and smiled with the easy grace and confidence of a man who had always been considered handsome and accomplished. But his earlier arrogance and manipulative charm were gone. His biting sarcasm had been replaced by a self-deprecating wit, and his conversation, rather than being myopically focused on himself, dealt with the attainments of his children and his relationships with people he loved, including Liddy.

In describing his illness, James said, "When I came out of the hospital, I felt frail and vulnerable and depressed. I had always thought of myself as a sort of golden boy. Everything came easily to me. I could cope with anything. I felt protected and invulnerable; but no more. When I came home, I couldn't even walk down to get the mail, and my recovery took much longer than anyone anticipated. I don't know what I'd have done without Liddy. I started to wonder what I was doing with my life, why I'd been on this crazy ego trip, why I was working so hard, and why I wasn't spending more time with the people I loved."

Both the middle-aged James and Liddy had become better people than when they were younger—less blaming, more thoughtful and kind and emotionally honest. And should Liddy say yes to James one day, the Pennybakers would have a good chance of making a new marriage work.

Their children felt that way, too. Despite Liddy's reluctance, Adam and Bethany remained optimistic about a reunion. At his twenty-year interview, Adam told me the two of them were planning "a full court press" on Liddy. "Mom's got to realize she and Dad are never going to meet people as perfectly suited for them as they are for each other," Adam said.

The small group of men who functioned well in a single state were men like Simon Russell, who often had functioned competently before marriage and who had many protective factors operating after the divorce. Simon had grown into an affable, slightly absentminded, just retired sixty-year-old when I saw him for his twenty-year interview. He had aged well. His thick curly hair had turned gray, but his face was unlined, and his manner more lively and responsive than it had been when he was younger. He was enthusiastic about retirement, looking forward to traveling and spending more time in community activities and with his family. The next week, Simon was leaving on a tour to study orchids in Latin America. He could barely contain his excitement about the trip.

Simon said, "Looking back on my life, I've been very fortunate. The only really bad times I had were when Connie left and I was separated from the children and then when Celia was raising hell as a teenager. I've never been happier than I am now. Michael and Celia have grown into fine young people and we're very close. And my grandson, he's a wonder." Simon beamed and whipped out a picture of Simon Junior to show me. "I sometimes think I should never have married; but then I wouldn't have had the children, and what a loss that would have been. I have no regrets about the divorce; in some ways it was a boon. It gave me a boot on the behind and made me see what a dull fellow I was. The divorce and the children helped push me into the outside world and made my life more interesting. I should probably thank Connie for leaving me."

Remarried Couples:
Those Who Survived the Early High-Risk Years

Our failure rate for second marriages proved roughly the same as the national average, 60 percent. However, there was a sliver of good news in these numbers. Most second marriages that fail, fail during the tumultuous early years of stepfamily life. Couples who are able to cope with the challenges of the early years usually are rewarded later for their perseverance. At the end of the study, couples in long-lasting stepfamily marriages looked a lot like those of a long-lasting first marriage. They were companionable, mutually supportive, and promoted personal well-being. Couples in both types of long-lasting marriages had low rates of depression, substance abuse, and health problems.

What qualified as long-lasting second marriages?

It usually took five to seven years for the tensions of stepfamily life to decline to the point where the couple's stress level matched that of a husband and wife in a first marriage. The period of destabilization was shorter for couples married when the children were young. Still, seven years is ample time for even adolescent stepchildren to grow up and move out of the home. And as boys and girls matured, and became absorbed in their own lives, they put less pressure on the remarriage. Most stepfamilies who got this far also had defined acceptable or at least tolerable roles for the stepparent. But for some of our long-established stepfamilies, especially complex stepfamilies, contentiousness continued and was still centered on children and finances even after the children had left home. Stepparents resented any kind of financial support of young adult children. They were less likely than biological parents to contribute money for going to college, establishing a new business, assisting in paying the down payment on a new house, or generally helping deal with the financial hurdles young people encounter when they move out of the family home.

The remarried couples, or for that matter any couples who make it to the seventh year of a marriage, can be considered marital survivors. They have survived the early high-risk years of marriage—of learning how to compromise, to be sensitive to each other's needs and feelings, and to support each other in difficult times. They also have learned how to deal with solvable problems and to avoid becoming fixated on unsolvable ones. Couples who stayed together were different in another way, too. They made sacrifices for each other and for the marriage. They invested in their marriages, and this investment often created a staying power. When the marriage hit a bad patch, as every marriage does, the couple rode it out.

This was what kept Nick Lang steadfast through the years of Leah's abuse. "After all the sweat and sacrifice I put into the marriage, I was damned if I was going to let a twelve-year-old drive me out of town," Nick said at the twenty-year interview.

I don't know whether time had been kind to Nick or he finally had become as old as he looked when I met first him, but the middle-aged Nick looked a lot like the young Nick. He was still squat, still had a double chin and a wide, beaming smile, and he still thought Janet was the best thing that ever happened to him. They were in fact the best thing that happened to each other.

In one way or another, most of what Nick had was connected to Janet. And that included not only his relationship to her children and his emotional well-being, but also his material well-being. After a decade of working as a bookkeeper for a supermarket chain, Nick joined "Janet's Garden" as a purchasing agent and accountant for the expanding company's six stores. At the twenty-year interview, fifty-year-old Nick and fifty-one-year-old Janet were enjoying a happy and affluent life.

They had bought a large, run-down house with eight fireplaces and an overgrown garden on Capitol Hill in Washington, which they were renovating. I picked my way over electrical cords and broken plaster as they toured me through the house and led me to a beautiful glass conservatory overlooking the back garden for our interviews. Janet and Nick's shared enthusiasm for their restoration project and for each other was apparent. They held hands as they described their plans.

Nick said, "Janet came home one day and said she had found the most wonderful eighteenth-century fixer-upper house. When I saw it, I told her it looked more like a faller-downer than a fixer-upper." They both laughed and Nick squeezed Janet's hand. Nick went on, "There'll be plenty of room for the kids to visit and we're doing the garden ourselves. We love to grub around in the garden together."

Since Michael had taken over most of the running of "Janet's Garden," Janet was free to pursue a more relaxed regime. Her current major passions were her grandchildren; her work at a shelter for abused women; and a recently adopted holistic lifestyle that explained Janet's gray hair.

"I've been using toxins since I was fourteen," she said. "I've decided it's time to start giving my body a break."

"Ms. Granola," Nick said, then turned to me. "I keep telling her, she's becoming the world's oldest hippie."

Janet and Nick had acquired all the characteristics of long-married couples—the practiced punch lines and cherished foibles, secret jokes and hidden messages in their playful patter. They had become what happily married couples eventually become: the world's greatest experts on each other.

Two decades ago, Janet was an unlikely candidate for such a happy ending. Other than the support of a single friend, Marcia, and a semester of community college, she left an abusive marriage and entered postdivorce life with few obvious protective factors. She didn't have a supportive parent like Liddy Pennybaker, nor did she have Liddy's attractiveness, or strong religious faith, or her education.

These differences are instructive because they highlight two alternate routes of change after a divorce. For Liddy, and for some other Enhancers, change took the form of the unfolding of personal resources not previously known. These women already possessed the requisite resources for personal fulfillment and career success, and they had a support system that allowed the resources to blossom in a relatively predictable way.

For other women, like Janet, their marked resiliency was unexpected, and the great driving force behind their self-invention was personal need. While such late bloomers were also provoked by need, for women like Janet who had few if any outside sources of support, the need was much deeper and more desperate.

Most of the skills Janet possessed at the end of the study were learned, and each was acquired to solve a concrete, often pressing problem. Janet needed money to support herself and her children, so she took a job at the flower shop. She wanted to make the most of her job, so she virtually recruited Gordon Cramer as a mentor. And she wanted to own her own business, so she learned about finance, marketing, and organizing and leading people—even people who intimidated her a little.

Janet required more time to learn about love. But after several false starts, she picked a mate who didn't intimidate her or pose a threat to her hard-won independence. There were some lingering insecurities: for all her success, Janet never entirely got over Richard Coleman. The scar he left on her grew shallower as the years passed, but it never quite disappeared.

If Nick and Janet represented the optimum in a second marriage, Connie Russell and Bob Keatly represent the mean. They were still getting along at the end of the study, but over the years certain qualifications and reservations had crept into their relationship. Most of these emanated from Bob, who was still tolerating Connie's idiosyncrasies and impulsivity, but a good deal less happily than he had before.

Connie's recent participation in a wet T-shirt contest had him agitated. "It was for charity," Bob said at his twenty-year interview. "The Policeman's Fund is trying to raise money. But still, Connie made me look like a fool. I mean, there she is up on the stage, strutting—and I mean strutting—her stuff and all my friends are 'oohing' and 'ahhing' over her boobs. I mean, Christ, any guy would be upset at that."

But Bob also knew that many of Connie's annoying habits were the flip side of the things he found exciting about her like her spontaneity and sense of fun. Which is why, at the twenty-year interview, he was still talking about "trade-offs." "After Connie stopped drinking, I thought I'd be able to help her pull the rest of her life together," he said. "I tried for about five years. I got on her about the house, and Celia and the way she dresses. You know what? Nothing changed. With Connie, you either take the good with the bad or you leave. Sometimes, she does things . . . I mean, you just want to brain her. But she's forty-four and she's still the most exciting and sexy woman I've ever met."

In truth, Connie had aged physically better than almost anyone in the study. A late-blooming athlete, she began working out after she stopped drinking, and a decade of aerobics and weightlifting had turned a good figure into an eye-popping one, which Connie was not at all shy about displaying.

"I suppose my hero Bob has been telling you I'm the anti–Martha Stewart," Connie said a few weeks later. "And I bet he also told you about the T-shirt contest. I want to go on the record, Mavis. I did it for charity, Bob's charity. And it was fun. I'm sorry he was embarrassed. But everything I do has always seemed to embarrass someone—either him, or Celia or Michael." Connie became more serious. "I never mean to hurt him. He's the most important thing in my life. I know he saved me and Celia. We wouldn't be here without him."

Thanks to Bob's support, Connie had managed to rise to the Good Enough category by the end of the study. But, in some areas, problems remained. Still a sensation-seeker, she tended to do things that hurt her marriage—like enter a wet T-shirt contest—still impulsive, she ran up credit card charges that were a problem with Bob's modest policeman's salary; and still lacking in self-discipline, she couldn't do something as basic as keep a clean house. But Connie with Bob's help had come a long way from her early postdivorce years. She no longer drank; she was a devoted, loving, and faithful wife; she had a job as a hostess in an upscale restaurant, which she was good at and enjoyed; she was gradually rebuilding her relationship with her children; and she had a wide circle of friends who found her zaniness endearing.

Some of the couples in our studies were in marriages and remarriages that had now lasted twenty years or more. There was a tranquility and comfort level in these marriages not found early in a marriage and not found in their own marriages when they were younger.

One long-married man said, "There's not the emotional extremes, the big highs and lows, the passion and the fighting we had when we were younger. It takes a lot to work us up. But I like the serenity now and the comfortable routines in our lives, the things we do together. I like us planning our days when we sit on the terrace drinking coffee in the morning and playing cribbage when we watch the evening news. I like being able to complain to Louise about a problem at the office or how our kids are raising our grandchildren. I just like the feeling of being best friends. I'd never want to trade it for our early years."

In the early years of a first marriage or remarriage, the best predictors of marital dissatisfaction and considering a breakup were high levels of contempt, hostile criticism, and withdrawal. We were surprised to find that frequent fighting produces temporary unhappiness but isn't a good long-term predictor of marital breakup. It was *how* people fought and whether they were able to resolve the problems that were undermining their relationship that was associated with marital breakup. Often, disagreements were constructive and were associated with egalitarianism in a marriage, with both the husband and wife feeling free to express their needs and opinions. But early in a marriage, all couples—even couples who had lived together before the marriage—had to negotiate many issues. Some of these were related to basic routines of family life—who carries out the garbage or pays the bills or does the laundry, or whether vegetarian meals or down-home cooking should be served. Others involve the more critical emotional nurturing of the marriage.

At the twenty-year point, what seems to have sustained long-enduring marriages were the more active positive aspects of the union: the mutual respect, friendship, and support of each other in difficult times. This finding was unexpected. Most investigators have emphasized that it is the lack of negative rather than the presence of positive behaviors that sustains a marriage. In the short run, that may be true, but not necessarily in the long run. Couples in happy, lasting marriages often spoke of the marriage as a partnership, in which both partners felt secure and valued, and both recognized and accepted their interdependencies. In the clinical literature, much has been written about the hazards of co-dependency and the importance of maintaining autonomy. Still, in most successful marriages, a trusting relationship develops that allows spouses to rely and lean on each other for support. Relationships with no interdependencies seldom endure because the couple don't need each other to sustain the lives they are living.

Co-dependent couples have the opposite problem. They are held together not so much by love as by fear and neurosis. Husband and wife are unable to function apart, to act independently, or to maintain an identity separate from one another.

Sequential Divorces

In our studies, the number of divorces experienced by participants ranged from none to five. Multiple divorces, in contrast to a single divorce, were more likely to be associated with serious personality problems or psychopathology in a parent and with high rates of problems in adjustment in children. Serious emotional or behavioral problems were found in only 20 percent of children whose parents had gone through a single divorce, but in 38 percent of those coping with multiple divorces. Since children usually lived with a divorced mother, her divorces were more important in undermining a child's well-being than were the divorces of fathers.

One boy whose mother had divorced three times and had had several cohabiting relationships said, "I don't know what to expect when I get up in the morning or when I come home from school in the afternoon. I don't know who's going to be there or if we're going to be packing for another move. I never know what's going to happen. I never feel safe. I never know when my life is going to fall apart."

Most multiple divorcers, propelled into successive breakups by their own immaturity, insensitivity, behavior problems, and lack of social skills, were leading lives as unhappy as those of their children. However, some, like Lucinda Fredericks, would view themselves as having led a life that was in the main happy and fulfilling. At the time of the twenty-year interview, Lucinda was a court date away from a fourth divorce, and was now involved with a country club golf pro who was almost a decade younger than she was.

"Dickie says I'm going to be arrested for contributing to the delinquency of a minor one of these days," Lucinda said with a laugh when I asked about her new relationship. "But why should men be the only ones who can have younger partners? I'm still attractive, and for once, I'm with a man who has a real paying job. So I don't have to support him."

Although they did well in gratifying their own needs, self-fulfilling egocentric women like Lucinda did less well by their children. When the study ended, these mothers were often thriving emotionally as well as materially. But their sons and daughters, who had been neglected throughout childhood and adolescence, were drifting aim-lessly through early adulthood, and often had difficulties in social and emotional relationships.

Some egocentric women were so wrapped up in their own careers or success that they genuinely neglected their children. Others, like Lucinda, had some protective factors that buffered them from their vul-nerabilities. Lucinda's physical attractiveness, social charm, and the gen-erous financial settlement she received from Charles, her second husband, had helped to protect her from the impulsivity, dependency, and helplessness that had made her first postdivorce period so painful. A new man was always waiting in the wings to provide solace and support for the lovely, wealthy Lucinda.

But the settlement, which freed Lucinda to do what she did best, focus on Lucinda, had hurt Richard, who felt increasingly neglected and lonely as his mother went from man to man to man. Without Ed Dooley, very likely, the adult Richard would have turned out quite differently.

Other multiple divorcers like Diana Taine were unhappy about their succession of marital breakups and bewildered about why they hap-pened, but they just didn't seem to learn by experience. In each of her three marriages, Diana was equally critical, contentious, dogmatic, and unyielding. At our twenty-year interview, I saw a considerably chas-tened Diana. Two weeks before, her third husband had fled, leaving only a note with a forwarding address on the hall table. "I don't understand it. We had some problems, but I thought we really cared for each other. He was the man I wanted to spend the rest of my life with," Diana said, turning away to hide the tears in her eyes. She still wasn't able to relate the cherished "fierceness" of the Taine women to her marital failures.

Families Old and New

Social scientists who study families are like economists prognosticating about economic trends: they are better at describing why past changes occurred than at accurately forecasting the future. Sociologists, demog-raphers, and psychologists all failed to predict the post–World War II move to traditional *Ozzie and Harriet*, white-picket-fence suburban marriages, and the baby boom. They didn't anticipate the soaring rates of divorce and teenage single births in the sixties and seventies, and they are equally baffled as to why these have recently declined.

However, some of the experiences of our parents, whom we first encountered in the early seventies, and their young adult children in the year 2000, reveal trends that can help us understand where the American family is going. Our parents were children of the baby boom, born into traditional families, but becoming adults and marrying at a time when the family was changing dramatically. The divorce rates had doubled in the past decade, family size was decreasing, teenage pregnancies and births to single women were increasing, mothers were going into the labor force at an unprecedented rate, and feminism was on the march. Many of the young men and women I saw in the seventies were confused and ambivalent about the changes in gender roles and in the family that they were confronting, with men generally clinging to a more traditional view.

Thirty years ago, some of our young women were swept along by books like Betty Friedan's *The Feminine Mystique*, which presented marriage as a prison for women; but at the same time, these women were apprehensive at the prospect of moving out on their own. They were singing "I am Woman" along with Helen Reddy, but were uncertain about just what kind of woman they wanted to be. They were confronting the recessions of the seventies and eighties when good jobs were hard to obtain and many women had neither the education nor the job skills to live well independently.

Our VLS parents had grown up in the 1960s, when anti-establishment protests and idealism were rampant, when social standards and institutions such as government and religion and marriage were all being questioned. Their children emerged a more self-serving, materialistic generation, dealing with a very different world from their parents'. Sexuality, cohabitation, childbearing, and marriage are less closely linked than they used to be. Sexual relations are freer and initiated at an earlier age. Half of our young people in comparison to 10 percent of their parents were sexually active by age fifteen. When their parents got pregnant, they usually married; someone who had an abortion or a child out of wedlock was a social pariah. However, almost 20 percent of our young women had a child while they were single, with the rates higher for those in divorced and remarried families, and over 58 percent had had an abortion. Still, fear of AIDS and other sexually transmitted diseases was a major concern for many of these "sexually liberated" young men and women. Less than 5 percent of the couples in our original 1970s sample had cohabited before marriage; almost half of their adult children at some time had. Eighty percent of our contemporary youths versus less than 20 percent of their parents said living together was a good trial run for marriage; but two thirds of the young couples' cohabiting relationships did not end in marriage.

The divorce rate has actually dropped slightly in the nineties, from a high of over 50 percent of marriages ending in divorce to about 43 percent currently. This is in part because cohabitation is increasingly seen as a substitute for marriage, particularly among young people who lack a firm commitment to their relationship. Thus, one high-risk group is not entering the marital pool. However, I believe more than that one factor is contributing to the leveling or slight decline in the divorce rate. The average age at which people divorce is moving up; as life expectancy has increased, more couples in their fifties and sixties are divorcing. Since our VLS youth in the year 2001 are only in their early thirties, we don't know what their ultimate divorce rates will be.

One man, on leaving a marriage of twenty-eight years for a relationship with a younger woman, said, "It wasn't that my wife had changed; that was the problem. I had changed and she just wasn't what I needed anymore. The children were gone and I thought I want to do something more exciting with the twenty years I have left."

In spite of the modest decline in the divorce rate in the past fifteen years, the American divorce rate remains among the highest in the Western industrialized world. Why? Is it because the value and quality of marriage has declined or because there are fewer barriers to divorce?

Our research reveals that people have become less satisfied with marriage over the past three decades. Over half of our couples in the parents' generation who were in the first seven years of a marriage reported themselves to be "very happy," versus one third in their children's generation. Twenty percent of the parents reported themselves to have had a serious marital problem in the past year versus 38 percent of their young adult children. Conflict, inability to resolve disagreements, and lack of mutual supportiveness were more common in our contemporary couples. Some of the difficulties in these couples were associated with trying to juggle family life and two careers. They complained about the lack of time spent together—especially time without children—and this new generation of better-educated, more economically self-sufficient young women were very vocal and resentful about inequities in the division of labor in the household.

The "happiness gap" between the married and unmarried has also declined. This is not only because the younger generation of men and women report themselves to be less happy with marriage than their mothers were, but also because divorced women like Liddy Pennybaker and single men and women who never married have become increasingly satisfied with their lives. As marriage has become less essential to having children, sexual satisfaction, economic security, and the maintenance of a home, it has increasingly become defined in romantic terms as a means of satisfying emotional needs. "It has to make me happy" is a fragile foundation on which to build a marriage—or indeed, any human relationship—yet increasingly, modern marriage is judged by a "happiness" standard. And with nothing to hold a couple together but their expectations, often a marriage is jettisoned when each fails to get the steady stream of emotional satisfaction, personal fulfillment, and companionship they were anticipating.

Points to Remember

- Twenty years after divorce, most men and women are coping reasonably well with their new situations. Divorce is now a shadowy memory, and one largely irrelevant to their current lives.
- Happy marriages are one of the most important buffers in dealing with life's stresses. Happily married couples are healthier, happier, wealthier, and sexier than are singles, especially single men.

- A substantial number of divorced women, but not men, eventually emerge enhanced by their divorces and are leading more constructive, fulfilling lives than women who remained in unhappy marriages.
- Multiple divorces are associated with problems in adjustment for both parents and children. To some extent, this may be because personality characteristics that erode a marriage and make someone difficult to live with are carried from one relationship to another.
- Although quarreling may contribute to immediate unhappiness in a marriage, frequency of conflict is not associated with long-term marital stability. It is how people disagree, how they resolve conflicts, and the positive things they do for each other that are important in the long run.
- Sexuality, cohabitation, childbearing, and marriage are less closely linked in the generation of contemporaries than in their parents' generation. Intimate relationships are less predictable, programmed, and stable, and young people are less satisfied in marriage and intimate relationships than their parents were.
- Ultimately, coping with marital transitions is an active, not a passive process for adults and children. It is not just the availability of resources but how people seek them out and use them and how stresses are dealt with that determine a win, lose, or draw after divorce and remarriage.
- Certain personality traits such as impulsivity, irritability, antisocial behavior, and depression that are at least partly genetically determined can contribute to marital instability, poor parenting, difficulties in intimate relationships, and behavior problems in children.
- Divorce is a high-risk situation, but the majority of divorced parents and their children are resilient and able to cope with the challenges in their postdivorce life. They emerge as reasonably happy, competent individuals.

13

Lessons Learned in Forty-five Years of Studying Families

*W*hat are the lessons my research colleagues and I have learned in over forty-five years of studying families over time? What have we learned about what sustains families and nurtures family members' well-being or leads to conflict, distress, and marital breakup? What helps or hurts adults and children as they deal with the changes and stresses in their lives associated with divorce, life in a single-parent household, and remarriage?

Lesson One: The Diversity Lesson

Be suspicious of averages and focus on diversity. Averages conceal the great variability in how individual men and women, boys and girls function in intimate relationships, and how they cope when these relationships alter or break down and they have to build a new life. It is the diversity rather than the predictability or inevitability of pathways in intimate relationships over the course of life that is striking. Although some kinds of marriages have a greater risk of marital failure, there is no single pattern of marital relations associated with happiness and fulfillment or with dissatisfaction and instability. To a large extent, success in a marriage depends on the goodness of fit between the expectations, needs, and behaviors of a husband and wife. It also depends on how they go about solving their problems, healing emotional rifts when they do occur, and supporting each other in difficult times. Similarly, there is great diversity in the routes taken after marital breakup, in life in a single-parent household, and in new cohabiting or remarried relationships.

Lesson Two: The Gender Lesson

In spite of the fact that the roles, opportunities, and attainments of men and women have become more similar over the past thirty years, notable gender differences still remain in how husbands and wives, sons and daughters function in close personal relationships. Men may not be from Mars or women from Venus; both have strong needs for being loved and valued by another person. But the way they express closeness, communicate, and deal with conflicts often differs significantly.

Lesson Three: The Change and Malleability Lesson

Marital transitions offer great opportunities for personal growth and change. As families are reorganized, and old relationships and roles between husbands and wives, parents and children, and siblings that sustain our notions of who we are and what is important in our lives alter or are peeled away, a window of change opens. Although the most notable changes are found in the years immediately surrounding divorce and remarriage, the window of change is always open—sometimes for the better, sometimes for the worse. The routes to well-being or defeat and unhappiness are rarely direct. Many bumps in the road are encountered as new stresses and challenges arise, resources alter, and new relationships are formed.

Lesson Four: The Active Participant Lesson

People are not passive pawns of fate, dragged down destructive or fulfilling pathways after a divorce. They play an active role in building their new life by making choices, planning for the future, developing new competencies, and seeking out and using available resources. Those who wallow in helplessness, self-pity, and inaction are left behind.

Lesson Five: The Past Is Present Lesson

Many of the difficulties that are blamed on divorce—such as depression, antisocial behavior, poor interpersonal relationships, and lack of problem-solving skills in parents; inept parenting; and emotional and behavior problems in children—are often present in dysfunctional families long before the divorce occurs. Although divorce and remarriage usually contribute to temporary disruptions in family relationships, and require personal readjustment as parents and children deal with the new challenges in their lives, a move from an unhappy, stressful, conflicted family situation to a more harmonious, less stressful situation eventually benefits both parents and children. Conversely, the move into a situation that brings increased stresses, few resources, continuing acrimony, and deteriorating parent-child relationships can exacerbate adjustment problems that were present earlier and promote the development of new difficulties.

Lesson Six: The Risk and Protective Factors Lesson

Divorce and remarriage are usually very stressful transitions. How well adults and children deal with these transitions is related to the balance between risk factors that undermine both their ability to cope with stress and their well-being, and protective factors that help buffer them from adversity. Some of these factors are attributes of the individual, such as intelligence, ability, or personality characteristics; some lie in relationships in the family; and some in relationships and experiences outside the family. Over the course of a life, the presence and effectiveness of risk and protective factors shift as people's needs and situations change.

Lesson Seven: The Biology and Behavior Lesson

In Western cultures, the emphasis has been on nurture over nature in development, as reflected in the plethora of books on parenting and self-improvement, and the propensity to attribute such factors as antisocial behavior or low attainment to stressful experiences like poverty. Most people, including social scientists, also have emphasized the role that environment, personal experiences, family background, and stresses play in precipitating divorce. Twenty years ago, the idea that genetics might play a role in divorce would have been greeted with considerable skepticism; even now, no one is suggesting that there is a divorce gene. Still, there is accumulating evidence that personality characteristics such as impulsivity, antisocial behavior, irritability, neuroticism, and depression that are destructive in intimate relations and lead to divorce are at least partially genetically determined. Furthermore, these same characteristics in parents may be associated with irascible, inconsistent, inept parenting and with the same personality problems emerging in the children of divorced parents. Thus, the whole chain of events we have been discussing in this book—marital problems and divorce, difficulties in parent-child relations, higher rates of divorce in remarried families, behavior problems in children from divorced families, and the higher risk of divorce in offspring from divorced families—may to some extent have an underlying genetic basis.

This is not to say these underlying high-risk personality characteristics cannot be modified by experience. They can. A temperamentally difficult, irritable, impulsive child is less likely to develop into an explosive, unregulated adult if he or she has authoritative parents. The personalities, interaction styles, behaviors, and risk of divorce of young adults from divorced families are modified by the kind of mate they select. Biology is not destiny. Still, genetic predispositions to some extent influence the way other people respond to us, the stresses we encounter and supports available to us, the quality of our intimate relationships, and our chances of these relationships being stable and fulfilling, or short-lived, turbulent, and unhappy.

Lesson Eight: The Intimate Relations Lesson

Close, supportive intimate relations, whether with husbands and wives, lovers, parents and children, siblings, or outside the family, play the most important role in buffering people from stressful events. None of our children flourished without the presence of a caring, involved adult in their lives, and the formation of a new intimate relationship was the most notable positive turning point for divorced adults. Even most of our Competent Loners didn't want to be alone. They enjoyed relationships with friends, family, children, and new lovers. They just didn't find marriage desirable or essential for their happiness.

Lesson Nine: The Resiliency Lesson

The Resiliency Lesson is probably the most important lesson we have learned about divorce. Divorce and remarriage initially are experienced as stressful transitions by both children and adults. Looking back, many parents and adult offspring describe divorce as the most painful event in their lives, but they also say that they were able to adapt to their new situation and are currently leading reasonably gratifying lives. About 75 to 80 percent of adults and children show few serious long-term problems in adjustment following divorce and are functioning within the normal range. Many who have long-term problems after a divorce had problems that preceded the breakup. Moreover, a substantial group of our divorced women and some daughters were actually strengthened by developing new competencies to deal with the pressing demands that followed divorce and life in a single-parent family.

There seems to be a strong "self-righting" tendency in development, a striving to adapt and cope positively with the challenges that confront us, including those of divorce, life in a single-parent family, and remarriage. After all, adaptability is central to human survival.

Divorce and remarriage certainly often put both children and adults at risk for encountering stresses that may contribute to problems in economic and educational attainment, in social, emotional, and behavioral adjustment, and in the formation of stable intimate relationships. The easiest family setting in which to raise happy, competent children is one in which two mature, mutually supportive adults are committed to protecting and promoting the well-being of their children in a harmonious environment. A caring partner who shares the responsibilities and joys of raising children, and who is there for advice and support when problems arise, is the most potent protective factor a parent can have. But happy, competent children can and do develop in all types of nurturant, well-functioning families, including divorced, single-parent, and remarried families, through the courageous, selfless, and frequently dedicated caregiving of parents.

The current narrow focus in the media and some of the clinical literature on the hazards of divorce and remarriage, and problems in children whose parents have gone through marital transitions, is a disservice to the majority of those individuals who, often with heroic effort, are leading constructive lives. It isn't a matter of whether the glass is half empty or half full. In the long run, after a divorce, the glass is three-quarters full of reasonably happy and competent adults and children, who have been resilient in coping with the challenges of divorce.

Divorce should not be undertaken lightly; it is a high-risk situation. Every effort should be made to sustain marriages with some strengths and satisfactions, or marriages going through perturbations because of temporary stresses such as the birth of a difficult child, a job loss, or a casual affair. But divorce is a reasonable solution to an unhappy, acrimonious, destructive marital relationship. It can be a gateway to pathways associated with joy, satisfaction, and attainments, not just with loss, pain, and failure. At each step along the path, at each major transition, choices made and new directions taken can lead to a more fulfilling life or to desolation and despair. The most important steps in this voyage of personal discovery are those involving intimate relationships, which must be built and nurtured with care and sensitivity if the final destination is to be one of resiliency, enhancement, and happiness.

Appendix

The Three Studies

*T*he findings in this book were based on the results of three longitudinal studies of marriage, divorce, and remarriage: Study I: The Virginia Longitudinal Study of Divorce and Remarriage (Hetherington, 1989, 1991, 1993, 1998, 1999; Hetherington & Jodl, 1994). Study II: The Hetherington and Clingempeel Study of Divorce and Remarriage (Hetherington & Clingempeel, 1992). And Study III: The National Study of Nonshared Environment (Hetherington, Henderson, & Reiss, 1999; Reiss, Neiderhiser, Hetherington, & Plomin, 2000). Although all of these studies used a family systems life span framework, similar constructs, and often the same or similar measures, each contributed unique information about family functioning, individual adjustment, and adaptation in diverse family types. The use of similar measures often permitted us to pool data from multiple studies in our analyses. All three studies were approximately evenly divided across male and female children and had non-divorced families as comparison groups.

The Design of the Studies

Study I: The Virginia Longitudinal Study of Divorce and Remarriage

Study I was originally intended only as a comparative study of family functioning and adjustment in recently divorced, mother-custody, and non-divorced families. But remarried stepfamilies emerged over time as families remarried and the sample in later waves of the study was expanded and balanced to include equal numbers of divorced single-parent, remarried, and non-divorced households. The initial sample consisted of 144 middle-class white families, half non-divorced, half divorced, with a "target child" four years of age. Children and families were studied at two months, one year, two years, six years, eight years (truncated assessment), eleven years, and twenty years after divorce, when the offspring in these families were twenty-four years of age. Additional assessments were made when the young people married, cohabited for more than six months, or had a child. Thus, some of these families were followed and are continuing to be followed for as long as twenty-eight years. Of the original 144 families, 122 are continuing to participate in the study.

However, it was obvious that if we took our risk and resiliency approach to coping with marital transitions over time and wanted to examine diverse life pathways, we would need a larger sample. At the six-year follow-up, when the children were ten, the sample was expanded to include 180 families; when the children were fifteen, it was expanded to include 300 families; and when they were young people of twenty-four, it was expanded to include 450 families. In addition, although some examination of sibling relationships had been included in all waves, beginning at age ten a full assessment was done of the sibling closest in age. So, at the twenty-year assessment, we were studying 450 families and 900 youths distributed across non-divorced, divorced, and remarried families.

In this study and in our other studies, divorces and remarriages were occurring throughout the period under review. This gave us an opportunity to examine family functioning and the adjustment of family members both before and after a marital transition occurred. It also permitted us to examine whether there were times at which these transitions were easier or more harmful.

Study II: The Hetherington and Clingempeel Study of Divorce and Remarriage

Some of my research in other studies was beginning to indicate that early adolescence was an especially difficult time at which to have a remarriage take place. This study was designed to examine adaptation in stepfamilies with a young adolescent child three times over the course of the first twenty-six months of remarriage. It might be viewed as a study of the initial crisis period following a second marriage. It had a comparison group of non-divorced families and one of divorced non-remarried mother-headed families, where the mother had been divorced for the same length of time as the mothers who had remarried in the stepfamilies. This provided an opportunity to study how families at the same point in their postdivorce lives are benefited or harmed by a new marriage.

The 202 families in the study were white middle-class families, living in Philadelphia and its suburbs. The stepfamilies were studied at four months, seventeen months, and twenty-six months after remarriage, with the non-divorced and divorced families studied at equivalent intervals.

Study III: The National Study of Nonshared Environment

The primary aim of the National Study of Nonshared Environment was to examine the contribution of genetics, shared environment, and nonshared environment—that is, experiences that differ for siblings in the same family—to the development of both competence and psychopathology during adolescence. However, this study also offered an unusual opportunity to examine the functioning and development of children in different kinds of stepfamilies (Hetherington et al., 1999). A national sample comprised of 720 two-parent families with a pair of same-sex adolescent siblings no more than four years apart in age was obtained. It consisted of six groups of families with siblings of varying degrees of genetic relatedness. These six family types were: (1) families with dizygotic twins; (2) families with monozygotic twins; (3) stepfamilies with full siblings where both children were from the mother's previous marriage; (4) stepfamilies with half siblings where one child was from the mother's previous marriage and one was born in the new marriage; (5) blended stepfamilies with unrelated siblings (one from the mother's previous marriage and one from the father's previous marriage); and (6) non-divorced families with full siblings (intact). The stepfamilies were stabilized stepfamilies that had been remarried for an average of almost nine years.

This gave us an opportunity to examine not only different kinds of sibling relationships, but also simple and complex stepfamilies. In this study, simple stepfamilies are those in which only children from the mother's previous marriage are present in the family. Complex stepfamilies are those in which siblings in the family vary in biological relatedness to the mother and father.

It was expected that more complex relationships would be associated with more problems in the parent-child relationship and in the adjustment of children. In contrast, the quality of the sibling relationship was expected to be influenced by the biological relationship of the specific sibling pair rather than the complexity in biological relationships among all family members. Four years after the initial assessment, a second assessment of 404 families in which both adolescents still remained in the home was conducted. The drop in sample size was due to one adolescent having left the home rather than refusal to participate. Refusals were less than 10 percent.

Constructs and Measures

I have always been suspicious of studies involving only one source of information, whether it be clinical interviews, parent or child reports, or observations. All methods and informants have their shortcomings and strengths. Although a parent's or an adolescent's report of how they view their family situation is interesting in understanding their perspective, it may not be accurate in presenting what is actually going on in the family. By using multiple sources of information in all the studies, we attempted to derive convergent measures that would be more valid and reliable than any single measure. Multiple measures, multiple methods, and multiple informants were used to gather information on family functioning and children's adjustment in all three longitudinal studies. Each wave of data collection involved a large set of interviews, questionnaires, standardized test measures, and observations of family problem-solving sessions in various combinations of parents, siblings, and target children.

In Study I, observations with younger children and parents included unstructured play; structured observations of parents and children; observations of family relationships from the time children got home from school until they went to bed; and observations of children in school and in peer interactions. Studies I and II also included observations of the family at the dinner table. Information on marital, sibling, and parent-child relationships, as well as on children's competence and behavior problems, was obtained from a variety of sources, including children, parents, siblings, and teachers. In addition, data were collected on other variables outside the home, such as school quality, peer networks, social support, life events and stresses, and relationships with grandparents and non-residential fathers. In Study I, as the younger generation grew up, formed intimate relationships, and had children, their interactions in marital relations, with friends, cohabiting partners, and children were assessed through observations, and their life experiences and relationships were also assessed through multiple informants.

Certain common areas or constructs were assessed in all the studies. In the marital relationship, marital satisfaction, areas of conflict, family tasks and roles, warmth/support, and conflict/negativity in the couple's relationship were measured. Marital instability was also assessed in Studies I and III. In the parent-child relationship, the child's negative/coercive/conflictual behavior, as well as warm, congenial behavior and feelings of closeness with the parent, were assessed. Four parenting dimensions were central in these three longitudinal studies of marital transitions: warmth/involvement; negativity/conflict; monitoring; and control.

Sibling relationships were assessed through observations and parents' and siblings' reports on standardized inventories: sibling aggression, avoidance/embarrassment, rivalry, involvement/companionship, teaching/guidance, and empathy were measured.

Assessments of children's adjustment included multiple measures of externalizing antisocial behavior, internalizing depressed anxious behaviors, social and academic competence, social responsibility, and self-esteem.

The parents' personalities were assessed through standardized tests, interviews, and observations. The assessments were broadest in Study I, and included such areas as depression, anxiety, antisocial behavior, sensation-seeking, locus of control, social responsibility, and traditionalism.

In analyzing the data from all three studies, a wide variety of analytic techniques was used to assess differences in the average levels of family functioning and adjustment in men and women, boys and girls, and different types of families, and in an attempt to identify the functional and causal relationships that contributed to changes in family relations and the adjustment of family members over time. Cluster analyses were used to identify the types of marital relationships, sibling relationships, parent-child relationships, and patterns of adjustment that have to a large extent been the focus of this book. For example, the parenting styles of authoritative, permissive, authoritarian, and neglecting parents were identified in this way. Observations were assessed through multiple ratings and coding systems.

Composite variables of different constructs were made by combining information from various informants and measures. So, mothers', fathers', and adolescents' reports and ratings by observers were combined to form composite measures of such factors as parent-child conflict, parental warmth or control, or child antisocial behavior. Such combined measures are more reliable and better predictors of later behavior than are single measures. However, reports from individual informants were also examined in order to understand the different perspectives of individual family members.

More details about research methods and data analyses are presented in the works cited in the Selected References. Over two hundred theses, dissertations, papers, and books have been based on data drawn from these studies.

I would like to express my appreciation to the hundreds of undergraduate and graduate students and staff without whose dedication and effort these studies could not have been completed. I am also grateful to the families who gave so freely of their time and allowed us to come into their homes and observe their interactions. Finally, my thanks go out to the National Institute of Mental Health, the Grant Foundation, and the MacArthur Foundation for their generous support of this research.

Selected References

The Virginia Longitudinal Study of Divorce and Remarriage

Hetherington, E. M. (1989). "Coping with Family Transitions: Winners, Losers and Survivors," *Child Development*, 60, 1–15.

———— (1991). The Role of Individual Differences and Family Relationships in Children's Coping with Divorce and Remarriage. In P. Cowan and E. M. Hetherington, eds., *Advances in Family Research. Vol. 2: Family Transitions*. Hillsdale, NJ: Lawrence Erlbaum Associates.

———— (1991). "Families, Lies, and Videotapes," *Journal of Research on Adolescence*, 1(4), 323–48.

———— (1993). "A Review of the Virginia Longitudinal Study of Divorce and Remarriage: A Focus on Early Adolescence," *Journal of Family Psychology*, 7, 39–56.

———— (1998). Social Capital and the Development of Youth from Nondivorced, Divorced and Remarried Families. In A. Collins and R. Laursen, eds., *Relationships as Developmental Contexts. Minnesota Symposium of Child Development*, 30, 177–210.

———— (1999). Should We Stay Together for the Sake of the Children? In Hetherington, ed., *Coping in Divorced, Single Parent and Remarried Families: A Risk and Resiliency Perspective*. Hillsdale, NJ: Lawrence Erlbaum Associates.

Hetherington, E. M., & K. M. Jodl (1994). Stepfamilies as Settings for Child Development. In A. Booth & J. Dunn, eds., *Stepfamilies: Who Benefits? Who Does Not?* Hillsdale, NJ: Lawrence Erlbaum Associates.

The Hetherington and Clingempeel Study of Divorce and Remarriage

Hetherington, E. M., & W. G. Clingempeel (1992). *Coping with Marital Transitions: A Family Systems Perspective. Monographs of the Society for Research in Child Development,* 57.

Vuchinich, S., E. M. Hetherington, R. A. Vuchinich, & W. G. Clingempeel (1991). "Parent-Child Interaction and Gender Differences in Early Adolescents' Adaptation to Stepfamilies," *Developmental Psychology,* 27, 618–26.

Clingempeel, W. G., J. J. Colyar, E. Brand, & E. M. Hetherington (1992). "Children's Relationships with Maternal Grandparents: A Longitudinal Study of Family Structure and Pubertal Status Effects," *Child Development,* 63(6), 1404–22.

Miller, N. B., P. A. Cowan, C. P. Cowan, E. M. Hetherington, & W. G. Clingempeel (1993). "Externalizing in Preschoolers and Early Adolescents: A Cross-Study Replication of a Family Model," *Developmental Psychology,* 29, 3–18.

O'Connor, T. G., E. M. Hetherington, & W. G. Clingempeel (1997). "Systems and Bidirectional Influences in Families," *Journal of Social and Personal Relationships,* 14, 491–504.

The Nonshared Environment Study

Henderson, S. H., E. M. Hetherington, D. Mekos, & D. Reiss (1996). Stress, Parenting, and Adolescent Psychopathology: A Within-Family Perspective. In E. M. Hetherington & E. A. Blechman, eds., *Advances in Family Research. Vol. 5: Stress, Coping, and Resiliency in Children and Families.* Hillsdale, NJ: Lawrence Erlbaum Associates.

Mekos, D., E. M. Hetherington, & D. Reiss (1966). "Sibling Differences in Problem Behavior and Parental Treatment in Nondivorced and Remarried Families," *Child Development,* 67, 2148–65.

O'Connor, T. G., E. M. Hetherington, & D. Reiss (1998). "Family Systems and Adolescent Development: Shared and Nonshared Risk and Protective Factors in Nondivorced and Remarried Families," *Development and Psychopathology,* 10, 353–75.

Kim, J. E., E. M. Hetherington, & D. Reiss (1999). "Relations Between Family, Peers and Adolescents' Externalizing Behaviors: Gender and Family Type Differences," *Child Development*, 70, 1209–30.

Hetherington, E. M., S. Henderson, & D. Reiss (1999). *Adolescent Siblings in Stepfamilies: Family Functioning and Adolescent Adjustment. Monographs of the Society for Research in Child Development*, 63, no. 4.

Reiss, D., J. Neiderhiser, E. M. Hetherington, & R. Plomin (2000). *The Relationship Code: Genetic and Social Analysis of Adolescent Adjustment.* Cambridge, MA: Harvard University Press.

General Reviews of the Research Literature

Hetherington, E. M., M. Bridges, & G. Insabella (1998). "What Matters, What Doesn't. Five Perspectives on the Association Between Divorce and Remarriage and Children's Adjustment," *American Psychologist*, 53, 167–83.

Hetherington, E. M., & M. M. Stanley-Hagan (1998). Divorce. In A. E. Kazdin, ed., *Encyclopedia of Psychology.* New York: American Psychological Association and Oxford University Press.

———— (1999). "The Adjustment of Children with Divorced Parents: A Risk and Resiliency Perspective," *Journal of Child Psychology and Psychiatry*, 40, 129–40.

———— (2000). Diversity Among Stepfamilies. In D. H. Demo, M. A. Fine, & K. R. Allen, eds., *Handbook of Family Diversity.* New York: Oxford University Press.

———— (2001). Parenting in Divorced and Remarried Families. In M. H. Bornstein, ed., *Handbook of Parenting.* 2nd ed. Hillsdale, NJ: Lawrence Erlbaum Associates.

Index